Praise for

The Mysterious Case of Rudolf Diesel

"Brunt is very good at drawing out the political tensions that swirled around Diesel during his life. . . . A dynamic detective story."

—*The New York Times*

"Excellent . . . a well-researched and well-written biography."

—*The Wall Street Journal*

"[A] thrilling investigation . . . Brunt's audacious yet surprisingly tenable theory makes for a wildly enjoyable outing."

—*Publishers Weekly* (starred review)

"A terrific whodunit, there's everything to love about this book."

—Mike Rowe

"The author's interest in history and politics shines through in his well-researched, engaging book . . . fascinating . . . a worthy read."

—*Kirkus Reviews*

"*The Mysterious Case of Rudolf Diesel* sheds light on one of the most perplexing mysteries of the twentieth century. Written with the intensity of a thriller, this brilliant work will ensure the reader and the world will long remember Rudolf Diesel."

—Jack Carr, former Navy SEAL sniper and
#1 *New York Times* bestselling author of *Only the Dead*

"Equal parts Walter Isaacson and Sherlock Holmes, *The Mysterious Case of Rudolf Diesel* yanks back the curtain on the greatest caper of the twentieth century in this riveting history."

—Jay Winik, *New York Times* bestselling author of
1944: FDR and the Year That Changed History

"Outstanding—Brunt mixes a historian's respect for research with a novelist's eye for character, adds fascinating context and connections, and reaches a conclusion worthy of James Bond."

—Lee Child, #1 *New York Times* bestselling author

"The best kind of historical detective work . . . hard to put down."

—Gareth Russell, *The Spectator* (UK), Best Books of 2023

"A riveting, impressive, history-changing book. I couldn't put it down and gasped at the conclusion."

—Zibby Owens, host of *Moms Don't Have Time to Read Books* and
author of *Bookends* and *Blank*

"This fascinating story, told in the most vivid fashion, about a name so many recognize has been missed by true crime aficionados and historians alike—until now. An important addition to twentieth-century history."

—Dan Abrams, *New York Times* bestselling author of
Lincoln's Last Trial

"Insightful, suspenseful, and thoroughly enjoyable, you will be absolutely captivated!"

—Brad Thor, #1 *New York Times* bestselling author of *Dead Fall*

"Absolutely riveting."

—Chris Bohjalian, #1 *New York Times* bestselling author of
The Flight Attendant and *The Lioness*

"A textured and sensitive portrayal of Diesel's personality in its private and public aspects."

—*Booklist*

THE MYSTERIOUS CASE OF RUDOLF DIESEL

Genius, Power, and
Deception on the Eve of
World War I

DOUGLAS BRUNT

ATRIA PAPERBACK

NEW YORK ■ LONDON ■ TORONTO ■ SYDNEY ■ NEW DELHI

ATRIA
PAPERBACK

An Imprint of Simon & Schuster, LLC
1230 Avenue of the Americas
New York, NY 10020

First Atria Paperback edition October 2024

ATRIA PAPERBACK and colophon are trademarks of Simon & Schuster, LLC

Simon & Schuster: Celebrating 100 Years of Publishing in 2024

For information about special discounts for bulk purchases, please contact Simon & Schuster Special Sales at 1-866-506-1949 or business@simonandschuster.com.

The Simon & Schuster Speakers Bureau can bring authors to your live event. For more information or to book an event, contact the Simon & Schuster Speakers Bureau at 1-866-248-3049 or visit our website at www.simonspeakers.com.

Interior design by Dana Sloan

Manufactured in the United States of America

1 3 5 7 9 10 8 6 4 2

Library of Congress Cataloging-in-Publication Data has been applied for.

ISBN 978-1-9821-6990-9
ISBN 978-1-9821-6991-6 (pbk)
ISBN 978-1-9821-6992-3 (ebook)

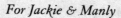

For Jackie & Manly

CONTENTS

AUTHOR'S NOTE

THIS BOOK BEGAN in 2015 when I bought an old boat. It was a thirty-eight-foot runabout built in 1996 with the original gasoline engines. I stood on the dock by my new purchase and spoke with the gentleman who owned the boatyard. He'd run the yard for decades, having taken it over from his father, and the whole place appeared frozen in the 1950s. The man's face was rough and tanned from the sun and salt air, his fingers like stones. He rolled his own cigarettes. I asked him what he thought I should do to fix up the boat.

He said that a boat like this should have Diesel engines, not gasoline. I had always thought one engine delivered on the same promise as any other, so I asked him why. He launched into his reasons: that on my two-hundred-gallon fuel tank I'd get twice the range; that I wouldn't breathe noxious fumes from the Diesel fuel the way I would with gasoline; that nearly all boat fires came from gasoline engines and none from Diesel. He held up the stub of his cigarette, which looked like a splinter pinched between his fingers, and said, "I could drop this lit cigarette into a barrel of Diesel fuel and nothing would happen. Gasoline engines start with an electric spark, but not Diesel. Diesel fuel's not flammable and the engine doesn't use a spark. The fuel needs to be pressurized *inside* the engine first. Diesel is a different engine. A better one." I followed the old salt's advice and repowered the boat with Diesels.

A year later, in the strange lull between having finished one novel and not having started my next, I was doing what I always do to connect with a new idea. I was on my computer, exploring anything and everything, plucking the threads of random discovery that bring me to different eras and geographies. As I clicked my way down threads, sometimes following one for a great distance, then hopping to a new thread, I came upon a list of "mysterious disappearances at sea." Down the list a bit I saw the name Rudolf Diesel and wondered if there was any connection between this person and my new Diesel marine engines. I clicked to a summary of the events of September 29, 1913, and began the extraordinary voyage that led to this book.

PROLOGUE

———

O CTOBER 11, 1913.

There was something in the water.

Crew members of the Dutch pilot steamer *Coertzen* approached the object that had caught their attention. There, near the mouth of the Scheldt River along the eastern edge of the English Channel, in the rippling black, the men on the small vessel realized what they'd seen.

It was a body.

Though the decomposition was ghastly, the sailors noticed the fine quality of the clothing that still wrapped the body. Pulling the remains alongside the boat, they plucked four items from the pockets of the deceased before releasing the rotting corpse back into the waves: a coin purse, a penknife, an eyeglass case, and an enameled pillbox. The steamer then made its scheduled call to the Dutch port city of Vlissingen, where the crew reported the discovery and turned over the items.

Harbor officials immediately wondered if the report from the *Coertzen* could be connected to the missing person case that had been in the headlines of newspapers in every major city in Europe and America. Officials sent word to the missing man's son, who arrived in Vlissingen from Germany the next day. As soon as he saw the items, Eugen Diesel confirmed that they belonged to his father, Rudolf.

Rudolf Diesel, the inventor of the revolutionary engine that bears his name, had disappeared almost two weeks earlier during an overnight crossing of the English Channel on his way from Belgium to London. The captain of the passenger ferry had reported Herr Diesel

missing at sea, in international waters where there was no legal jurisdiction and no investigatory authority. Since there was no body, there
had been no coroner's report. There was no trial by admiralty nor even
a company hearing. There had been no official investigation at all.

NO RAY OF LIGHT
ON DIESEL MYSTERY

German Inventor Was a Millionaire and His Home
Was Happy.

From the front page of the New York Times, *October 2, 1913.*

Rudolf Diesel grew up during an industrial boom. In America it became known as the Gilded Age, in France it was called the Belle
Époque. Economies flourished and urban centers developed at unprecedented rates. Through his childhood, Diesel witnessed this expansion from the vantage of an impoverished immigrant. His nomadic
family scratched out a living in cities across Europe, until a relative
recognized the boy's gifted mind and offered him a hand up.

At the age of twelve, Diesel took the modest opportunity for an
education and made the most of it. With natural ability and the determination of the most desperate, he excelled at his studies, and by his early
twenties he inhabited the most revered circle of engineers in Germany.
His scientific peers were Edison, Tesla, Bell, Marconi, Ford, Einstein,
the Wright Brothers, names that would achieve cultural immortality.
These geniuses delivered innumerable advances in science, spawned
new industries and destroyed existing ones, have been the subject of
books, films, and other tributes, and have been the shoulders upon which
countless others have stood. Yet Rudolf Diesel is missing from this list.

Throughout history, the world has often adopted technological
advances in ways the inventor never imagined, and certainly never

intended. The advances wrought by Diesel and his contemporaries changed their world from a place of decentralized rural economies to a place of mass industry, from the age of steam power to the age of oil, from battles fought at close range between men bludgeoning each other to mechanized warfare. As empires, both political and corporate, applied revolutionary technologies to accelerate their advance, the unintended consequences of an inventor's brainchild could wreak havoc and terror.

In the time before Diesel's engine became ubiquitous, the great battleships such as the British *Dreadnought* and the great passenger ships like the *Lusitania* and *Titanic* were equipped with steam engines. The steam technology pioneered by James Watt was as old as America and was the genesis of the Industrial Revolution. Shipbuilders installed a giant boiler filled with water, a coal-burning furnace stoked by teams of men to turn the water to steam, the steam pressure turned the gears of the engine, and finally a chimney and funnel that released black towers of smog from the coal furnace. It was rudimentary technology. A ship "raising steam" from the cool water in the boiler of an idle engine took hours to get under way, and the tons of coal needed to feed the furnace took up valuable cargo space. The dozens of men living on the ship to shovel the coal took up more space and needed to be fed as well. The massive and inefficient engines required the ships to hop from port to port around the globe to acquire more coal, announcing their advance with a smoke-stained sky visible for a hundred miles.

The Diesel engine didn't require hours to boil water. It operated immediately from a cold start. Nor did it require teams of men to stoke the fires, but simply drew liquid fuel automatically from a tank. The compact engine had no boiler, no furnace nor chimney apparatus at all. Diesel burned a viscous fuel that had no fumes, was safe to store, and the engine consumed its fuel so efficiently that a ship could circumnavigate the globe without stopping to refuel, and it did so with no discernable exhaust to give away the ship's presence on the horizon. What's more, the fuel for a Diesel engine came from the natural resources that were abundant nearly everywhere. Diesel's design was a quantum leap forward in humankind's ability to convert a substance into power. His engine became the most disruptive technology in history.

Diesel intended for his compact, safe, and efficient engine to lift up rural and urban economies alike, to do the work previously done by the backs of men, to advance the quality of life for all. But his intention was not to be.

When Rudolf Diesel went missing in 1913, the major newspapers from New York to Moscow ran front-page stories about the great scientist's disappearance. Though suicide by drowning was the working theory, the press also advanced the theory of foul play, and named two of the most famous men on the planet as the prime suspects.

One theory pointed to the German emperor, Kaiser Wilhelm II, and his agents, hypothesizing that the kaiser was so enraged by Diesel's rumored business dealings with the British that he had ordered the inventor's murder. One headline read, "Inventor Thrown into the Sea to Stop Sale of Patents to the British Government."

The other high-profile person who some suggested could be behind Diesel's death was the world's richest man, John D. Rockefeller. Rockefeller and his cohorts viewed Diesel's revolutionary technology—an engine that didn't require gasoline or any product derived from crude oil—to be an existential threat to their business empires. Another headline claimed that Rudolf Diesel was "Murdered by Agents from Big Oil Trusts."

In death, Rudolf Diesel, the genius inventor, was at the center of a great mystery. Only one year earlier, in 1912, major figures on the world stage had lauded the emergence of Diesel's game-changing technology. Thomas Edison pronounced the Diesel engine "one of the great achievements of mankind." Winston Churchill, an early admirer and advocate of Diesel motors, declared a new class of Diesel-powered cargo ship to be "the most perfect maritime masterpiece of the century." Now Rudolf Diesel, the man whom the famed British journalist W. T. Stead described in 1912 as "the great magician of the world," was gone.

In an industrial age nothing moves without a motor. It is the beating heart of nations, and no inventor was more disruptive to the established order than Rudolf Diesel. The terrible irony is that Rudolf Diesel abhorred the societal evolutions that his engine wrought. He opposed economic centralization to urban centers, he despised global dependence on the oil monopolies, and he loathed mechanized warfare. His aim from the start had been to invent a compact and economical source of power to revitalize the artisan class and liberate the factory workers of the Industrial Age. He envisioned an engine that burned the natural resources that nearly all countries possessed, and did so cleanly, ridding the earth of smogging pollutants.

The story of Rudolf Diesel's effort to change the world is one of the most important of the twentieth century, yet most people know little about it. His engine has persisted and thrived through the decades, and incredibly, the fundamental concept of the engine's design is practically the same today as the engine Rudolf first unveiled in 1897.

But the man seems deliberately scrubbed from history, so much so that Diesel is often misspelled with a lowercase "d." When has Ford been spelled with a lowercase "f"? Chrysler or Benz?

Today, people around the world pass within a few yards of the word *Diesel* many times each day: written on the side of a passenger train, a marine engine, at a fueling station, or on one of the five hundred million Diesel motor vehicles traveling the roads.* But few know that the word refers to a person. That he started out an impoverished immigrant. That he seized a sliver of opportunity to escape London's slums. That he believed in the rigors of capitalism, and also stood for peace, equality, the artisan class, a clean environment, and humane working conditions in an era of increasing exploitation. That he believed an engineer had a dual role as both a scientist and social theorist.

---

* WardsAuto estimates there were 1.4 billion automobiles in the world as of 2020, approximately 35 percent of these are Diesel. This excludes off-road and heavy machinery, almost all of which are powered by Diesel.

Diesel's genius set him on a collision course with an emperor and a tycoon. The result of this collision changed the course of the Great War and the fate of the modern world, yet history has failed to recognize that these figures are intertwined. Four people are key to understanding the quarter century leading up to the Great War: John D. Rockefeller, Kaiser Wilhelm II, Winston Churchill, and—overlooked until now—Rudolf Diesel. By walking the paths of these men in the decades before the war and connecting facts previously thought to be unrelated, a shroud of mystery dissolves to reveal the truth about Rudolf Diesel's fate.

———

On September 28, 1913, the day before he disappeared, Diesel penned a letter to his wife, Martha. In his final hours before boarding the passenger ferry *Dresden* bound for London, he wrote "Do you feel how I love you? I would think that even from a great distance you must feel it, as a gentle quivering in you, as the receiver of a wireless telegraph machine."

One day later, Diesel was gone. While his disappearance and the eventual discovery of his body were front-page news for a time, earthshaking events were unfolding that would push all else aside. It was the eve of a global conflict that would see thirty-two nations declare war and claim forty million casualties. Investigators ceased to pursue the peculiar actions of the players involved in Diesel's last days, the press failed to resolve the conflicting news reports in the weeks after his disappearance. The outbreak of brutal calamity only months after Diesel's presumed suicide demanded attention to the exclusion of nearly everything else. And the world forgot about Rudolf Diesel.

PART I

WAR & OIL ENGINES

1858–1897

CHAPTER 1

An International Identity

EUROPEAN WARS WOULD bookend Rudolf Diesel's life.

He was twelve years old in August 1870 when the French government decreed that all immigrants of Germanic origin must leave the country. The hostility toward the German peoples that had been brewing for years in France had reached a boiling point, and the countries were now at war. Rudolf fled with his family from their home in Paris.

The Diesels were of Bavarian descent, but the family felt a kinship with their Parisian neighbors, among whom they'd lived for more than a decade. The Diesels were participants in the flourishing cultural life of the great city, had sunk Parisian roots. But the Kingdom of Bavaria was one of thirty-nine loosely affiliated Germanic states led by Prussia that had formed a confederation and had gone to war with France. The Diesels found themselves designated as belligerents in their adopted French home.

The streets of Paris were in chaos, swollen with panicked newcomers as rural families streamed inside the city limits to seek refuge from the advancing Prussian armies. Theodor and Elise Diesel gathered their son, Rudolf, and his two sisters, Louise and Emma, packed what few possessions they could carry, and abandoned their modest residence and workshop to the inevitable looting mobs and certain ruin. Theodor had attempted to secure a loan but failed in the hostile climate. They fled Paris nearly penniless.

Theodor Diesel, Rudolf's father, was a third-generation craftsman, working mainly with leather as a bookbinder, though he also crafted children's toys, purses with delicate silk linings, and holsters for guns. He was born in 1830 in Augsburg, one of Germany's oldest cities, in the Kingdom of Bavaria. At the age of twenty, he emigrated to Paris with his brother in search of greater fortune. They were disciplined and ambitious men, used to a life of struggle and long workdays.

In Paris, Theodor met Elise Strobel, the daughter of a Nuremburg merchant. She was four years his senior. The couple wed in 1855 and had three children in orderly succession: Louise (b. 1856), Rudolf (b. 1858), and Emma (b. 1860).

Elise had a gentler nature than her husband. When she was younger, Elise had lived and worked in London as a governess teaching English, French, German, and music. When her father passed away unexpectedly, she returned home for several years to care for her seven younger siblings. She then settled in Paris and was working as a teacher of music and language when she met Theodor. The Diesel family lived with few luxuries, but Elise instilled in Rudolf a love of music and art.

His observant mother recalled to friends that she knew even from his infancy that Rudolf was unlike her other children. Her first indication was that though she breast-fed her two daughters, she was vexed in nursing her son. She couldn't get the strong-willed baby to comply, so soon after his birth she hired a wet nurse who cared for Rudolf until he was nine months old.

In these early years, the family noticed other ways in which Rudolf was different from his siblings and other boys his age. He would shrink away from boisterous play—games of tag or races in the street—and withdraw in solitude to a corner of their home where he would disassemble and analyze toys made by his father or draw sketches of mechanical devices. At an early age he possessed a level of sustained focus that amazed his sisters and mother, but Rudolf's father found his son's analytical nature troubling. Like Elise, Theodor recognized that Rudolf's relentless curiosity could lead him to a life beyond the tradition of his father's humble workshop—and from Theodor's vantage, the workshop was where Rudolf belonged.

Theodor's business occupied the ground floor of the family home at 38, rue Notre-Dame de Nazareth in Paris's third arrondissement. During the first years after Rudolf's birth, the workshop was a busy place with enough customers to keep Theodor and two apprentices employed. The smell of leather, oils, and grease drifted up the stairs to the shared bedrooms on the second and third floors where Elise tutored the children in language and music.

One morning while his father worked, seven-year-old Rudolf's curiosity carried him away. Accustomed to playing with toys crafted in the home, he pulled the family's prized possession, a cuckoo clock, to the floor with him. Determined to discover the clock's inner workings, he pulled apart the clock to its component pieces.

At first confident that he could put the clock back together before his father found him, he soon realized he was out of his depth. He sat and awaited his father's fury, which did come. That afternoon, the Diesels had a family outing planned. After Theodor yelled at Rudolf and lashed him with a leather strap, the rest of the family went on their excursion. Seven-year-old Rudolf spent the day alone at home, shackled to a heavy sofa.

———

The Paris of Rudolf Diesel's youth had already earned its name *La Ville Lumière*, the City of Light. In 1667, Louis XIV had decreed that lanterns should brighten the city to promote safety, making Paris one of the first cities to adopt streetlighting. At the dawn of the Age of Enlightenment, generally considered to be the year of the Sun King's death in 1715, Paris became the center of this intellectual and philosophical movement, and so the city's nickname took on both a literal and meta-phorical meaning.

The first gas streetlamps appeared along the Champs-Élysées in 1828. By the 1860s, the gas lamps were commonplace throughout the city, and by 1900 more than fifty thousand of them sparkled in the Paris night.

This innovation added to the gaiety of outdoor Parisian life and allowed evening activity that otherwise could not exist. On a typical Sunday afternoon, working-class Parisians would dress up and gather in outdoor spaces for parties to dance, drink, and eat. The parties lasted into the night under the dizzying new illumination. Renoir's *Bal du moulin de la Galette* (1876) gives an Impressionist snapshot of the real-life festivities in the Montmartre area of the Right Bank's eigh-teenth arrondissement. Renoir depicts the weekend scene under the lights at this famous hub of restaurants and cafés, only a fifteen-minute walk from the Diesel home. During the early 1860s, when Theodor's workshop was still bustling and the Diesel family hovered precari-ously above the threshold between the working and middle classes, Theodor and the musically inclined Elise would often stroll to Mont-martre to enjoy music and wine. While Paris had an undeniable and inimitable charm during these decades, it was far from perfect. A typ-ical nineteenth-century European city of 500,000 people might have been home to 100,000 horses, each one dropping thirty-three pounds of manure and more than two gallons of urine per day on the city streets. Worse, the manure attracted hosts of flies that bore typhus, taking the lives of thousands each year.

The population of France was second only to Russia at the time, and the capital was dense with people. According to the 1861 census, Diesel's district alone, the third arrondissement, was home to an astounding 99,000 people (nearly triple the arrondissement's population of 34,000 in 2017).*

Horse-pulled carriages and buses filled the streets, some intersec-

---

* The overall population of Paris in 1870 was in excess of 1 million people, and as the outer arrondissements grew, the city reached a peak of 2.9 million people in 1921. The population has gradually declined since World War II to the current level of 2.2 million.

tions so heavily trafficked that they were considered wonders of the world. Through this bustle, beauty, and bile, Rudolf pushed his wheelbarrow to deliver his father's homemade goods, traveling from the family workshop only a mile from Notre-Dame Cathedral to the homes of some of the city's wealthiest aristocrats.

———

Much of the city Rudolf walked had been recently transformed by the new head of state. Charles-Louis Napoléon (Napoléon III), nephew of Napoléon Bonaparte, was elected to be the first president of the French Second Republic in 1848. French constitutional law prohibited reelection, so the arrogant and power-hungry president overthrew the government and appointed himself emperor in 1851.

He wanted the capital to reflect the glamorous image he desired for his regime, so he made the beautification of Paris a priority. The new emperor ordered the construction of broad and straight boulevards, expansive parks, majestic monuments, and breathtaking government buildings. The engineering works beneath the city were no less of a masterpiece. There were millions of pipes for water, drainage, and gas. Engineers built a subterranean sewer wide enough for a rowboat. And high above the city, hot-air balloons floated across the skies, carrying wealthy sightseers in wicker baskets. This high-altitude mode of transportation was a marvelous amusement, and in times of war, provided a method to scout enemy positions and drop incendiaries.

Young Diesel and his peers in Paris were familiar with photography, aluminum for use in jewelry and fine cutlery, soaring airships, and engines that burned gaseous fuels like methane or natural gas. The world was experiencing a period of rapid innovation unlike any in history. Startling technical achievements continuously altered the way people traveled, communicated, and worked. Advances in metallurgy enabled the construction of machines and buildings never before possible.

The excitement surrounding this acceleration in human knowledge and achievement was reflected in the advent of the Exposition

Universelle—also known as the World's Fair—the first of which was held in Paris in 1855. The very idea that society could undergo such rapid change was a change in itself, and something to celebrate.

Rudolf attended the Paris World's Fair of 1867, the second fair hosted in Paris. The event ran from April 1 to November 3 and attracted fifteen million visitors, including Tsar Alexander II of Russia, Wilhelm I and Otto von Bismarck of Prussia, Emperor Franz Joseph of Austria, and Sultan Abdülaziz of the Ottoman Empire.

The government commissioned Victor Hugo and Alexandre Dumas to write promotional materials for the event. Jules Verne attended to witness the astonishing exhibits demonstrating electricity that inspired his novel *Twenty Thousand Leagues Under the Sea* (published in 1870).

In wide-eyed wonder, nine-year-old Rudolf strolled the Champ de Mars, the 119-acre stretch of land housing the fair that was ordinarily used as military parade grounds. More than fifty thousand exhibitors in concentric ovals were arranged by category of innovation and region of origin. He stopped to listen to the glorious tones of the Steinway piano from an American exhibit that sparked a global piano craze. He stood transfixed in front of the exhibit of the Krupp foundry from Prussia, studying the terrible dimensions of the fifty-ton cannon made of steel using the latest metalworking techniques, so that he could later sketch it.

He stopped at the unusual exhibits of the Japanese who, at the invitation of Napoléon III, participated in a World's Fair for the first time, bringing paintings, ornately decorated folding screens, swords, ceramics, and sculptures that intrigued the Europeans.

But a different exhibit garnered the most attention at the fair that year, and certainly the most attention from young Diesel. In 1867, the World's Fair's Grand Prix went to the coal-gas engine designed by Nicolaus Otto. Otto and his partner Eugen Langen won the prize for their engineering of a motor that was safer and more compact and fuel efficient than traditional steam-powered engines. Otto's new creation was an *internal* combustion engine burning gaseous fuels, unlike the *external* combustion steam engines burning coal that had provided power for almost every industrial use since the dawn of the Industrial Age one hundred years before when James Watt first developed a practical steam engine.

———————

To imagine the traditional steam engine (external combustion), think of the famous scene from the film *Titanic* when the captain says, "Let's stretch her legs" and passes the order for "all ahead full." The camera then enters the engine room where dozens of sweating men working with shovels heap tons of coal into the fierce orange glow of the blazing furnaces in the belly of the massive ship. The actual *Titanic* had more than 150 engine stokers aboard to feed the fires around the clock. These furnaces heated boilers full of water to create steam, the same principle as a pot on a stove. The steam was captured in airtight pipes and the expanding pressure of the steam created incredible force, which moved the gears of the engine, the gears then turning the ship's propellor. The coal fires in the furnace never touched the engine. The fires heated the boilers full of water that were external to the engine, and the water was an intermediary substance between the fuel and the engine. The pressure captured from the resulting steam then moved the engine to deliver the work.*

A chimney apparatus connected to the furnace captured the thick, sooty smoke of the coal fire and released the exhaust through funnels mounted on top of the ship's deck. The steam engine requires two substances—fuel (usually coal or wood) and water (to make steam).

———————

* The scientific definition of *work* refers to the transfer of energy into force that creates motion, or displacement. The early steam engines of the mid-1700s converted about 0.5 percent of fuel to usable work. The innovations of James Watt in the late 1700s improved efficiency to about 2 percent. These early steam engines were constrained by the state of metalworking technology. A great deal of energy was lost due to the inability to capture the pressure of expanding gases. Engine frames were made of wood timbers, metal fittings were hand-forged by blacksmiths, and pipes were packed with rope to make a seal, their valves capped with leather fittings. Pressure leaks and inefficiencies were inevitable.

Only the steam touches the engine. Primitive forms of steam engines existed even in ancient times—Egyptians used steam power to move heavy stone doors—though it was the pioneering advances of James Watt and others in the 1770s that brought the technology into industrial use.

Otto's *internal* combustion engine changed the design so that the combustion could occur inside the engine chamber and move the pistons directly. Otto didn't use an external furnace and boiler with water for steam. He did away with the intermediary substance (water) altogether.

Internal combustion engines explode the fuel directly inside the engine cylinder. Rather than the expanding pressure of steam, the expanding pressure of the combusting fuel itself moves the engine parts (the piston and crankshaft) to deliver work.

The origins of the internal combustion engine date back to the invention of the cannon in the twelfth century. With each combustion of gunpowder, the piston fired off at a single power stroke in the form of a cannonball. By the seventeenth century, scientists were experimenting with a closed cylinder containing a piston attached to a crankshaft (instead of a cannonball). Otto succeeded in delivering a useful engine with this concept.

The fuels for early internal combustion engines were unstable and highly flammable. Otto commonly used gases such as propane, hydrogen, benzene, or coal gas, and he experimented with liquid fuels such as kerosene, also highly flammable. As fuel combustion *inside* the cylinder moves the piston back and forth, the crankshaft turns a wheel to deliver the work. Collectively, internal and external combustion engines are in the broad category of "heat engines," which convert heat, or thermal energy, into mechanical energy for work.*

For stationary purposes on land, the massive steam engine could

---

* Thermodynamics is the study of the relations between different forms of energy (heat/thermal, mechanical, electrical, chemical, etc.). "Heat Engine" is a broader category that includes both internal and external combustion engines.

pump water from mines, turn wheels to grind wheat or stone. Different designs of the steam engine could be used for transportation, providing power for large ships or trains. Steam engines were behemoths though, and required teams of men to tend them, constantly shoveling enormous quantities of coal into the furnace. This technology was especially challenging for marine and rail use because of its massive engine, boiler, and chimney apparatus, and because stores of fuel needed to be carried with the ship or train. The engine also required regular maintenance of the inevitable burst valves and tubes that conducted the steam pressure. Further, the nineteenth-century steam engine was still grossly inefficient, converting only 6 to 7 percent of the energy in fuel to usable work.

Because Otto's new engine did away with the external furnace and boiler, it was much more compact than the steam engine. But a shortcoming of Otto's engine was that it was puny by comparison, both in size and the amount of power it could deliver. The new internal combustion engine typically delivered only a few horsepower, nowhere near the many hundreds required to drive a ship. But Otto's engine was more efficient in the amount of work it derived from a given amount of fuel, achieving approximately 12 percent fuel efficiency in 1867, double that of steam. In the rapidly expanding Industrial Age, the judges in Paris recognized the wealth of potential applications for this new power source and honored Otto and Langen with the grand prize.

Otto had a decades-long head start on his young admirer, who hurried home to sketch this new type of engine.

———

Later that summer, nine-year-old Rudolf and his father took a weekend stroll through Paris that resulted in a story retold by generations of the Diesel family. Sundays were typically reserved for relaxation and family time, as the other six days of the week Theodor worked in his shop from dawn to dusk.

Taking a pleasant stroll down the city streets, through parks, blooming gardens such as the Tuileries and Luxembourg, and alongside the River Seine was the most common pastime of the era. There were no commuter trains or motorcars of any kind. The Paris Métro wouldn't begin operation until 1900.

The father and son started on a pleasant walk under the warming sun. Up ahead they saw a crowd of onlookers gathered around a tree, talking excitedly in disturbed tones. As the pair got closer, they realized the attraction was a body hanging from a branch of the tree. An apparent suicide.

After observing the body for a moment, Theodor Diesel stepped forward from the milling crowd, drew his knife that he used to shape leather in his workshop, and cut the rope so that the body dropped in a heap. He had found the crowd's hysteria to be disrespectful and had put an end to it.

Theodor gathered his boy and wordlessly continued the walk. Minutes later, from a path atop a hill that overlooked a pond, Theodor gently put his hand on his son's shoulder. From this initial feint of affection, he then stuck his foot to the side to trip the boy's legs and forcefully shoved him down the hill toward the pond. Rudolf went sprawling down the hill, landing in water and mud. Shaken and bruised, Rudolf stood, covered in filth, now a spectacle himself to a new crop of onlookers. The startled and ashamed nine-year-old asked his father why he had done such a thing.

Theodor answered simply that it was a lesson in the hard knocks life had in store.

This was harsh parenting, even in the context of the period. Theodor's tactics were brutal and had the effect of exacerbating the boy's natural shyness.

———

A talent for invention ran in the Diesel family. Theodor showed creative flair, adding velvet to his leather pocketbooks, and he produced innovative games and toys for children. He invented a "light shedder" as housing to place over a burning gas flame, his invention predating by several years the glass cylinder that later became a standard lighting fixture of the time.

Theodor produced quality goods, but the family business was struggling by the late 1860s. Though the Diesels did not consider themselves to be a party to the Prussian aggression, French customers began to feel differently.

An increasing sense of anti-German sentiment had set in, and many of Theodor's French clients were either delinquent in paying their accounts or ceased to do business with him altogether. Theodor often dispatched young Rudolf to collect fees from clients.

Theodor's customers ranged from people of modest means to Paris's most well-to-do. Rudolf covered the span of the city on foot and wrote in his journal that he came to know the city streets "like the inside of my pocket." This exposure gave the boy an early education in the full spectrum of the social classes.

Theodor had good reason to place his son in the customer-facing role. Unlike Theodor with his heavy German accent, Rudolf spoke perfect French, and had a natural charm despite his reclusive nature. He was called not only handsome but beautiful, and Diesel biographer Charles Wilson (who met Rudolf years later in America) declared that Rudolf was considered "quite possibly one of the most beautiful young males in Paris."

Rudolf would later write that these early years in Paris, pressed into service as the bill collector for his father's struggling business, formed his views of money and poverty. Rudolf dreaded the task of bill collecting and often shirked the duty, then attempted to cover up his truancy with lies to his father.

———

Rudolf found ways to escape the confines of their home on the Right Bank. From his front door, turning right on rue Notre-Dame de Nazareth, he would walk less than a thousand feet to rue Saint-Martin and the Conservatoire national des arts et métiers, the oldest technical museum in Paris. The dank and dingy museum was the converted abbey of Saint-

Martin-des-Champs (Saint Martin in the Fields), which was used as a prison during the revolution then reopened as a museum in 1802. It housed a strange assortment of exhibits that ignited Rudolf's imagination: agricultural tools, models of ships, and some of the earliest steam engines.

Foremost among the exhibits was the *fardier à vapeur* (steam car), the world's first automobile, designed by Nicholas-Joseph Cugnot in 1770. Cugnot mounted an enormous teapot-shaped boiler on the front of the three-wheeled vehicle that in all weighed two and a half tons. Though it could move only two miles per hour and was grossly fuel inefficient, it was a marvel of the age.*

Diesel was a familiar face to the museum curators. He sat in the quiet, musty corridors and filled his sketchbooks with drawings that captured the nuances of the machine. At home, he escaped to the attic to sketch replicas of oil paintings he'd seen at the museum, or scenes from the Paris streets, or engineering contraptions far wilder than anything the old abbey held. As an adult, he often said to his friends, "Drawing is an engineer's right hand."

———————

One summer day in 1869, eleven-year-old Rudolf sat on the warm, flat rocks in the sun along the banks of the Seine. He'd climbed to a quiet place amid the active shores of the river. Reports of the looming Prussian threat had grown more frequent, though a sense of true danger was still hard for the boy to conjure. He took a pencil from his leather pouch and opened the sketchbook in his lap. In the pages of the book he had drawn the ships that passed on the river before him, the hot-air

———————

* The fate of Cugnot's engine had a particular foreshadowing of the fate of Diesel's engine more than a century later. During the 1770s, as Cugnot's engine got so much attention, Louis XVI ruled France. Louis was the last French monarch before the revolution, and the king prioritized technical innovation for military purposes over civil use. At the king's direction, the French army took possession of Cugnot's car and set it up to haul cannon. Once loaded with its cargo, the primitive machine went out of control and demolished a large stone wall. Badly damaged from the collision, the steam car eventually found its way to Rudolf Diesel's childhood museum in Paris. This example of the military co-opting technology repeats throughout history, so perhaps Diesel should have read his own fate early on.

balloons he'd seen overhead, horses, carriages—all with extraordinary precision for a boy not yet in his teens. He had precious few empty pages available in his book. Two beautiful women in fine dresses and elaborate hats walked the path above him, and he privately chose them to be the next subject to hone his skill as a draftsman.

As he worked, he barely noticed the group of bathers splashing in the river below him, or the old man on the opposite bank who fished for trout and Atlantic salmon. These were the happy childhood moments he lived for.

However, that morning his father had given him several addresses to visit and collect the fees for work. Rudolf couldn't bring himself to do it. He felt embarrassed calling on customers in his threadbare clothes that bore the hallmarks of a mother's mending. When he would arrive at a client's home, he could feel his voice abandon him and his eyes well up from the flood of anxiety. The request for the fees was made all the more humiliating by his family's obvious need.

Today he hadn't gone to the addresses his father had given him. Instead, he'd taken his pouch of pencil stubs and his sketchbook and walked to the Seine.

Rudolf finished his drafting when the sun was low. It was time to return home—without the money. With the obstinacy of a dreamer, he hadn't acknowledged the storm that awaited him. Back at the workshop, Theodor asked his son for the money. Rudolf said he had tried, and the clients promised to pay at a future date—but Rudolf was no good with lies, and when Theodor uncovered the truth, more old-country discipline lay in store. Theodor pulled the sketchbook and pouch from Rudolf's grip, the moment emphasizing the stark contrast between the hands of father and son. Rudolf's were soft, gentle, almost feminine next to his father's stony, calloused hands that were stained dark by the oils he used to work with leather and wood. Theodor then reached for the strap.

After excruciating lashes, he made Rudolf design a large placard that read *Je suis un menteur* (I am a liar) and forced the boy to wear it around his neck through the following school day.

A sketch of Jesus Christ made by the artistic Rudolf Diesel in September 1874, when Diesel was sixteen years old.

Life for the Diesels in Paris continued to grow worse through the late 1860s. By 1870, Theodor was unable to sell anything to French customers. He had placed all his products through the German-owned department store in Paris called Kellers of Solingen, but this strategy worked little better than selling direct. Then in July of that year, war was upon them.

Many of the peoples of the loosely formed German confederation, such as the Bavarians and Saxons, preferred peace and were friendly toward the French. But Prussia in particular was still bitter over the thrashing they'd taken at the hands of the first Napoléon. They were eager for revenge, if not against the original Napoléon, then the obnoxious facsimile Napoléon III would do. Eventually, Bavaria gave in to the will of Prussia and allied with it in the war against France.

On September 4, 1870, news of the Battle of Sedan reached Paris. The battle just two days earlier had been a devastating defeat for the

French army. Along with the surrender of the French forces, Prussia captured the disgraced Napoléon III.

Paris erupted in bedlam. Mobs tore down the many likenesses and tributes to the showy emperor throughout the city. Shops that had once proudly displayed insignias to designate service to the royal house were threatened and sacked.

It was an unsafe place, especially for anyone of Germanic heritage. On September 5, as the Prussians advanced on Paris from the east, the Diesel family boarded a refugee train headed west to the coast. From there, they boarded a steamship to cross the English Channel, bound for London.

Forced to evacuate in haste, the Diesel family left behind their home and workshop along with most of their possessions. They had little in cash and brought only what they could carry on their backs. As Theodor's grandson Eugen later related, Theodor managed to procure "a loaf of bread and a bar of chocolate" to feed the family of five on the channel crossing.

They were bound for an uncertain future among the throngs of immigrants pouring into England, competing for work and shelter.

———

Behind them the battle raged. France was falling to the disciplined Prussian forces with humiliating ease, and Paris was soon surrounded by Prussian troops, cut off from the outside world. Chancellor Otto von Bismarck had already led Prussia to quick victories over Denmark and Austria, and a decisive victory over France was the next and final military campaign of his political strategy. Bismarck's chief aim was to unify the Germanic peoples into a single powerful German state with Prussia at the helm. A rapid defeat of France would secure his goal.

The end of the Franco-Prussian War in 1871 marked the founding of the modern German state as the twentieth century would come to know it. Germany was immediately a feared rival of the major European powers, with the most lethal land-based military in the world.

The Germans imposed harsh peace terms on the French, including massive reparations payments and seizure of the prized territory of Alsace-Lorraine. The German seizure of these French assets in 1871 created a long-standing political enmity between the two nations that would come to have a profound effect on Rudolf Diesel's life.

CHAPTER 2

———

A Brief Stay in London

As the Prussian advance toward Paris continued, fleeing families packed themselves aboard overfilled steamships bound for England. The five members of the Diesel family huddled together, suffering seasickness as their steamer tossed in the rough seas of the English Channel. Winds whipped the ocean spray across the decks. Theodor did his best to protect their few possessions from the desperate people around them. They took a spot on the deck near the rail as the children became violently ill from the motion of the ship. Rudolf was old enough to register the raw fear that came with their new circumstances.

After a harrowing seven-hour crossing, the Diesels arrived in Newhaven, England. They spent the first night cramped in a cheap room at the London & Paris Hotel. Two days later, they reached London by train.

Theodor and Elise left the children on a bench at the train station as they set off to begin the overwhelming task of starting a new life in a strange city. The first requirement was a roof over their heads. They returned several hours later having found nothing.

The family of five then set out together, dragging their boxed possessions through the streets. Finally, nearly exhausted, they found a simple two-room flat at 20 Herbert Street in the district of Hoxton. The three children slept on a couch and the parents in the bed. The small boxes they had brought along as luggage were used for chairs, a table, and a washstand.

Hoxton is part of historic East London with roots dating back to the fifteenth century, though from the outset of the Industrial Age, a gradual displacement of the residents had been underway due to the encroachment of factories and warehouses. This is the London of *Oliver Twist*. And in 1870, twelve-year-old Rudolf arrived at precisely the age of Dickens's title character. Hoxton is in the Borough of Hackney, a name associated with a lower-class "Hackney," or Cockney, accent. The sudden relocation from Paris to this dangerous new home was an unsparing deterioration in their already modest circumstances, traumatizing for both the adults and the children.

Rather than falling in with any artful dodgers, the introverted Rudolf immediately tried to replicate his pastimes from Paris, and found his way to the British Museum and the South Kensington Museum, where there were exhibits of engines to study and sketch. As a silver lining, he realized the good fortune he had to live in the two cities of the world that most honored the tradition of the engineer.

But he also encountered horrors in London that haunted him the rest of his life: tenement housing of the London industry laborers, factories with poor lighting and no ventilation, the foul smells of wretched humans mixed with the smog of coal smoke from belching machines.

Worst of all was the immoral use of children pressed into labor. Rudolf was only twelve years old, and children his age and younger were marched off to factories rather than schools. Floggings of children were routine, and in his Hoxton neighborhood Rudolf witnessed children with prison pallor and open, bleeding welts. Rudolf was so disturbed by these encounters that years later he recounted the experiences in detail to his children, and his son Eugen included the stories of Rudolf's time in London in the family biography he published.

On a brisk autumn afternoon Rudolf began a walk across London

Bridge, spanning the River Thames. Midway across, he stopped and gazed across the horizon that was blotted with the rising black plumes of coal exhaust from ships, cranes, pile drivers, and factories scattered over the landscape. Smoking chimneys and trails of steam smudged the horizon. Rudolf had been in London only a month and had already seen the inhumane conditions that existed at the points of origin of those smoky plumes. Whether his German immigrant craftsman father could find work in this new city amid a throng of other refugees was all that separated Rudolf from the factory and the whip.

Passersby on the bridge would have barely noticed his slender frame standing by the rail. The young boy was a bit odd, a loner, a dreamer who had a gifted but untrained mind for engineering, and who also loved the arts due mainly to his mother's gentle touch. Though the source of his next meal was uncertain, he was, for the moment, more fortunate that the ill-fated children bound for the factories. The naive and optimistic youth who filled his time drawing sketches of contraptions he'd seen in exhibits, or more fantastical ones from his imagination, determined in that moment that he could create a better machine. As he stood on the bridge, he committed himself to the vague ambition of making something that could change the circumstances of working-class people like him and his family.*

He pushed back from the rail of the stone-arched bridge with an erect posture that he would maintain throughout his life, his skinny limbs draped in clothes even more threadbare and ill-fitting than in his Paris days. Rudolf contrasted the smog before him in the London sky with what he had experienced in his father's Paris workshop. The mechanized society that had begun in England had made its way to the continent and tilted the economic scales overwhelmingly in favor of big urban industry over smaller rural businesses.

The advent of industry on this new scale seemed a form of

---

* The moment on the bridge was indelible to Rudolf and the story entered Diesel family lore. He recounted the vivid memory to his children many times, and eventually his son Eugen wrote out the story in a family biography published in 1937.

enslavement. Businesses relied on an army of pliant workers and behemoth machines fueled by warehouses of coal. These resources to power the Industrial Age were antithetical to the small proprietorships that had been the norm of Diesel's youth in Paris.

Rudolf's observations and experiences in London and Paris during these years became ingredients for invention. A thousand times he had sketched in his notebooks the ravenous coal-devouring machines that were both beyond the means of the independent craftsman and counter to the tradition of custom workmanship. But, he thought, perhaps there could be a new engine design that could distribute power to rural communities, an engine that could fit in a corner of a workshop rather than the colossal apparatus that was larger than the workshop itself. Otto had already revealed an engine design that was a small step in this direction only three years prior.

Rudolf walked to the other side of the bridge, ideas swirling in his head. He had a goal, a vision that would matter to artisans like his father.

———

Theodor was an immigrant in London, without his own shop, without prospects for work at all. Louise, the eldest Diesel child, managed to find a job teaching language and music at a small private school. Her income helped put food on the table, but the Diesels were only barely eking out a living. The three children were as close as ever, bonded in the family struggle. Though destitute, the family unit remained intact.

Theodor's brother (also named Rudolf) had left Paris several years earlier and returned to Germany. Theodor wrote to his brother in Augsburg to inquire about prospects there, but his brother replied that employment conditions in Germany were no better.

And then came a lifeline for Rudolf. Theodor's cousin Betty in Augsburg was married to a mathematics teacher, Christoph Barnickel. These relatives offered to have Rudolf come to Augsburg, where he could attend the Royal County Trade School. Barnickel offered to board Rudolf in their home along with several other students.

Even if they didn't always show it with displays of tenderness,

Theodor and Elise loved their son, as letters between them over the next several years attest. They also recognized that their son had a gifted mind. Life in Augsburg with the Barnickels would open doors for Rudolf that would be firmly shut to him in London.

Theodor was loath to humble himself by accepting charity, but he knew an education like this could lift twelve-year-old Rudolf out of the day-to-day struggle to survive. His son could have a stable home life and the opportunity for an education, after which, Theodor assumed, Rudolf could return and join his father in a reconstituted workshop.*

Rudolf spent less than three months in London, but that stay would have a major impact on his life and worldview. In late November 1870, traveling alone under a sky of steel gray and in the biting cold, he boarded a ship with one change of clothes, a few coins, and a basket packed by his mother with enough food to last several days.

The trip to Augsburg took eight days. Weather delayed his crossing. From Rotterdam he took trains taking him through Emmerich, Cologne, Frankfurt, and Würzburg. He stayed in cheap inns along the way, sharing rooms with strangers, fearful the entire time of being robbed of the little he had. During one severely cold night, he sipped a glass of schnapps that a stranger offered, and he wrote to his parents that he enjoyed the drink, but suffered from a sore throat, toothache, and earache for the remainder of the trip.

When he arrived at the Barnickels' home, he was exhausted, ill, and homesick. He was worried about his sisters and whether his father had found any prospects for work.

Upon seeing the boy, Christoph Barnickel remarked that he was "more like a mature adult than a twelve-year-old boy" and that he was a youngster "to whom anyone could immediately lose his heart." Barnickel kept Rudolf home for three days to rest and recover.

But while his body rested, his mind remained unbridled. Fresh

---

* Theodor promised to pay the Barnickels 1,000 marks per year (approximately $6,000 today), which was the regular boarding fee, though this was not paid until some years later by Rudolf once he started earning his own money.

from his first experience riding long stretches in railway cars, he became fascinated by trains. Barnickel remarked that during the boy's three-day rest period he "made a railroad out of cigar boxes, complete with marshalling yard. He nailed wooden rails to the cigar-box boards. The switches, which actually moved, were connected to the signal box by hairpin wires."

Barnickel, an educator of many promising youths, was immediately impressed, and determined to nurture Rudolf's obvious gifts. Once ensconced with the Barnickels, Rudolf began the formal education that would set the trajectory for his life's work. In Augsburg, the seed of Rudolf Diesel's vision began to grow.

Rudolf's son Eugen later summarized the benefits of his father's nomadic youth from an engineering perspective. "Paris kindled in him an enthusiasm for technical and scientific things under the aspect of that special genius peculiar to the French. London showed him the classical origins of the age of the heat engine, as well as the vast scale of operations of a great world power . . . Germany brought him in contact with the solidity and logic of the Swabian* school of German workmanship."

Throughout his life, Rudolf pursued the parallel efforts of the engineer and the social theorist. His early years, shadowed by war and dislocation, developed in him truly international sensibilities. When he returned to the home of his ancestors in 1870, he had already lived in the capitals of Germany's two greatest rivals, spoke three languages, and had spent twelve years immersed in Anglo-French culture, politics, and educational systems.

But the prevailing and indelible lesson, learned through traumatic personal experience, was his understanding of the fragility of a family's security. War and industrial innovation could destroy the life a family had made for itself.

---

* Swabia was a medieval duchy that eventually became part of the Kingdom of Bavaria in 1803. Cultural stereotypes portray Swabians as frugal, entrepreneurial, and hardworking. The stereotype exists to the present day, evidenced in a remark by Chancellor Angela Merkel praising the "thrifty Swabian housewife" (*The Guardian*, September 17, 2012).

CHAPTER 3

A New Empire in Europe

A<small>T THE TIME</small> of Rudolf's arrival, Augsburg was a modest-sized city of 50,000 people. (The population of Berlin at this time was 820,000 and Munich about 180,000, though these urban centers were experiencing a period of rapid growth.) Sprawling canals were lined with waterwheels that had powered early forms of industry for centuries. It was one of Europe's oldest cities and had been an important trade route for ancient Rome. The original name of the city at its founding, Augusta Vindelicorum, was in tribute to the Roman emperor Augustus.

By the 1800s, it was a place of textile manufacturers and factories, tobacco mills, and was home to all types of tradespeople. In 1838, Carl Buz, a German railroad engineer, directed the construction of a fifty-mile rail line to connect Augsburg and Munich, which brought another surge of industry to the ancient city.

When Buz had completed the railway, he decided Augsburg was the perfect town for a young engineer like himself. He met a talented, well-connected potential partner in Carl August Reichenbach, whose uncle had invented the flatbed printing press in 1811.

In 1844, the two men purchased an existing manufacturing plant in Augsburg and Buz soon founded Maschinenfabrik Augsburg (M.A.), where he focused on building heavy machinery for industry: steam engines, steam boilers, and water turbines.

In 1864, control of the company passed to Carl's son, Heinrich Buz, whose savvy and daring business acumen established M.A. as a leader of German industry, just as Germany was emerging as a world industrial power. By the time Diesel arrived in Augsburg in November 1870, Heinrich Buz had earned his nickname "the Bismarck of German Industry." Augsburg was a hotbed for rising engineering talent, and in Germany during the late nineteenth century, if an engineer wanted to bring concept to reality, Heinrich Buz of Maschinenfabrik Augsburg was the man to see.

For the prior hundred years, the greatest engineering advances had come from France and England, but this was now changing. Germany was enjoying rapid economic expansion, and Rudolf found himself in the seat of Germany's rising engineering power.

———————

War and industry have always had a symbiotic relationship. The nature of the political regime within which a scientist works can have a determining effect on the direction and application of his work, and a scientist must find his place. The reason for Germany's industrial surge was in large part due to the political and military triumph of the Prussian leadership. After the Prussian-led victory over France, Augsburg was no longer simply a city in the Kingdom of Bavaria. When Rudolf arrived, Augsburg had become a city within the German Empire.

To understand the political and social climate within which Diesel lived and later worked, it is important first to understand how the German Empire was created, and how Kaiser Wilhelm and later his grandson Kaiser Wilhelm II exercised their power. At the time of Rudolf's arrival, the nascent German Empire was still forming its identity.

Upon victory in the Franco-Prussian War in 1871, Wilhelm I became the first German emperor. Otto von Bismarck, the minister-president of Prussia, assumed the title "Chancellor of the German Empire," along with the nickname "the Iron Chancellor." The emperor's grandson, a prince the same age as Rudolf Diesel, cheered on the victorious German military.

Chancellor Bismarck became the dominant political figure of Germany. Standing over six feet tall with broad shoulders, an imposing figure in every sense, Bismarck bent even the aging emperor to his will. Kings and ministers around the world revered and feared Bismarck, who now presided over the most powerful army on the continent. For the next two decades, he would continue to pull the strings of international diplomacy. Not since Charlamagne in the ninth century had any one leader so ably implemented his vision over the expanse of Europe.

France had been the third and final of Bismarck's strategic wars to forge the German Empire. He fought a successful nine-month war against Denmark in 1864 and defeated Austria in 1866. By ousting France as a rival and threat, Bismarck had won the political capital and public goodwill to obtain the prize of German unification. Bismarck had surmised all along, and declared in an 1862 speech that "[The German states do] not look to Prussia's liberalism but to her strength . . . The great questions of the day will not be decided by speeches and resolutions of majorities . . . but by iron and blood." On the road to unification, he had defeated two emperors and created a third.

Bismarck wrote the new German constitution. Though the German Empire was nominally a constitutional monarchy, as was Great Britain, Bismarck was far more conservative in his allocation of government powers, and granted greater authority to his emperor, and to himself, than was the case for Britain's monarch. As the global trend saw democracy on the rise and autocracy on the wane, Bismarck designed a government of the autocratic old world. This fundamental political difference would echo through generations.

What even Bismarck could not control or predict were the wild twists in the dynastic lines of power of royal families. In an era of rapidly shifting international alliances, marriages among the ruling classes were a strategic tool. In 1858, Wilhelm I's son, Frederick III, married Victoria, Princess Royal ("Vicki"), the eldest child of Britain's Queen Victoria. Their son Wilhelm II was Queen Victoria's eldest and favorite grandchild, and through the complex web of royal connections this meant that Wilhelm II was a first cousin to King George V, against whom he would eventually go to war.

But in these halcyon last decades of the nineteenth century, England and Germany were on friendly terms. Several German states had joined England as allies against Russia in the Crimean War (1853–1856), and before that as part of the allied coalition in the Napoleonic Wars (1803–1815). Queen Victoria was of German descent, and had chosen a German, Prince Albert of Saxe-Coburg and Gotha, for her husband and consort. With delight, the Queen agreed to the marriage of her favorite daughter, Vicki, to the German crown prince, Frederick.

Vicki and Frederick's first child, Frederick William Victor Albert, was born on January 27, 1859, in Berlin, capital of the Kingdom of Prussia. He was second in line for the German throne (after his father) and just ten months younger than Rudolf Diesel.

Wilhelm was born with a physical deformity; his left arm was six inches shorter than his right. In the hypermasculine Prussian culture, this enfeeblement caused him great embarrassment. Sadly for the boy, the withered arm was also a source of embarrassment for his mother, who wrote to her own mother in England, "He would be a very pretty boy were it not for that wretched, unhappy arm which shows more and more, spoils his face . . . his carriage, walk and figure, makes him awkward in all his movements . . . not being able to do a single thing for himself. . . . To me it remains an inexpressible source of sorrow."

Wilhelm's greatest torment in his youth was learning to ride, a skill his mother insisted that, as heir to the throne, he must learn. The riding instructor who supervised Wilhelm later wrote, "The weeping prince was set on his horse, without stirrups and compelled to go through the paces. He fell off continually; every time, despite his prayers and tears, he was lifted and set upon its back again."

Reflecting years later, Wilhelm confirmed, "The thought that I should not be able to ride was intolerable [to my mother]. But I felt I was not fit for it because of my disability. I was worried and afraid. When there was nobody near, I wept."

Vicki blamed herself. Wilhelm's birth had been a complicated breech, and the baby's arm was crushed during the delivery. The child would not resemble his tall, handsome, strapping father. Vicki's obsession with the handicap only served to exacerbate the problem for the boy. She wrote to Queen Victoria in May 1870 that Wilhelm "begins to feel being behind much smaller boys in every exercise of the body—he cannot run fast because he has no balance, nor ride, nor climb, nor cut his food . . ."

Wilhelm's arm, and his mother's obsession with it, contributed to his lifelong feelings of insecurity. Throughout his life he attempted to conceal the withered arm behind his back in photographs.

Despite her dismay over her son's arm, Vicki remained devoted to Wilhelm's overall development and took charge of his general education. She did so in a decidedly British manner. Vicki found German culture and German education to be boorish. This won her few friends among the German nobility, but she didn't mind the absence of affection from those she looked down upon.

Her distaste for things German extended to politics and Bismarck's autocratic form of government, which she found to be unmodern, nearly medieval. She wrote to Queen Victoria, "Prince Bismarck remains the sole and omnipotent ruler of our destinies. His will alone is law here."

Throughout this period, Vicki guided and educated her son. Many of the boy's fondest childhood memories were lengthy visits to Buckingham Palace or to his grandmother's summer retreat at Osborne House on the Isle of Wight. The most lasting impression on Wilhelm from these visits was the magnificence of the Royal Navy. The boy was awestruck by the splendor and massive bulk of the capital ships that ensured Great Britain's domestic security and her hold on her global possessions.

Not only were these visits frequent, but Vicki, to her last days, in all her correspondence referred to England as "Home."* Vicki's way of life was thoroughly British, and by conscious and subconscious influence, she tried to instill in Wilhelm the notion that the ways of the English were superior to those of the Germans. Her husband, Crown Prince Frederick (who in 1888 would ascend to the throne for a period of only ninety-nine days before dying of throat cancer), while a devoted German, was also a devoted husband. He supported a liberal education for his son, and he preferred a liberal form of government that was less autocratic than what Bismarck had crafted for the German Empire.

As the years passed and the more docile Wilhelm I grew old, Frederick and Vicki moved ever closer to the throne. Bismarck recognized the liberal threat that Frederick and Vicki represented, but he also recognized a new potential ally to combat the ascending couple.

When young Wilhelm, alternately spoiled and aggressively disciplined, reached his early teenage years, Bismarck and his ministers gradually asserted more influence in the direction of the boy's professional education, slowly wresting control from Vicki. Bismarck's aim was to steep the boy in conservative principles and instill in him a Prussian sense of regimen. Bismarck already held sway with the German public and ministers. As insurance, he wanted to fortify the young prince in the struggle he foresaw once the boy's father ascended to the throne.

Bismarck, the master manipulator, succeeded. The boy's worldview, even his nature, began to change. No longer did he yearn for the

* In her final days in 1901, Vicki left two dying wishes. First, that her body be returned to England for burial. Second, that she be buried unclothed and wrapped in the English flag. Wilhelm, by this time thoroughly embittered by his mother's pro-English sentiments, refused the first, feeling it would be a disgrace to Germany, but in a moment of sentimentality he granted the second.

playful visits to his mother's homeland, nor did he subscribe to Vicki's political beliefs. And as he spurned her entreaties, he fully embraced his German roots and placed the grand Prussian achievement of German unification on a pedestal. Wilhelm set aside his own parents and came to idolize his grandfather. He referred to Wilhelm I as "Wilhelm the Great" and fostered a cult of the first German emperor. Even his manner took on the brusque, clipped bearing of the Prussian military, and his relationship with his mother grew increasingly distant.

Reflecting on the origins of his physical deformity, he recounted that Vicki had allowed only English physicians to care for him as a child because she felt the German doctors did not have equal ability. He came to view her dismissal of the German doctors as an insult. In 1889, Wilhelm remembered his youth in an outburst that revealed his pent-up loathing. "An English doctor killed my father, and an English doctor crippled my arm—which is the fault of my mother."

Hardened as he had become, inside Wilhelm was still that little boy who stared with fascination at the grandeur of the Royal Navy, who happily played at the feet of his adoring grandmother, who esteemed British manners, traditions, and sophistication. Biographer David Fromkin observed, "The half-German side of him was at war with the half-English side. He was wildly jealous of the British, wanting to be British, wanting to be better at being British than the British were, while at the same time hating them and resenting them because he could never be fully accepted by them."

Many people find strength in having an identity that is a blend of ethnicities and cultures. For Wilhelm, his dual identities were a source of confusion and conflict. For Rudolf Diesel, the blend of cultural influences led to a certain balance in his character. His mother had taught language and arts as a governess in London. His father embodied the stern, almost militaristic, discipline of the German old country. Rudolf spent his youth in both France and Germany, indifferent to the fact that the antagonism between the two nations led to the greatest political rivalry in Europe. Rudolf embraced both places as home. He appreciated his Bavarian roots as well as the cultures of his adopted cities, in particular Paris. He happily declared himself to be a "citizen of the world." Wilhelm could not find such peace in duality. In his case, the military culture of Prussia came to the fore, to the exclusion of the fond feelings he once had for his mother, Vicki, and his grandmother, Queen Victoria.

———

Eugen Diesel, Rudolf's son, became one of Germany's preeminent writers on the topics of culture and technology. He would later write of Bismarck's influence on the empire, "Germany's lodestar was the soldier. And Prussia, the embodiment of militarism, became the ideal in which the German love of order and organization could find full satisfaction. Germany became an astounding piece of organization, strong in every measure of defense, weak only in the national culture which was to be defended. Germany had risen by the sword; by the sword, then, it would continue to live. In military rigor lay the path to success."

But Bismarck's leadership was more nuanced than what Eugen describes. His plan was tempered with specific, strategic goals. Having achieved German unification, Bismarck was finished with the sword for the moment and preferred to maintain a pragmatic peace while he focused on growing Germany's economy. Politically, he recognized that France would be a perpetual antagonist so long as Germany held Alsace-Lorraine, and therefore France must be politically isolated. Thus, the key to Germany's success was to remain always on good terms with the other great powers.

Bismarck had the world's most powerful army, yet as Germany had no significant navy to speak of, Britain was unperturbed by these land forces. (Even the navies of France and Russia were a distant second and third at this time—Britain ruled the sea.) The Royal Navy rendered continental armies impotent, making them just as unlikely to reach English shores as had been the armies of Napoléon at the start of the century.* Bismarck had no wish to develop a navy and pursue colonial expansion overseas, which he felt would only antagonize his neighbors.

Bismarck's focus was domestic, and as he artfully crafted a web of alliances to secure peace, German industry grew at a rate that stunned the nations of the world. In 1871, Great Britain was the center of the Industrial Revolution and by far the world's leading coal producer, delivering 112 million tons of coal. Germany produced a mere 34 million tons in the same year. Though Great Britain maintained healthy growth, by 1911, astonishingly, the coal output of the two nations was equal.

The growth of German steel production, critical for war and heavy industry, was even more astounding. In 1871, German production of steel was negligible compared to Great Britain. By 1890, Germany moved closer, producing 2.4 million tons of steel compared to Great Britain's 3.6 million, and by 1896, German steel production surpassed Great Britain's. By 1914, Germany produced *more than two times* Great Britain's steel output (14 million tons to Britain's 6.5 million). Germany's rate of population growth, also essential for industry and war, outstripped the other European nations by a similar proportion.

The Germany that Bismarck created was very different from the place Theodor Diesel had left in 1850. By the time Rudolf returned to the land of his ancestors only twenty years after his father had left, all of Germany was united under the political sway of Bismarck and Wilhelm I. Success was in the air. Urban centers grew and modernized. German industry thrived under Bismarck's stewardship, but it was

---

* Napoléon's Grande Armée was vastly superior to the English army and he planned to invade the British Isles, but the French Navy was never able to provide safe passage across the channel for the French troops due to the strength of the British fleet. Eventually the Royal Navy met the combined French and Spanish navies on October 21, 1805, in the Battle of Trafalgar. The Royal Navy, led by Vice-Admiral Horatio Nelson in the flagship HMS *Victory*, triumphed, which definitively established Britain as the world's dominant sea power.

with an undercurrent of nationalism and a focus on maintaining a dominant military force. These were exhilarating times for a twelve-year-old prince waiting in the wings off the throne room, and for a twelve-year-old student determined to change the world with his intellect.

CHAPTER 4

Is Anyone Truly Self-Made?

Only a few city blocks from Heinrich Buz and his bustling Maschinenfabrik factory, Rudolf Diesel dedicated himself to the classrooms of Augsburg's Royal County Trade School. He'd escaped from the xenophobic discrimination and war in Paris to the terrors of extreme poverty and industrial enslavement in London. Through a stroke of good fortune and a family connection, now he was free. He lived in a stable home with loving relatives, and through wonderful serendipity, he found himself in a place perfectly designed to nurture his gifts for math and engineering. Eugen later recounted that his father "heard the names of the top executives and leading engineers [at Maschinenfabrik], and his youthful imagination added fire to his enthusiasm for the famous company."

Rudolf entered a three-year program at the Royal County Trade School, located on the second floor of a former cloister. The first floor of the cloister housed a small but impressive art gallery that included works by van Dyck and da Vinci. Diesel routinely circled the gallery below his school, indulging his fondness for the arts, thinking of his mother, then returning to his room to write letters to her describing what he'd seen.

Education in Germany, and most European countries at the time, followed a tracking system. Educators assessed the abilities of children at a very early age, then set the children on paths that strictly determined their future opportunities.

Many children were sent to vocational school that, for example, did not teach any foreign or classical languages. Others qualified for the *Gymnasium*, a humanist education that led to a career in law or government. Diesel, because of his engineering aptitude and because his uncle was a mathematics teacher in Augsburg, qualified for the more technically oriented *Realgymnasium*. Though this school offered no Greek, it did require limited study in philosophy and literature to complement the technical coursework.

Rudolf knew that an education was his ticket to a better life. Perhaps having experienced greater hardship than many of his classroom peers, he demurred at the recreations other boys enjoyed. He attended every lecture and studied exhaustively. An hour of piano practice each day and an occasional long walk or tour through the art gallery were his only distractions. He declared in letters to his parents that his aim was to be top in his class.

Rudolf received no funds from Theodor but was eventually able to take odd jobs and tutor in French and English to earn spending money. The Barnickels provided the rest.

Back in London, the Diesel family's circumstances were worsening. A January 1871 entry in the diary of Rudolf's sister Louise reveals that "provisions are diminishing" and that her parents were uncertain whether they could continue in London. On January 14, a relatively happy day, Louise wrote, "I went with father to explore some of the most important streets in London, Regent Street and the streets around there, but they are not even half as beautiful as the boulevards in Paris. What a difference between Paris and London. The streets here are so dirty and there is almost always fog. I like Paris so much better; it is so gay and gracious."

Her next entry says that Theodor is exhausted to the bone, and that her mother "is indisposed and suffers regular migraines."

Theodor, Elise, and their daughters eventually returned to Paris after the conclusion of the Franco-Prussian War. On September 11, 1872, Rudolf wrote to them of his academic plans, "Now I shall be for one year in the Koniglichen Kreisgwerbschule [Royal County Trade School, his third of three years]. Then I must go two years to the industrial school of Augsburg, and then I must go some years to the Polyteknikum of Munchen."

Rudolf and Louise frequently corresponded during his absence. Trying to keep things bright, they shared exciting new discoveries in their mutual love of music and the arts, made the occasional amused observation of the quirks of their parents as they helped each other to unload the stressful burden of challenging circumstances in the way a person can do only with a loved one. His older sister was a crucial outlet and source of intimacy for the lonely youth far away from his family.

Though the Barnickels had given Rudolf a great boost by rescuing him from a life of toil in a London factory, Theodor was set against any plan for his son to continue his studies. He wanted their fourteen-year-old back home, and he told Rudolf that the sooner he quit school, the sooner he could rejoin the family and become a wage earner, working with his hands as a craftsman. Theodor explained to Rudolf that there was honor to be found in working with one's hands.

Rudolf decided he needed to visit his family in Paris to change their minds. He was determined to persuade them of the merits of his continued education. Should he follow Theodor's direction to abandon his studies and begin as a craftsman, he would start a three-year unpaid apprenticeship, the custom of the day. Whether he chose school or work, he faced three years without a wage. What was the point then of abandoning his schooling?

He traveled forty hours from Augsburg to Paris by the cheapest train. It was 1874 and he hadn't seen his family in more than three years.

The reunion was bittersweet, marked by tense and unhappy conversations. The Diesel family had established their home and workshop at 127, boulevard Voltaire in the eleventh arrondissement, still on the Right Bank, though farther from the river and significantly less comfortable than their previous Paris home. The family's financial conditions were little better than what they'd been in London. Rudolf's musically talented older sister Louise was still giving piano lessons to contribute to the meager family funds. Theodor and Elise wanted their son back in Paris to help.

Rudolf, now sixteen, entered the family home with a mixture of anger and desperation. The hallowed halls of a German university were within his reach. The escapist daydreams of his Paris youth spent in technical museums had become his daily reality in Augsburg. Yet his parents, still not fully aware of his extraordinary gifts, couldn't grasp what they were asking him to give up. In his agitated state, Rudolf raised his voice to his mother, protesting that his parents had always been opposed to science and math, and that their lack of support for his education now, based on immediate financial concerns, was absurd. Rudolf told them he was certain to win a scholarship to the university, and from there he could accomplish great things.

Theodor came thundering to the defense of Elise, "Didn't she try to awaken your interest with child's games and stories? Do you think a man is what he is simply because of himself or does the education provided by his parents play a role?"

———

Tempers flared during the visit, neither side willing to budge. Then tragedy struck. Rudolf had been home only a few weeks when his older sister Louise, still a teenager herself, suddenly died. Family records from the time suggest she suffered from a heart condition. Rudolf's loving pen pal and confidante, the person to whom he felt most connected, was gone.

It was a terrible blow. From the time of Louise's death, Rudolf committed himself to playing the piano as a way to honor her.

Theodor's grief took a more bizarre turn. Initially he fell into deep despondence. As he slowly made his way back into the world, he did so as a changed man. He renounced his Christian faith and embraced a form of spiritualism. He declared himself a mystic and would conduct séances to connect with his daughter in the afterlife.

Theodor eventually made mysticism his career and assumed the title "Practicing Magnetopath." A few years later, in 1882, he published a book, *Magnetotherapie: Der animalische oder Lebens-Magnetismus.* He explained that magnetism is a form of electricity in the human nervous system. Some people, like himself, possessed excess magnetism and could transmit it to those with a deficiency, thereby healing illness. Rudolf described his father as having become delusional.

———————

Two letters from Augsburg arrived in Paris to help settle the argument in favor of Rudolf's return to Germany. The first was from Christoph Barnickel inviting Rudolf to return to Augsburg and stay in their home again and offering to sponsor him through the rest of his education. Christoph urged the Diesels to see that Rudolf had a gifted mind that should not be deprived of further education.

A second letter arrived from the head of the Augsburg school offering the family a stipend to cover Rudolf's travel and enrollment expenses.

Rudolf made his own wishes clear. Theodor and Elise relented. The Barnickels rescued him again, and the teen returned to Augsburg. He knew he could never count on financial support from his parents. They simply had none to give.

CHAPTER 5

Petroleum Upends the Game

ACROSS THE ATLANTIC, education and opportunity had a very different tenor from the regimented, feudal traditions of the Old World. In America, it was boom time. Towns and cities sprung from the dirt that bore little resemblance to the metropolises of Europe. While Paris had a subterranean infrastructure that supported millions of people, America's ramshackle towns appeared virtually overnight upon freshly cleared virgin lands. Buildings only a few decades old passed for historic landmarks, urban centers were supported by nascent or nonexistent infrastructure. Often the law enforcement and educational systems in these towns were equally underdeveloped. The new nation was in a period of hyper growth and continental expansion that emphasized speed and quantity over quality. America's focus was inward, managing the opportunity for expansion within the bounds of its own continent. There was hardly a care for the nationalist and cultural divides of Europe that had kept Diesel on the move throughout his adolescence.

The process of invention is inherently linked to the social and economic challenges of the time, and inventors like Rudolf Diesel were generally working in response to forces beyond their control. Amid

America's breakneck pace, one man would emerge above all others as the dominant force of industry. To understand the environment in which Diesel worked, it's important to understand John D. Rockefeller—the man who controlled much of the world's fossil-fuel production in the late nineteenth and early twentieth centuries, and who would accumulate more wealth than any man in history.

John was born in Richford, New York, in July 1839, nineteen years before Rudolf Diesel's birth in Paris. His father, William Avery "Big Bill" Rockefeller, was largely absent. John lived with his mother, Eliza Davison Rockefeller, older sister, Lucy, and four younger siblings, William Jr., Mary, and twins Franklin and Frances. In a nearby town, Big Bill had fathered half sisters to John, one a year older and one a year younger. The record is unclear as to whether John knew of these illegitimate relations.

With a parenting style reminiscent of Theodor Diesel's when he intentionally pushed young Rudolf down a hill, Bill once remarked, "I cheat my boys every chance I get. I want to make 'em sharp."

———————

John would later say of his father that he liked to carry as much as $1,000 in cash and he knew how to handle himself. When Bill returned from the road, he would spoil his children with gifts and money, as any narcissist craving adoration might do.

If Diesel came from an imperfect home, Rockefeller came from a broken one. Big Bill was a charlatan. He made his living as a con artist and peddler of patent medicines, usually traveling far from home to commit his frauds, then returning merrily with cash in hand.

Big Bill had another home, another wife, and other children, far away in a town near Ontario, Canada. He used a different name— Dr. William Levingston—when he was with his Ontario family.

Though he was no doctor of any kind, when riding into a new town far from either of his families to sell his phony wares, he posted a sign reading, "Dr. William A. Levingston appearing for one day only. All cases of cancer cured unless they are too far gone and then they can be greatly benefitted." It is interesting to note that the fathers of both Rudolf Diesel and John Rockefeller would end up making a living by selling phony medical remedies.

In 1843, the Rockefellers moved to Moravia, New York, a town of barely two thousand people, where Bill built a two-story clapboard home heated by a stovepipe from the kitchen. The walls were not plastered and the winter winds came whipping through seams between the boards. It was hard and gritty frontier living, especially when Bill was away. But the children could play in the fields, fish in the lake, farm a small plot of land, and they managed to get by.

In 1850, they moved to Oswego, New York, a port city trading post on Lake Ontario that had been connected to the Erie Canal in 1829. Fort Ontario, rebuilt in the decade before John arrived, was one of the few masonry structures in the town that was otherwise constructed mainly from local timber. Oswego had more bustle and opportunity than Moravia, but the family stayed there only three years. New York had had enough of Big Bill, and he'd had enough of New York. Due to debts and legal problems stemming from a paternity claim, Bill needed to leave the state altogether.

John was fourteen years old when the family moved to Strongville, Ohio, in 1853. As Augsburg held the ingredients to launch the career of Rudolf Diesel, the ground of Ohio held treasures for young Rockefeller in a literal sense. In Ohio, he established the foundation of his empire.

———————

Once the family was in Ohio, Bill became even less of a presence. He married the mother of his second family, while still married to John's mother, and several years after moving his first family to Ohio he returned there to announce a more formal separation. He never ceased contact completely, but John knew that he and his family could no longer count on Bill for anything. John became the de facto head of household, obliged to provide for his entire family.

In 1856, at age seventeen, Rockefeller landed a job as a financial records clerk for Hewitt & Tuttle, a grain-commission merchant company. John was quick with numbers, reliable, disciplined, and earnest. He dressed in a way that was proper and professional, though not extravagant.

A natural entrepreneur, he saved a bit of money and began to trade on the commodities market for his own account, making successful transactions in wheat and pork.

John started to earn a name for himself around the growing business district in Cleveland. When he was eighteen, he befriended Maurice Clark, a twenty-eight-year-old Englishman who worked at a produce house down the street from John's office. Clark remarked that Rockefeller already had "the reputation of being a young bookkeeper of more than ordinary ability and reliability."

John had been working three and a half years at Hewitt & Tuttle when Tuttle retired. John capably took on the responsibilities. Tuttle had been making $2,000 annually, but for the same work Hewitt refused to pay young Rockefeller more than $700.

Rockefeller already had a sense of his own worth. He felt underpaid, undervalued, and resentful. Here, his friendship with Clark presented a way out.

Clark approached Rockefeller with a partnership proposal. They would each invest $2,000 to organize a trading company to buy and sell produce. Frugal and hardworking, John had already socked away $800, but was still well short of the necessary investment.

Then Big Bill made another appearance in John's life and his behavior was predictable. He told John that he'd always planned to give each of his children $1,000 upon their twenty-first birthday, and the occasion was now only months away for John. He said he'd be willing to advance the sum. He added, "But, John, the rate is ten."

Ten percent was nearly double the market interest rate of the time. John knew there was no sense in negotiating terms with his father. It was a scheme, and he could either play or not. He decided that it was quick money on offer, and he was confident that he could grow it then pay off the usurious loan. He took the money.

Clark and Rockefeller had talent and drive, but they needed more capital. They took meetings with potential investors who had noticed the ambitious pair, including George W. Gardner.

Gardner came from an elite Cleveland family. He brought money, connections to banking and law, as well as an additional air of respectability to this young upstart partnership. The three men agreed on terms and Gardner bought in.

Rockefeller was nearly ten years younger than either of his partners. Though he'd argued that age was an unimportant ingredient to value, not only was John relegated to third place in stature, but his name was dropped from the firm altogether. The firm was renamed Clark, Gardner & Company—a powerful sting to the proud young man.

But Rockefeller proved there was one thing more important to him than recognition or any superficial accolade that serves pride. What mattered was money.

What began at Clark, Gardner & Company initiated a pattern that would continue for the rest of Rockefeller's life. When he accumulated wealth, he went to great lengths to conceal it, an instinct opposite that of his father, who would flash bundles of cash in public. He also instructed those who became wealthy through their professional associations with him that they should conceal their new fortunes too. Any flaunting of riches by his executives earned a penalty. Not because he had any aversion to the finer things, but because the attention attracted by showiness could make earning additional money more difficult.

Rockefeller recognized that his apparent subordinate status at the new firm had the merit of good business sense. Clark and Gardner were the names the bankers knew and respected, and so he accepted the change to the firm's name.

What he found increasingly intolerable though was Gardner's bon vivant lifestyle. One afternoon while Rockefeller dutifully worked on the firm's books, Gardner breezed through the office and announced that he'd just bought a new yacht for $2,000. In a friendly, sporting way he suggested that John put down the ledgers and join him and a few others for an afternoon pleasure cruise.

Rockefeller's response is emblematic of what earned him money, enemies, and very few intimates—unless they shared his puritanical discipline and love of earning: "George Gardner, you're the most extravagant man I ever knew! The idea of a young man like you, just getting a start in life, owning an interest in a yacht! You're injuring your credit at the banks—your credit and mine. . . . No, I won't go on your yacht. I don't even want to see it!"

Wealth in plain sight infuriated him. It was bad for business.

The third leg of the partnership stool was also a problem for Rockefeller. Maurice Clark had more in common with Big Bill than he did with John. Clark smoked, drank, swore, had no use for religion, and was on the run from the law in his home country of England. Conversely, John cared deeply for family, was religious and tempered. Having a fugitive and a bon vivant as his partners was untenable.

Despite these differences Clark, Gardner & Company thrived through the Civil War years. Because John was the primary wage earner for his siblings and mother, he was able to defer military service. He was a "$300 man," paying that sum to the government in lieu of joining the war effort.

The commodities firm branched out from produce to trading in oil, which was locally abundant, and with earnings from successful trades they invested in a refinery. Despite the financial successes, the clashes among the partners grew fiercer. Again, Rockefeller knew his worth, and he knew he didn't need Clark and Gardner to succeed. He needed only more capital.

Rockefeller finally determined that complete dissolution of the partnership was the only way forward for him. He lined up financial backing from Sam Andrews, a local businessman who had been a client of the firm. When the next conflagration with his partners occurred, Rockefeller called their bluff to carry on without him. The threat of dissolution had been merely a tactic that Clark and Gardner used to try to contain their ambitious partner, but this time, with capital behind him, Rockefeller insisted on seeing the dissolution through. He forced his partners to a best-bid auction for the firm—winner take all.

Of course, Rockefeller won. His best-bid of $72,500 (approximately $1,300,000 in 2022) seemed an exorbitant amount at the time. In February 1865, he reconstituted the firm as Rockefeller & Andrews. Among its other businesses, the firm already owned one of the larger oil refineries in Cleveland, though it was just one of many in Cleveland. Rockefeller was now captain of his own ship, and though oil was for the time only a side business, he was beginning to see the potential of the petroleum market.

Mark Twain named the remaining decades of the nineteenth century after the Civil War the Gilded Age. With the exception of a recession from 1882 to 1885, this was a period of hyper economic growth. Industry, landmark patents, and business innovations flourished right alongside tricksters, hustlers, and charlatans. Markets were active and saw a steady increase in value. The banker Thomas Mellon later noted of the decade from 1863 to 1873, "One had only to buy anything and wait, to sell it at a profit."

Markets were grossly inefficient though, and regulations were slow to keep pace with the rapid growth. Industry became less fragmented. The small-business model of proprietor and apprentice, like Theodor Diesel's workshop, evolved into a more centralized form of industry. The multitude of small businesses began to give way to large corporate entities with market influence and thousands of employees. These corporate trusts enjoyed enormous advantages of scale over small-business competitors. With regard to the labor force, the well-organized trusts established an imbalance of power over the working class that was, as yet, entirely unorganized in this new economic environment. Clever men, particularly in industries such as oil, steel, tobacco, and sugar, obtained labor cheaply, which padded profits, ushering in the age of the robber baron.

In 1867, Rockefeller finally met the business partner with whom his fortunes would soar—Henry Flagler. Flagler had wealth and connections, and he wanted in on the oil game. Rockefeller and Andrews owned the largest refinery in Cleveland and needed more capital to grow their business, so they teamed up with Flagler and renamed the enterprise Rockefeller, Andrews & Flagler.

Flagler practiced strict self-discipline, was a churchgoer, a devoted husband, didn't drink, and prioritized business above all else. A ruthless form of business.

He and Rockefeller shared a philosophy that they should live with stability at home so that they could be revolutionary in the office.* And it was in the office that this team became a fierce and indomitable force. Flagler would be Rockefeller's most trusted colleague for the rest of his life.

Flagler had no formal legal training, but nonetheless was the designated lawyer of the group. In 1870, as Rudolf Diesel fled Paris for London then Augsburg, Flagler wrote the act of incorporation to create the legal entity Standard Oil. It was a document of remarkable brevity, less than two hundred words, simply declaring their right to do business. This founding document set the course for what became the most powerful company in history. So powerful that it could control international markets, promote or stifle related innovations, and influence global wars.

Rockefeller later said that he decided he must go all in for the oil business after learning the story of Pithole, Pennsylvania.

In January 1865, a middle-aged farmer named Thomas Brown strolled alongside Pithole Creek on a frosty afternoon. As he walked,

---

* Novelist Gustave Flaubert advised, "Be regular and orderly in your life, so that you may be violent and original in your work."

he held a twig in front of him to use as a sort of divining rod for petroleum, then sought after primarily as a fuel for illumination. When the twig bent to the ground, Brown began to dig in that spot.

With the luck of a blind squirrel, days later he struck a subterranean oil reserve that delivered two hundred barrels of crude per day.

News of Brown's strike spread like wildfire. Prospectors flocked in.

By May, wooden oil derricks littered the landscape along the creek.

By June, there was a town. Two streets lined with shops, saloons, offices, and dance halls.

By December, there were fifty hotels, several schools, churches, gambling halls, and banks. The population soared above fifteen thousand.

As the armies of the Civil War disbanded, soldiers moved into this type of oil town. Pithole was home to lieutenants, captains, and even several colonels. The growth of the town was faster than law and order could manage. In less than a year, what had been a barren stretch of landscape with undisturbed wildlife was suddenly a frenzied, near-lawless frontier town that produced more than six thousand barrels of oil every twenty-four hours.

Lamps burning kerosene refined from crude oil had become the dominant form of illumination around the world, and Rockefeller became convinced that he must dedicate his efforts exclusively to the petroleum business.*

The key to dominance, especially in a commodity business, is advantageous distribution. Rockefeller needed to reach new markets with his oil, and he needed to do so at a cost lower than his competition.

While Rockefeller owned many oil wells himself, he came to dominate the refining stage of the petroleum business, which was his first step in building a superior position over his rivals. Already owning the

---

* Within four years, the Pithole oil reserves ran dry. Most of the construction was sold as scrap and used to build the homes and offices in nearby towns. By the end of the decade, Pithole had an official population of six people.

largest refinery in Cleveland, Rockefeller had the advantage of scale when negotiating transportation contracts with the railroads for the kerosene from his refineries. He knew that if he could lower Standard's cost of doing business, he could reduce the price of his product, if only temporarily, to a level where his competition couldn't turn a profit. Rockefeller dispatched Flagler to negotiate secret agreements with the heads of the railroads for better transportation pricing for his product over the rail lines. Once he secured an advantageous deal with the railroads, he could drive his competition out of business.

This ruthless pricing scheme came in the form of "rebates."

Oil refineries and the railroads suffered from the same problem. Both were commodity industries. One barrel of Cleveland crude was the same as any other, just as passage for that barrel from the Pennsylvania fields to New York was the same on one rail as another. There was no differentiation on quality, which is the very definition of commodity.* The only way to differentiate was on price. Rockefeller and the overlords of the rail system realized they could solve this problem to mutual advantage.

Both the refineries and the rail system suffered from excess capacity and suicidal price wars. The way to fix this problem was through collusion.

In 1872, Tom Scott of the Pennsylvania Railroad gathered his competitors from the New York Central and the Erie Railroad, and together they reached an exclusive deal with Standard Oil. They made the agreement in utter secrecy.

Each of the four firms became a shareholder in the South Improvement Company (SIC), a type of shell organization the federal government had introduced just after the Civil War to promote rebuilding. The shareholders pre-agreed to an amount of oil to ship in set proportions across the three rail systems. This halted the price competition among the railroads.

---

* Years later, crude oil from regions of Mexico and Russia was of a lower quality, but the oil from this region of America was generally of the same quality.

Standard, the only refinery in the scheme, committed to shipping a massive amount of oil. With this committed load for oil, the railroads could now simplify their operations by sending trains with only oil tanker cars, rather than an assortment of cargo cars, which further improved the bottom line for the railroads.

In return, Standard Oil received large price rebates from the railroads, so that the cost to Standard was 50 percent the rate paid by all other refineries. In a commodity business competing on price, this massive cost advantage allowed Standard to obliterate the competition.

And, because Standard owned the transport commitment for *all* oil going over the rails, Rockefeller was able to resell excess rail passage to other refineries at the full price, then collect the rebate. Standard Oil made rebate money even on the oil that wasn't from its own refineries.

It was a brutal scheme, brilliantly negotiated with questionable ethics. Biographers and the press called the results of this advantage the "Cleveland Massacre." Standard Oil either absorbed or ruined every other refinery in Cleveland. Ida Tarbell, the antagonistic biographer of Rockefeller who produced award-winning journalism covering Standard Oil in subsequent years, called the South Improvement Company scheme the "original sin" of Rockefeller and Standard Oil.

Rockefeller gave the ultimatum, join us or perish, to every competing Cleveland refinery. He even said the same to his own younger brother Frank, who owned a small refinery in Cleveland. "We have a partnership with the railroads. We are going to buy out all the refineries in Cleveland. We will give everyone a chance to come in. We will give you a chance. Those who refuse will be crushed."

Rockefeller's defense of his business practices reveals his sense of mandate for his no-holds-barred tactics. "I believe the power to make money is a gift from God—just as are the instincts for art, music, literature, the doctor's talent, the nurse's . . ." He believed, or would have others believe, that he saved the oil industry, that other men were less suited to build it than he.

Through the 1870s and '80s, Standard Oil invested in the construction of pipelines to connect the wells of the oil fields with the refineries. Enormous profits gave the firm the capital to invest in staying steps ahead of the competition. A gang of twenty-eight men could bury a six-inch pipe in a ditch at a pace of two-thirds of a mile per day. By this method, Standard Oil built a pipeline network connecting Philadelphia, Baltimore, Buffalo, Pittsburgh, and Cleveland to the oil fields of Pennsylvania. They even connected Bayonne, New Jersey, to a refinery on Long Island with a pipe that ran under the Hudson River, across the southern edge of Manhattan's Central Park, and under the East River.

Anyone looking to move crude oil from the wells had to go through Standard Oil.

Rockefeller then moved into the retail market in the 1880s. Standard Oil wagons pulled by horses moved across country lanes and city streets bringing kerosene for cooking and lighting directly to people's homes.

By the early 1880s, the goal of monopoly in America was complete. Though Rockefeller declared his ability to make money was a gift from God, he was very careful not to show it off. Secrecy was tantamount. Once when Rockefeller was riding a train back to Cleveland, a fellow passenger remarked on a beautiful and extravagant mansion on a hill, visible from the train. The home was owned by a senior executive at Standard Oil.

Upon arrival at the Cleveland office, Rockefeller reviewed the payroll books, determined the executive was overpaid, and reduced his salary. Rockefeller knew that great wealth attracted competition, negative coverage in the press, and the unwanted attention of the federal government.

Rockefeller invested enormous capital to build the infrastructure that would ensure the massive and steady supply of oil to the world.

What he relied upon, but could not control, was the world's steady demand for his product.

———————

John D. Rockefeller's early years are a great contrast to those of Rudolf Diesel. In their youths, though born nineteen years and an ocean apart, they both endured family instability, moving from place to place, scraping for a better life. Both witnessed harsh poverty and suffered it themselves. But in their early teens they encountered very different circumstances that set them on divergent trajectories.

Rudolf had Theodor as his head of house. Though Theodor struggled in the role, he loved his son and valued his son getting an education. When the opportunity arose to give his son a better chance, he begrudgingly took it, even though it meant the loss of having Rudolf's assistance at home. Rudolf had endured a difficult childhood, but once the Barnickels took him in, he was no longer at risk of falling into poverty or being sent to join a child labor force. He could view the world through a philosophical, academic lens. This was a luxury Rockefeller did not have.

Rockefeller did not pursue schooling; there was no one to offer him a route to higher education. As his family's sole breadwinner, he had a family to feed, and he got right to work. Rather than seeking a formal education, he pursued corporate success and learned on the job. Rather than observing industrial growth through a moral lens and working to improve conditions, he fed the growth of industry and rationalized making money as doing God's work.

This early, critical difference between the childhoods of Rockefeller and Diesel proved to have lasting effect. Beginning with his arrival in Ohio, Rockefeller spent a lifetime chasing wealth, recognizing how economic and political systems worked then playing the systems to his advantage. Conversely, Diesel believed a higher education could ensure him a position of long-term security from which he could then pursue engineering and social solutions to address the problems he recognized in economic and political systems.

Yet Rockefeller was no less an innovator than Diesel. Throughout his career he would have to manage the threat of alternative technologies that could disrupt his control of the oil supply and the global demand for it. History has judged his methods to be unsparing, and often criminal. The methods behind his epoch-making success set the stage for a rivalry with Rudolf Diesel which, in the end, would make him a murder suspect.

———

In 1870, the world was in flux with regard to the types of fuels available for use, and the types of machines that could burn them.

At the time, there were three primary demands for fuel: illumination, heat, and work.

The riches of Standard Oil from the time of its founding to the early twentieth century came from the sale of kerosene for illumination. The process of refining crude oil to make valuable kerosene also produced the by-product gasoline, which was considered a worthless liquid to be discarded. Though in the present day most associate Rockefeller with oil and gasoline for the combustion engine, this market came much later.

Fuels for illumination prior to the nineteenth century were commonly animal- and plant-derived oils such as fish, whale, olive, or nut. By the 1800s, the more industrial regions of the world began to burn gaseous fuels such as hydrogen, methane, propane, butane, or natural gas for illumination because these were less messy and easier to acquire. (There is some evidence that more than a thousand years ago in some parts of China natural gas was burned and piped through bamboo reeds for illumination.) By the late 1800s, the liquid petroleum-derivative kerosene began to replace other fuels for lighting, then kerosene was in turn gradually replaced by electricity over the next century.

The second major market for fuels was heat, for which wood and coal were the main natural resources. Then, in 1882, Ludvig Nobel introduced his design for the first commercially viable oil-burning stove for heat to Europe.* The oil stove burned more safely and reliably, and with far less smoke clouding residential areas than did coal- and wood-burning stoves. A similar model became popular in America several years later. The new technology eventually replaced coal-heating stoves and created a second surge in global demand for petroleum.

The third major market, which began as the smallest and ultimately became the largest, was work. The earliest forms of work didn't come from machines at all, but from draft animals. This was the inspiration for the marketing technique devised by James Watt in the late 1700s to define a measure of power that could compare the output of his steam engine to the power of a draft horse. The world adopted this definition and thereafter used the term "horsepower" as a measure of engine power.†

The early engines to deliver work, such as the steam engine designed by Watt, were *external* combustion engines that burned wood or coal. The first *internal* combustion engines, like Otto's prizewinning engine of 1867, ran on the same gaseous fuels that could burn for illumination, typically coal gas, though by 1870 engineers had begun to experiment with internal combustion designs that could run on liquid fuels such as kerosene and, later, gasoline. These internal combustion engines burning liquid fuel were broadly referred to as "oil engines."

The first commercially viable oil engines (these were based on the Otto design) appeared in the mid- and late 1880s, such as the engine for Karl Benz's motor car. Eventually, the liquid fuel gasoline emerged as the preferred fuel. Though safer than gaseous fuels, gasoline is highly flammable, emits dangerous fumes that are potentially lethal in

---

* At the turn of the century, three players dominated the world's oil market: the Rockefellers; the Rothschilds, whose oil operations were in southern Russia along the Caspian Sea; and the Nobel family, whose headquarters were in Saint Petersburg, Russia.

† Watt calculated that a horse could pull with a force of 180 pounds. With such a force applied to a mill wheel that had a radius of twelve feet, the horse could turn the wheel 2.4 times per minute. To calculate power, Watt needed to account for the full circumference of the circle, or wheel ($2\pi r$), so the full equation is *1 horsepower = 180 pounds x 2.4 x 2π x 12 feet = 33,000 foot-pounds/minute*. (Watt rounded up.)

confined spaces, and is hazardous to store and transport. Though gasoline-powered engines became more common through the end of the nineteenth century, this was still a small market relative to the kerosene market for illumination, and in fact, global kerosene production was greater than gasoline production until 1916.

In contrast to light liquid fuels like gasoline and kerosene, heavy fuels, such as the viscous oils drawn from nuts, vegetables, coal, or even other petroleum derivatives, are safe to store and not flammable unless at extremely high temperature. However, these safer and far less expensive oils were impractical as a fuel in the early combustion engines of the Otto design. Otto's design could burn only the easily combusted light fuels.

The inventors of engines that Diesel admired in museums and classrooms had to take into account the real-world constraints such as the availability of metals to construct the engine as well as the fuels to power it. When Cugnot built the engine for his steam car in 1770, he did not have access to precise metal fittings and had to use rope and leather to seal valves. And though an engineer may prefer a certain type of fuel, technical decisions about the engine must be determined based on which fuels will be in steady supply. For example, by 1870, coal was in abundance in Great Britain, and therefore the British rail system ran almost entirely with locomotive engines that burned coal. By contrast, in American in 1870, with its virgin forests, the rail system ran mostly with engines burning wood, until deforestation became a problem.

In the second half of the nineteenth century when America (then other nations) tapped into massive stores of petroleum and perfected refining techniques to produce kerosene and gasoline, the sudden and phenomenal abundance of this fuel that was more easily transportable than coal not only had economic and geopolitical implications but also implications for engineering designs. Those who were building the engines of the future had to consider which fuels were attainable.

The behavior of the firms competing to supply fuels was guided by corporate profit, self-interest, and, often, corruption. Rockefeller aimed to get the world addicted to kerosene as the fuel for illumination. When he penetrated markets in China that were using nut and vegetable oils for illumination, as had been the case there for centuries, Rockefeller dumped cheap kerosene on the Chinese market, undercutting the prices of the nut and vegetable oil producers, even supplying free lamps designed to burn kerosene. Once consumers had adapted to lighting devices that burned kerosene and Rockefeller had his hooks in, he was free to hike prices. It was a clear example of supply dictating the form of demand. Because Rockefeller could leverage his control of the fuel supply, he was effectively able to dictate the type of machine people would use. His success in China was fortunate for the manufacturers of kerosene-burning lamps and unfortunate for the manufacturers of lamps that burned nut oil. The skill of the engineers who designed and manufactured either lamp had little to do with the success or failure of their project.

The engineering arena that Rudolf Diesel entered as a young boy in Augsburg was not so simple as a one-to-one relationship between an inventor and his customer. Even to achieve his vision for a more compact, efficient, and cleaner engine might not be enough to win the day. The other stakeholders—customers, competitors, and fuel suppliers—would have great influence over how any new technology was embraced—or rejected—by the marketplace. As Diesel finished his education and prepared to enter the real world, he would find that he wasn't playing a one-to-one game with the customer, but a game of poker that pitted him against industrialists, monopolies, governments, and competing engineers, each with their own interests.

CHAPTER 6

Pursuit of the Ideal

RUDOLF'S NOTEBOOKS WERE filled with sketches of family members, engines, and descriptions of science experiments he intended to try. He committed two pages under the heading "*Jeffersons Zehn Gebote fur das Praktische Leben*" (Thomas Jefferson's Ten Rules for a Useful Life), the first rule being "Never put off till tomorrow what you can do today." Following Jefferson's advice, Diesel studied relentlessly.

In 1875, he graduated from the Augsburg polytechnic school with the highest marks in the history of the school. For Rudolf this was not just a matter of pride. He knew the living conditions that his family presently endured also awaited him should his schooling reach a dead end. If he could excel in school and win a scholarship, he could avoid the round-trip back to abject poverty.

He had been assured entry to Munich's esteemed university Technische Hochschule München (prior to 1868 called Polytechnische Hochschule), if only he could pay for it. From Munich, the head of school, Professor Karl von Bauernfeind, had heard of Rudolf's academic achievements and traveled to Augsburg so he could examine the seventeen-year-old himself.

After meeting with Rudolf, he was so impressed that he granted the young student a scholarship of 500 gulden (1,000 German marks, or about $6,000 today) per year for Rudolf to attend the university. Rudolf accepted.

In Munich, he became friends with and studied alongside many of the most talented engineering minds in Germany. One guest lecturer had a particularly powerful influence. Carl von Linde, pioneer of refrigeration, a successful industrialist, and one of the great inventors of the day, was Rudolf's thermodynamics lecturer and would later become his mentor.

In 1872, Linde had designed a concept for mechanical refrigeration that would eliminate the need for ice to be hauled from frozen ponds and lakes then stored in ice houses. The keen eye of Heinrich Buz took note of Linde's work. Buz brought Linde into the fold at M.A. and sponsored his research from 1873 to 1877, when Linde released a reliable refrigerator using compressed ammonia as the cooling agent. The pair then founded Linde AG in 1879 to promote the invention and execute international licensing arrangements for the technology, the business model typically followed by inventors of the era.

Right away, Linde identified Diesel as a rising star and admired his brilliance, his work ethic, and his humility. Diesel spent countless hours in the school's laboratory and machine shop, and to keep his single suit clean for Sundays he reported to his classes and lectures wearing his sturdy blue work clothes that were the traditional uniform of the Bavarian working class.

In his youth, Rudolf had seemed so different from his father, but something of Theodor's grinding work ethic, his rolled-up sleeves, and calloused, black-stained hands had passed to Rudolf. The young scholar made for an interesting sight when compared to his more formally dressed peers who had money for nice clothes and a propensity for well-manicured appearances.

In January 1877, while attending the university, eighteen-year-old Rudolf became a German citizen. The German military authority granted him a "scholar's deferment" from the compulsory three-year military service.*

Rudolf taught math and French to fellow students in his spare time, and soon earned enough to rent a piano to play for recreation. But he dedicated most of his hours to his studies. In his coursework, Diesel naturally gravitated to thermodynamics—particularly the study of the relationship between heat and mechanical energy. He investigated the theories of Nicolas Carnot (1796–1832), the French engineer and pioneer of thermodynamics.

Carnot acknowledged that the steam engine required massive and heavy metal vessels, like the three-ton teapot of the *fardier à vapeur* (the 1770 design of the steam car), to contain the combusting gases at high temperatures and pressures. Carnot wrote in his 1824 treatise, "We are obliged to limit ourselves to the use of a slight fall of caloric heat, while the combustion of the coal furnishes the means of procuring a very great one."

Basically, Carnot is admitting the gross inefficiency of the steam engine. Large amounts of energy were not directed to useful work but were lost as the heat and pressure were used to move the large and cumbersome engine parts, or as the pressure and heat simply leaked from the engine. Carnot had proved a theoretical capability for great efficiency, but the steam engine did not achieve anything close to what was possible in theory. Diesel marveled at this disparity and became obsessed with eliminating it.

On July 11, 1878, Diesel sat among forty peers, high in the rows of the stadium-style lecture hall, as though a spectator at a Spanish bull-

---

* Rudolf was pleased to have German citizenship because the status facilitated his educational opportunities and access to scholarship money. Since Rudolf was born in Paris and hadn't registered for citizenship in Germany (nor set foot there for his first twelve years), his citizenship was previously unsettled. Theodor had frequently considered attaining French citizenship, and Rudolf had pleaded with his father not to do so, as the father's status would transfer to the children. A French citizenship would have hindered Rudolf's education in Germany, and French compulsory military service at the time was for a period of nine years.

fight. Professor Linde's voice rang from below, through the auditorium. He reviewed the calculations written on the chalkboard that explained the ideal Carnot cycle, which was the crux of his lecture on theoretical machine design.

Linde then revealed calculations demonstrating that the best steam engines converted only 6 to 10 percent of the ideal theorized by Carnot. In a flash, the vague notion that Rudolf had felt on the London Bridge came into sharper focus. He bolted forward in his chair, hanging on each word from his professor. In an excited flurry, Rudolf wrote in the margin of his student notebook, which is now in the Maschinenfabrik (M.A.N.) archives, "Can one build steam engines which realize the perfect cycle process without their being very complicated?"

Diesel came to be obsessed with engine inefficiency. Finding the answer to the question he'd scribbled in the margin of his notebook motivated his life's work. Later in his career, he referenced this moment as the inception of his engine design effort. In 1913, he wrote of the effect of Linde's 1878 lecture, "The wish to realize the ideal Carnot process ruled my existence from then on . . . the idea followed me uninterruptedly."

His comments in a notebook months later note that the challenge was to find a way for an engine to do useful work without first having to generate steam, and in a way that was more efficient and could deliver more power than the still relatively new Otto engine. "But how is it practically feasible? That is precisely to discover!!"

His inclination to dispense with water and steam as an intermediary step is fundamental to internal combustion, and though Otto had explored this change, there was as yet no reliable engine for industry other than steam. But the question remained: Could Diesel design an engine better than the one Otto had? Otto's engine (which burned gaseous fuels) was more compact given that it required no boiler for water and steam, no furnace or chimney apparatus, but it was limited to small power operations, typically under a few horsepower. And Otto's fuel efficiency, though a doubling of steam power, was still a paltry 12 to 14 percent.

Diesel began his work at the dawn of the age of oil, in an area of the world where oil was naturally scarce. Augsburg was fertile ground for an engineer, but it had no oil, as was the case for much of Western Europe. This natural disadvantage elevated the importance of engine efficiency and the prospect of alternative fuels. European industrialists and military leaders, and therefore Diesel, wanted to avoid dependence on foreign oil tycoons who controlled supply. Though Diesel would have other breakthroughs, engine efficiency, in part driven by this scarcity, was his chief aim from the outset.

———————

Diesel was on track to graduate from the university in July 1879, but an epidemic of typhoid fever ripped through Munich that summer. Rudolf fell seriously ill with the disease. He spent months fighting the fever, then recovered the strength to work again, but had missed the window for his final exams and needed to wait to reschedule.

Linde offered a helping hand. He recommended Rudolf to the machinery company Sulzer Brothers for an interim job. Sulzer had a manufacturing plant in Winterthur, Switzerland, that built Linde products as well as steam engines and boilers.*

After three months in Winterthur, where Rudolf got valuable factory job training and made what would become important industry connections, he returned to Munich to prepare for his final examination. The test was entirely oral, consisting of discourse and questions with each of his professors. On January 15, 1880, Diesel completed the grueling examinations. As had become his habit, he received the highest grades in the history of the institution.

Rudolf was no longer the skinny adolescent in threadbare clothes who fearfully crossed national borders with empty hands and empty pockets, without even a resolved status of citizenship. By 1880, he was at the very top of the elite German university system. This young refugee was now a dynamo ready to make his mark.

———————

* The Sulzers became lifelong friends of Diesel, and thirty-four years later offered his son Eugen a similar internship.

CHAPTER 7

——+——

Meant for More Than a Salary

DIESEL'S NATURAL GENIUS was now university-trained and, for the first time in his life, he had no trouble making money. As soon as he has passed his exams, Linde offered him a job.

The ice machines manufactured by Sulzer Brothers were selling well in Germany and Switzerland. Linde decided that Diesel, with his Parisian roots, was a natural fit to join the new plant in Paris that handled sales and service of the machines in France. Baron Moritz von Hirsch had purchased the rights to Linde's French patents and built a manufacturing plant on the Quai de Grenelle, near the future site of the Eiffel Tower. Diesel joined as an apprentice on March 20, 1880, at a salary of 1,200 francs per year, a modest but livable wage.

By December, Linde promoted Diesel to "direktor" of the Paris plant and doubled his salary. By August 1881, Linde doubled the salary again to 4,800 francs per year.

Sulzer manufactured the component parts and sent them to Diesel, who was responsible for the design, fabrication, and installation of the machines. It was an enormous responsibility for a twenty-three-year-old, but commensurate with his talents.

————

Customers of Linde's machines used the ice for industrial purposes, to chill brewery tanks or refrigerate meat and other perishables. There was no element of the process to maintain purity of the water so that the resulting ice would be potable. Diesel recognized the market need for table ice at restaurants and in the home. Ice pure enough to put in a drink.

In a year, Diesel earned his first patent. On September 24, 1881, France issued the patent for *carafes frappes transparentes* ("bottled clear ice"). A month later came his French patent for potable ice in blocks. Seemingly incongruous, the future inventor of the Diesel engine also invented the ice cube. Diesel capably held down his day job while also indulging his natural craving for innovation. All the while he continued to ponder the puzzle of engine efficiency that first intrigued him in his university days.

————

With a bit of money in his pocket, Diesel became a sharp dresser. He wore a Stetson top hat, popular in America at the time (not a cowboy hat, closer to a bowler), and neatly tailored suits. Rudolf had always had a view from afar to the wealthy class—many of his fellow students came from wealthy families, his mentor Linde was already fabulously rich, even his father's well-heeled customers during his early years in Paris had caught Rudolf's eye. Having spent his youth in frayed clothing mended by his mother, once Rudolf had disposable income, he satisfied his pent-up demand for some of the finer things.

The purchase of a Stetson may have been influenced by his first love affair. An American artist and divorcée living in Paris named Mrs. Fullerton captured his heart. The two were introduced in 1880 by Rudolf's sister Emma.

On December 5, 1880, Fullerton wrote to Emma of Diesel, "He is a nice, modest, refined young man! He has an artistic temperament—a poetic temperament—and a mind far above the generality of young men. I think I understand him pretty well."

Months later when Mrs. Fullerton decided to return to America, Diesel nearly abandoned his work with Linde to follow her there. He wrote to his sister that his lover attracted his heart "as the needle of a magnet to the North Pole." But in the end, Fullerton returned alone and Diesel remained in Paris.

Most Thursday evenings Diesel visited the home of his German-born friend Ernest Brandes, a prosperous merchant in Paris. One Thursday not long after Fullerton's departure, he was surprised to meet a beautiful woman at his friend's home. Her name was Martha Flasche and Brandes had just hired her to come from Germany to be the governess for his children. This blond-haired, blue-eyed woman with a striking figure was witty and charming. She loved to play piano, and sang beautifully in English, French, and German. She'd read the latest novels from Britain and the philosophers from France, and she held a deep appreciation for the arts. She was also the supervisor of the children's education, refined and well educated herself, just as Rudolf's own mother had been in her role as governess prior to her marriage.

In the coming weeks, Rudolf didn't miss another Thursday at the Brandes home, and soon added a few more weekday evenings as an eager participant singing along with Martha and accompanying her on the piano. Rudolf observed that the two were "broadly and voraciously interested in the arts."

They fell in love. But not all Rudolf's friends were enthusiastic about the match. Rudolf spoke French without a trace of a foreign accent, he had come to be accepted in Paris as a native, which indeed he was. But Martha's German heritage was instantly apparent to Rudolf's Parisian friends. With her heavily German-accented French, she had little hope of assimilation in France. As a career move for Rudolf, the marriage was disadvantageous.

But Rudolf never thought in such terms, neither in matters of work nor love. He intended to marry Martha.

In May 1883, while Rudolf began a busy summer of work, Martha left for an extended trip to Germany. She had been yearning to visit her family, as well as to build a relationship with Rudolf's parents, who had moved to Munich.

During the several months apart, a heartsick Rudolf wrote a series of letters to Martha that seem to be the work of a poet rather than a scientist. On May 16, he wrote to her relating his daydream of hearing her voice:

> *I feel as if my body becomes lighter and lighter, lifts itself up from the earth, no longer physical, and [with] a sweet, sweet angel voice, saying, "Rudolf, I love you."*

Weeks later, Rudolf wrote again, revealing his poetic side, to describe the way Martha provided a certain balance in his otherwise arduous and work-filled existence by infusing his life with light and happiness:

> *Be my little star and lighten the darkness, the deep darkness of my heart, my heart is like an unlighted lake, surrounded by black fir and rocks, which is so black at night that one cannot see it. But when such a little star comes with its golden sheen, then he mirrors it a thousandfold in his waves and it is not dark anymore, but shimmering and alive from the light of its star.*

Rudolf added, "Only two or three more letters, and I will then only write, I come, I fly to you, into your arms, out of which I will then never go for the rest of my life.

"No woman is ever more loved than you by me, no one, and no man has ever had more expectations for joy than I since you told me you wanted to give me your love, your heart and your life."

Rudolf married Louise "Martha" Flasche on November 24, 1883, in Munich. Theodor and Elise attended the small ceremony, along with Christoph Barnickel and his new wife, Emma, Rudolf's sister, who was twenty-seven years younger than her husband. Barnickel's first wife, Theodor's cousin Betty, had died of typhus (outbreaks of typhus were common in that era) two years earlier.

Barnickel's remarriage had the effect of altering his relationship to Rudolf from uncle to brother-in-law. The match also brought Diesel even closer to his sister and Barnickel. Emma partially filled the void that his older sister Louise's death had left. He and Emma corresponded, in particular about the increasingly strange behavior of their parents, who had become financially dependent on Rudolf, a situation Rudolf accepted with resignation. Theodor wrote frequent letters to Rudolf asking for money. Rudolf was willing to provide funds to help his parents live more comfortably but was frustrated to learn that the funds enabled Theodor's continued pursuit of mysticism. He and Emma exchanged letters in which they shared their irritation with their father. Rudolf also wrote to Martha of his annoyance with Theodor, "I know from experience that one-sided spiritualist studies can turn men into real fools . . ."

In the same 1883 letter to Martha, he added his belief in the value of free and undogmatic thinking: "One does not have to be a spiritualist, a Protestant, a Catholic, or a Jew in order to feel true love of humanity in his breast and to practice it to the best of his ability. The less one adheres to specific opinions, the more one is open, the freer are his opinions and the more tolerant and loving toward his fellow man."

However, among Parisians at that time there was not a feeling of tolerance and love for Germans. Rudolf began to feel social and professional strains in the city. His French friends in the arts began to drift away, mostly as a reaction to his German bride. The country was in the midst of another swing of rising French nationalism. In the mid-1880s, political candidates won office on platforms of outrage, stoking the fires of bitterness at the 5-billion-franc war reparation and the loss of Alsace-Lorraine agreed to as conditions of peace ending the Franco-Prussian War. After a brief and rather tenuous reprieve from negative attitudes toward German nationals in the immediate wake of Napoléon III's capitulation in 1871, the climate in Paris had become hostile toward Germans yet again.

But these were small problems, easily addressed. Rudolf could handle his parents, and he could always leave Paris if he chose.

There was a much greater matter. The ambition he'd set in Augsburg to design a more efficient heat engine still preoccupied him.

Diesel knew that selling and servicing ice machines for Linde was not the future he wanted for himself. Staying on with Linde would earn him a good income and a measure of prestige as an engineer. On this wage he could provide for his wife and future children, and even for his parents, with money to spare. But Diesel felt he was meant for more.

Rudolf's ambition expanded beyond merely the scientific achievement of engine efficiency. As he thought about the applications of such an engine, he returned to the memory of standing on London Bridge as a young boy. He believed a design for a compact and economical engine could provide an affordable power source for small businesses in rural areas. Such an engine could disrupt the trend for massive factories centralized in urban areas with thousands of workers crowded in filthy living conditions all while rural economies sagged. Rudolf conceived a corresponding social goal to accompany his engineering one. Success would mean that not only would he personally avoid a return to tenement housing but that he would break the mold of tenement housing altogether.

In a June 1883 letter to Martha he wrote, "Our goal should not be to better the *future* happiness of men through intolerance and externals. Rather we should help our brothers on *this* earth, improve the situation of mankind, and redress poverty to the best of our ability. This seems to me better understood religion than that which neglects the earthly in favor of an unknown future. Jesus taught neither Protestantism, Catholicism, nor churchgoing and preaching. He taught love of mankind."

Diesel could not serve both Linde and this separate ambition for long. He was distracted from his work at Linde's factory by his theoretical concepts for a more efficient motor and how such a motor could level the balance of power between large and small businesses.

———

Diesel's later detractors joked at his expense. How can a man with scientific roots in refrigeration build a heat engine? Diesel made the nerdy rejoinder that the temperature of absolute zero is -273 degrees Celsius. Anything above that is heat.

Diesel's experience with refrigeration, specifically with highly compressed gases, paved the way for his unorthodox approach and resulting revolutionary engine design. Looking back from the perspective of 1913, he wrote, "How is an idea created? Maybe sometimes it strikes like lightning, but mostly it will develop slowly through intensive search under numerous mistakes."

While still living in Paris and managing the plant for Linde, Diesel worked from 1883 to 1889 on his heat engine side project using compressed ammonia gas. Though working on an external combustion design, his aim was to increase engine efficiency. He was initially attracted to ammonia because of his familiarity in working with the gas for refrigeration, and because ammonia has a lower boiling point than water and therefore requires less energy to create steam. By substituting ammonia for water, he could save energy by reducing the amount of heat required to generate steam pressure.

But ammonia is a volatile and dangerous gas. Additionally, this concept still required an external heat source to generate the steam. This period of experimentation was valuable to Rudolf's overall thinking on engine design, and a worthy cause in that an improved steam engine was useful as there was still no industrial-strength *internal* combustion engine. (In 1886, Karl Benz unveiled his three-wheeled Motorwagen with its $2/3$ horsepower engine—hardly useful in a factory.) But Rudolf's ultimate goal was not to make an improved external combustion steam engine but to design a practical *internal* combustion engine. An indistinct notion from his university days nagged at Diesel, telling him that he was not on the right course.

Torn between his passion project and his day job for Linde, Rudolf began to feel the strain. In a letter to Martha dated July 28, 1884, Diesel wrote, "I've had it with repairing machines. I'm short of temper even when I shouldn't be."

And the pay began to dwindle. The winter of 1884–85 was extremely cold. This offered an abundance of natural ice, which meant poor sales for Linde's ice machine. And French nationalism was still on the rise, making a harsh environment for a German man to sell a German product in French territory. An increasingly cash-strapped Diesel soldiered on with his experiments on the ammonia-fueled heat engine.

Still toiling between two masters, two years later, on November 27, 1886, he wrote to Martha (who frequently visited family in Germany while Rudolf worked in Paris), "I am tormented by severe insomnia that makes me feel like I am living in a dream."

But Diesel's goal was coming into focus. He had a vague concept of a new design for his heat engine, and an increasingly specific plan for the social and industrial application of it. In May 1887, he wrote a four-page list of commercial applications for craftsmen and small businesses using his compact, efficient (if still only theoretical) engine. The list included "dentistry, jewelry making, weaving, woodworking, printing, household tasks, restaurants, small boats, water pumps, and hospitals." His aim was to give small artisans, such as his father, access to a power source equal to what only large industry presently enjoyed. The vision was in place, but turning the vision into reality remained frustratingly distant.

That July he wrote a letter to Martha about his work on the ammonia engine that reflected the anguish common to genius inventors in a period of struggle: "I am gone the whole day, eat lunch out, and return late in the evening. After dinner I write down my impressions of the day. I'm not sleeping at all well; I lie awake half the night and mull things over and over in my mind. If it's only a success, it will seem like a salvation to me after years of imprisonment. I'm now living in desperate agitation."

On December 25, 1887, he again wrote to Martha, "I definitely feel my connection with Linde's company is rapidly coming to an end and that I must undertake something new in the future—but what?"

Of course, the "what" that he hoped to undertake was the heat engine, but even he didn't have the audacity to make the project his full-time endeavor at that time.

Linde, finally recognizing the irrevocable course of his protégé, offered a solution. He knew Rudolf couldn't serve as shop steward for someone else, no matter how well paid, so he offered Rudolf the opportunity to become an independent merchant. Rudolf would effectively run his own business and could still make an income by exclusively selling and servicing Linde products in France but would no longer have the burden of managing Linde's plant. The change was the first professional fissure between the two, but it further cemented their personal bond.

As an independent merchant, Rudolf now had more time to commit to the design of a new engine. He had bursts of optimism and bursts of despair. In one burst of optimism, he reserved space at the upcoming 1889 World's Fair in Paris to show his ammonia-fueled heat engine. During this time, Rudolf wrote to his parents in Munich that he occasionally saw Gustave Eiffel out in the city, taking short breaks from the construction of his tower. He wrote of his admiration for the fellow engineer.

But only weeks after making his reservation at the fair, he withdrew it. In his notes he wrote, "To be delayed is not to give up. I go back to jump forward."

Diesel did in fact exhibit at the 1889 World's Fair, which boasted the Eiffel Tower, though not as he had originally intended. With twenty-eight million people in attendance, he showed a Linde ice machine. He felt the bitter humiliation, now nearly ten years out of university, to be the secondhand peddler of someone else's achievement. Adding to his dejection, two other exhibitors at the fair created enormous excitement. Karl Benz showed the Benz Patent-Motorwagen and Gottlieb Daimler showed his four-stroke combustion engine, both running on refined gasoline. (There is no evidence that Daimler and Benz previously knew each other or were aware of each other's work.) These breakthroughs with motor technology happened adjacent to Diesel in his self-perceived ignominy over the Linde ice machine booth.

Throughout the run of the fair, business went from bad to worse for Diesel. In an echo of his childhood rush from Paris in 1870, Rudolf wrote to his parents living in Munich, "I must say that things here seem so unstable that I should always like to be ready to emigrate." In the letter, he heaped most of the blame for the war scare on Bismarck, who by 1889 was locked in a bitter struggle with the young kaiser Wilhelm II, his once hoped-for ally, for control of Germany.

Linde agreed with Rudolf that prospects for his company in Paris were dim, and though Linde was often reserved in expressing enthusiasm for Diesel's new ideas, he was ever the friend and supporter. Linde offered Diesel a job at his manufacturing plant in Berlin.

On February 21, 1890, Rudolf and Martha moved to the German capital with a family that now included three children: Rudolf Jr. (b. 1884), Hedwig, or Hedy (b. 1885), and Eugen (b. 1889).

Architecturally, Berlin was new but not beautiful, and already Europe's third-largest city. Most of its main buildings, streets, and squares had been built or rebuilt since 1870. Unter den Linden, a mile-long boulevard with a double row of trees that ended in the triumphal arch known as the Brandenburg Gate, was constructed with the purpose of being the biggest and most impressive boulevard in Europe.

Siemens began to lay electric cables under the streets for illumination. Locomotives running on precise schedules moved out from the city to all parts of the country. Even the horse-drawn carriages ran along iron rails. Berlin was a city unlike any Diesel had ever seen. Clean streets, bustling vitality, seemingly full of sophisticated industrialists, and a caste-like society dominated by military leaders and their wives, the highly visible pomp and ceremony of the army and navy so loved by the young kaiser, now twenty months into his reign.

Martha was far happier in Berlin, finally feeling accepted by society in a way she never was in Paris. Rudolf felt the opposite. He preferred the arts and culture of Paris to the stiff formality of Berlin. But he was too busy in his lab at 15 Bruckenallee to care very much about the city around him. He realized then that his ammonia engine, as Linde had suggested, was nothing out of the ordinary. His concept still required an external heat source, and, even if functioning properly, was only an alternate form of steam engine. Though he finally abandoned pursuit of ammonia as the key to engine efficiency, this period of work was undoubtedly an important part of what he later called his "intensive search."

He returned to the fundamental question he'd posed to himself as a student in Munich. He knew that one kilogram of coal contained seventy-five hundred calories, but steam engines captured less than 10 percent of that energy for work. The rest was heat lost to the environment, largely because the coal was not burned directly for work, but rather burned to heat water to steam, then the steam did the work. As an engineering student in 1878, he had written in his notebook, "It follows that one should convert this 7,500 Calories directly into work without intermediaries. But is that in fact possible?"

He expressed his confidence in moving away from ammonia and adopting a new approach in a letter to his mother dated November 15, 1891: "I feel myself ready for the next step . . . To err is human, I can deceive myself, but I have confidence in the cause. Twelve years have I with self-sacrifice tended a flower; now I will pick it up and enjoy its fragrance."

So Diesel picked up his flower while in Berlin in the early 1890s, and accelerated his grueling work schedule. He found himself in the capital of the German regime that was in the sway of its own nationalist movement. Kaiser Wilhelm II had a definite opinion about where Germany belonged on the world stage, and definite ideas about how to get there. Bismarck's domestic focus and emphasis on industrial growth of the previous two decades were about to change. The shift had implications for all Germans, including, and perhaps especially, the nation's scientists.

CHAPTER 8

Wilhelm II Envies a Navy

KAISER WILHELM I and his son, Frederick III, had both died in 1888, just prior to Rudolf's arrival in Berlin. Young prince Wilhelm lost his grandfather and then, only ninety-nine days later, his father. The headstrong twenty-nine-year-old began 1888 second in line for the throne. By June he was Wilhelm II, Emperor of Germany and King of Prussia.

His father, Frederick, had suffered from throat cancer. German doctors diagnosed the condition early and recommended surgery. Instead, Vicki spurned these doctors and sought a second opinion from the English physician Dr. Morell Mackenzie, recognized as the world's leading expert on diseases of the throat. Mackenzie declared that Frederick's ailment was not cancer, that surgery was a drastic mistake, and that simple rest in a temperate climate would cure the heir to the throne. The couple traveled to Queen Victoria's estate on the Isle of Wight where they spent three months. But Frederick's condition worsened. When Wilhelm I passed away just shy of his ninety-first birthday and Frederick was crowned the new emperor, the dashing fifty-six-year-old could no longer speak and was forced to communicate through the written word. By the time Mackenzie (who in the interim Queen Victoria knighted, at Vicki's request, for "saving" her beloved son-in-law's life) came around to agree with the cancer diagnosis of the German physicians, it was too late. Wilhelm II ascended the throne furious with both his mother and the English doctors whom he blamed for the death of his father.

While Frederick still lay in state in the palace, named Friedrichskron in his honor, the paranoid Wilhelm, now in charge, had his mother's rooms and closets searched by his royal guard, convinced that his mother planned to smuggle Frederick's private papers to London. Nothing was found. Days later he changed its name to Neues Palais (New Palace), a snub of, and deliberate departure from, his parents. Enraged, Vicki refused to attend the state funeral service for Frederick and held a separate service of her own. A chill came over the relationship between Wilhelm and his grandmother Queen Victoria.*

———————

Frederick's death meant that Wilhelm ascended the throne far sooner than anyone anticipated. Uncharacteristically, the person least prepared for the sudden change of monarchs was Chancellor Bismarck. Wilhelm had embraced the political ideal of autocratic rule and the divine right of kings just as Bismarck had tutored him. Dangerously for Europe, the new kaiser combined a proclivity for absolute power with bombastic, impulsive, and insecure tendencies.

With his uncle Bertie, the Prince of Wales† (King Edward VII

———————

* Afoul of both his mother and grandmother, Wilhelm had previously suffered a snub from another English woman. When a teenager, he had fallen in love with a maternal cousin, Princess Elisabeth of Hesse-Darmstadt, also a grandchild of Queen Victoria. Elisabeth found Wilhelm to be "overbearing," and the princess rebuffed him, despite a series of love poems he had written to her. She went on to marry Grand Duke Sergei Alexandrovich of Russia. Wilhelm went on to marry Augusta Victoria of Schleswig-Holstein on February 27, 1881. They remained married forty years, until her death in 1921, and had seven children.

† Queen Victoria and her husband, Albert, instructed that each generation reuse the names Victoria and Albert. Their first children were Victoria (Vicki, who married Frederick III of Prussia) and Albert (Prince of Wales, later Edward VII). To compound the confusion, the royal family also had the habit of recycling nicknames. Edward VII and his grandson George VI (portrayed by Colin Firth in *The King's Speech*) both had the childhood nickname "Bertie."

upon Victoria's death in 1901), who had been a friend and mentor to young Wilhelm, took on a lofty and superior tone. Despite Bertie's seniority in years, Wilhelm was first to become sovereign and, therefore, to Bertie's (and Queen Victoria's) surprise, demanded deference from his uncle during their formal meetings.

Wilhelm had an ambitious vision for Germany's future. Since the time of his birth, Germany's economic and political power had grown at a soaring pace. To Wilhelm, it was obvious that this growth was destined to extend beyond Germany's borders, just as the reach of the British Empire extended far beyond the borders of the small island nation. Wilhelm wanted colonies for advantageous access to the raw materials needed to feed German industry, in the same way that Great Britain enjoyed the benefits of a colonial system for trade and access to raw materials. Wilhelm didn't want to rely on friendly and familial relations with Britain, such as the current understanding that the Royal Navy would provide the German merchant fleet with escorts and protection from hostile powers or pirates. Wilhelm wanted a powerful navy of his own.

When Rudolf Diesel moved from Paris to Berlin, the empire's two leading figures were squaring off. Bismarck did not share Wilhelm's vision, and the two men were at odds from the start of Wilhelm's reign. They took long strolls together through the imperial gardens to argue foreign policy, striking an amusing image for onlookers. The tall, imposing elder statesman striding next to the short, youthful, handsome-albeit-handicapped kaiser. Bismarck had codified vast authority in the office of chancellor to manage the empire and its foreign policy. The key decisions rested with him, save one. In an unavoidable point of law, Bismarck's constitution granted to the emperor the duty to appoint the chancellor. Wilhelm could fire Bismarck.

Wilhelm I had never dared to dismiss Bismarck. To the contrary, just Bismarck's threat of resignation had always been enough to cow the sovereign. The Iron Chancellor held sway with ministers and had the love of the German population. But young Wilhelm was growing popular too, especially as anti-English sentiment was growing. Many Germans felt as Wilhelm did—that the British were an impediment to German growth and its destiny as an imperial power. And as Wilhelm was firmly conservative, unlike his more liberal father, he also had the support of Bismarck's base of conservative ministers. As the kaiser worked to win their loyalty, he found that Bismarck was not without his enemies.

In March, Wilhelm took the bold step of overthrowing the man who for twenty years had been the most powerful figure in all Europe. Bismarck, at age seventy-five, was forced to submit a letter of resignation to his kaiser.

From across the channel, Lord Salisbury, Britain's prime minister and leading conservative politician of the era, remarked in an echo of Shelley's *Frankenstein*, "It is a curious Nemisis on Bismarck. The very qualities which he fostered in the Emperor [Wilhelm II] in order to strengthen him when the Emperor Frederick should come to the throne have been the qualities by which he has been overthrown."

Wilhelm reached for the marionette strings of Europe that Bismarck had put in place. Over the previous two decades, Bismarck had managed a fragile peace through intricate dealings that often seemed at cross purposes. Bismarck had recognized that there were five great powers: Great Britain, France, Austria-Hungary, Russia, and Germany (Italy was then a distant sixth, the Ottoman Empire was already crumbling, and America was not yet a major power). In this fraught period when it was still customary for the major European powers to invade neighboring territory to acquire the resources they lacked, Bismarck believed that to maintain national security, Germany must be a party to an entente of three of the five powers. His constant goal had been to isolate France and remain in an alliance with two of the others. Austria-Hungary was firmly one of the allies. This left Great Britain and Russia from which to pick one more.

Britain refused to engage in a peacetime treaty with anyone. From Salisbury's perspective, British sea power was supreme, her shores were untouchable, and her government content with an isolationist foreign policy—a policy that England dubbed "splendid isolation." When Bismarck came with offers of alliance, Salisbury politely declined, explaining that future British Parliaments wouldn't necessarily adopt the agreements of the present one, and therefore Great Britain was unable to make peacetime treaties at all.

Bismarck then engaged Russia in secret alliance discussions, going behind the back of ally Austria (traditionally an enemy of Russia) to negotiate a defense treaty with Russia in 1887 called the Reinsurance Treaty, a pact unknown to the rest of Europe.

The complex structure of interlocking treaties crafted by Bismarck held European peace and German security. Wilhelm was wholly unprepared to step into what a contemporary German minister called a "criss-cross of commitments [that] resembles the tangle of tracks at a big railway station," with Bismarck as the yardmaster.

Upon taking charge, Wilhelm quickly tangled the delicate threads.

The Teutonic Germans and Slavic Russians had traditionally been at odds, and on a personal level Tsar Alexander III didn't much like Wilhelm. He privately mocked the young kaiser, and when rumors of Alexander's derision came to Wilhelm's attention, the new leader, still finding his footing, was extremely bitter. The antagonism became mutual.

In 1890, with Bismarck out of the way, Wilhelm refused to renew the Reinsurance Treaty with Russia. The implication from the cocksure kaiser was clear. Foreign policy from Berlin was about to change. Russia and France quickly formed an alliance due to a mutual fear of German aggression. The friendly talks between the two nations began in 1891, then developed further into a secret military and political pact called the Franco-Russian Alliance, established in 1894.

Wilhelm held the reins of the empire tightly, traveling Europe to meet personally with sovereigns, assuming more of a diplomatic role than was typical. He proclaimed to his uncle Bertie, "I am the sole master of German policy and my country must follow wherever I go." A concerned Queen Victoria wrote to Vicki that Wilhelm seemed "bent on a return to the oldest times of government." Bertie added derisively, "Wilhelm the Great needs to learn that he's living in the end of the nineteenth century and not in the Middle Ages." Hearing about these remarks, Wilhelm responded by calling his uncle a "peacock" and "Satan."

As Wilhelm traveled for state visits in his royal yacht *Hohenzollern*, a fleet followed. And as he disembarked, behind his person followed three valets, a hairdresser, and an assistant whose sole function was to appear at the proper time with a can of wax used to twist the ends of Wilhelm's mustache into their distinctive upward turns.

An increasingly paranoid Wilhelm founded the German espionage apparatus in 1889, the first year of his rule. Germany formed Sektion IIIb, the military intelligence group that focused on the land-based enemies Russia and France but ignored Great Britain. The Nachrichtenabteilung, also founded by Wilhelm in 1889, was the secret service branch of the German navy, focused exclusively on their island enemy.* Within a few years, Wilhelm built the largest and most active secret service operation in Europe of the prewar period, which practiced not only intelligence gathering but frequent sabotage.†

In keeping with his image as absolute sovereign, he involved himself directly in military affairs, often with embarrassing results. In 1890, the young kaiser took command of troops for army maneuvers in Silesia. Chancellor Leo von Caprivi, a former general who had replaced Bismarck, observed privately, "The General Staff had offered many traps and the Kaiser had gaily fallen into every single one of them."

---

* In 1882, Great Britain formed the Foreign Intelligence Committee (FIC) and in the same year the United States formed the Office of Naval Intelligence (ONI). Austria-Hungary created Europe's first permanent national secret service in 1848.

† Upon the outbreak of the Great War, many of these sabotage operations targeted the United States. While the US had not yet declared war, it did help the Allies against the Central Powers, sending food, supplies, and as many as a thousand horses per day to support the war effort. German agents operating on American soil planted explosives at munitions depots or on the transport ships. Historians describe these operations as the first domestic terror cells in America. The results stoked public outrage and hastened America's entry into the war.

The chief of the General Staff, Count Alfred von Waldersee, critiqued the maneuvers as tactfully as possible. He pointed out Wilhelm's numerous and clear mistakes to a large audience. Caprivi later noted that Wilhelm "tried to make excuses and became very feeble in his explanations." Three days later Waldersee was removed from his position. Ministers reported that Wilhelm afterward referred to Waldersee as a "traitor."

Wilhelm could not bridle his ambition to surpass Britain's naval power. This was a project that Bismarck had always been too pragmatic to undertake. Bismarck knew that with a weak navy but a strong army, Germany could still be the dominant continental player, but for Britain control of the seas was life or death. Britain lived with the fear that a rival navy could cut off the British Isles, starve it out.

Bismarck had viewed a powerful German fleet as an unnecessary provocation of the English. He was happy that the German merchant fleet enjoyed the protections of the Royal Navy. In fact, through the 1880s, the Royal Navy had even assisted in training the small German fleet. Through royal bloodlines, the Germans and English were natural allies, and England was no friend of France or Russia. Since the Middle Ages the English and French had persistently fought. England and Russia were also traditional antagonists and presently there was high friction over colonies in the Far East. But nothing mattered so much to England as a rival naval power, especially one located in her home waters of the North Sea. England considered this to be the single existential threat. Nonetheless, Wilhelm declared his determination to build a navy to rival and surpass the British fleet, and to establish colonies on foreign shores that would nourish German industry. He named his ambition Germany's "New Course." The aggressive policy led to an unlikely thaw in relations between England, France, and Russia. With France no longer isolated, Bismarck's party of three was breaking up.

If a continental power was determined to build a rival navy, then England could no longer have a passive approach to foreign policy with the other great powers. Queen Victoria, as always referring to herself in the third person, wrote to Prime Minister Salisbury, "Affairs now are so different from what they used to be that the Queen cannot help feeling that our *isolation* is dangerous." From retirement in Germany, Bismarck predicted that Wilhelm II would lead Germany to ruin.

Yet amid the political tensions that were largely created by Wilhelm's naval and imperial aspirations, the technologies required to build a navy that could master the sea lanes were changing. Conditions were already set for the critical role Rudolf Diesel would play in the power struggle between nations.

CHAPTER 9

The Birth of Diesel Power

THE CRUX OF a complex idea is often captured in a simple form. After abandoning his efforts with the ammonia engine, Diesel narrowed his focus and determined to eliminate the intermediary substance required in external combustion. He recalled the classroom demonstration of an old cigar lighter during his student days in Munich. This uncomplicated technology used to create a hot ember became the germ of his idea for a new combustion engine. Years later he asked his school to send him the very same fire starter, more technically called a pneumatic tinder igniter, that he had seen in class so that he could demonstrate the device to his children.

Eugen Diesel described the event in the biography he wrote of his father. The three children sat beside Rudolf in their living room while he held up the tinder lighter before them. It was the shape and approximate size of a modern bicycle tire pump, but with a glass cylinder so its contents were visible to all.

Highly compressed air generates heat. Even a bicycle tire pump gets warm after pumping up a few tires. The simple concept of the pneumatic igniter is that a person thrusts the plunger down on the

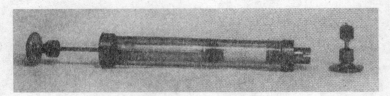

The fire starter, or pneumatic tinder igniter, that Rudolf Diesel saw as a student in Munich and later demonstrated to his children. The device resembled a bicycle pump. A rapid thrust of the pump compressed the air inside the glass cylinder, creating heat that ignited a tinder placed inside.

trapped air. The rapid compression of air generates heat that ignites a piece of tinder inside the chamber. Simple as that.

Rudolf sat in a chair by the eager children while holding the tinder lighter and pushed the plunger down with all his might, but with no result. A second dramatic thrust also had no effect. On the third thrust, the tinder began to glow red in the compressed air. Eugen wrote, "Seeing the tinder begin to glow and smolder without the agency of a flame of any kind had a magical effect upon the children."

Rudolf then said to his children, "Now just imagine that some petrol or petroleum or coal dust were in there instead of the tinder; of course it would have ignited, and the increased gas pressure from this combustion—because heat expands objects and air, too—would naturally push out the piston. The Diesel engine is no more than a pneumatic tinderbox like this one here, with the difference that the fuel does not get forced into the cylinder until after it is compressed. Then it ignites and performs the work."

This was the primary innovation of the Diesel engine. The engine started with the release of an air valve to make the piston's first downward stroke. This stroke of the engine's piston drew ordinary air into the cylinder, just like a bicycle pump. Then the upward thrust of the piston compressed this air against the cylinder head to a pressure of thirty-four atmospheres (or five hundred pounds per square inch) and this intense pressure heated the air to greater than 1,000 degrees Fahrenheit. At this precise moment, fuel was injected into the cylinder. The fuel ignited in the extreme heat, the explosion then driving the piston back out to achieve a power stroke. The engine required no spark ignition.* Due to metallurgy constraints, this high-compression design was impossible in Watt's era, and just shy of impossible in Diesel's. To make this design a reality, he would require the highest-quality metals, expertly forged to his exact specifications. But his calculations, if correct, showed that compression was the key to engine safety and efficiency. He believed he could take a fuel that was stable and without fumes at room temperature and from a cold start and with no spark-plug ignition introduce the fuel to highly compressed air to create internal combustion that would make use of approximately four times the amount of energy held in the fuel than did any other engine. If Diesel's calculation of the amount of power he could derive from a unit of fuel was correct, and if he could fabricate the engine parts to see his design through, he would effectively quadruple the power of the world's natural resources.

———

Diesel envisioned an engine with a cylinder pressure one hundred times greater than the Otto engines being sold. He calculated that such compression levels would generate high enough temperatures (approximately 800 degrees Celsius) to convert the fuel to usable work. Diesel calculated that burning fuel at a constant, very high temperature would extract the maximum energy. Instead of the 6 percent fuel efficiency of steam engines, or the 12 to 20 percent efficiency of other oil engines, Diesel predicted a theoretical 73 percent fuel efficiency for his engine.†

This was such a remarkable goal that most experts in 1890 believed

---

* See Appendix, Exhibit 1, for a diagram of the Diesel motor.

† Diesel's original patent filing in February 1892 contemplated a constant *temperature* engine. His subsequent patent filings during the development phase of the engine (1893–97) addressed his changed and, ultimately successful, approach to a constant *pressure* engine. Diesel's critics through the years have attempted to seize on the deviation from the original patent.

it was folly. Dugald Clerk, a Scottish engineer and engine expert, declared that the proposed increase in engine compression would require heavier, bulkier engine parts. The increase in weight of the engine itself would increase friction and lost energy that would more than offset any efficiencies gained. Diesel's engine did in fact require the highest-quality steel and other materials, which would make it not only heavier but more expensive to manufacture than competing combustion engines like Otto's.

Clerk did allow, "It is to be remembered, of course, that as yet engineers have had little experience in oil engines as compared with gas [here "gas" refers to gaseous fuels like benzene, coal gas, and natural gas, not gasoline] engines, and that probably with further development of detail the heat efficiency of the oil engine may yet be considerably increased."

———

Diesel felt certain his calculations were correct. Through 1891 he detailed his ideas in a sixty-four-page manuscript titled *Theory and Construction of a Rational Heat Engine to Replace the Steam Engine and Contemporary Internal Combustion Engine*. It had been fourteen years since he made the margin comment in his university lecture notebook.

Diesel published an edited version of the paper one year later, intending to lay the foundational work for a patent application and to attract the financial backing to build the engine from his concept. On February 11, 1892, Diesel sent a copy of the manuscript to Linde, his frequently skeptical mentor. He announced in his letter, "I have the pleasure to inform you that I have found an engine which theoretically uses only 10 percent of the fuel which today's best steam engines would use."

Linde's response was moderately encouraging. Linde complimented Diesel's overall approach, saying that "your direction is sharp and correct," but stated further, "I may not omit to add that in my opinion only in the best case perhaps one third of your theoretically calculated efficiency can actually be expected. . . . Nevertheless, the possibility exists to convert about 25 percent of the heat value of nearly all fuels into mechanical energy. That is somewhat more than is achieved today with special and expensive fuels."

Linde's letter also acknowledged that his young protégé's true calling was the rational heat engine, not Linde's ice machine. Though Linde remained skeptical of Diesel's boldest claims, he knew his young friend had hold of something potentially important, and that he wouldn't let it go.

Linde closed his letter saying, "You are very well prepared for this work and that the goal is worth every effort I do not doubt, so I cannot dissuade you from devoting yourself to this cause. . . . When you decide to follow up on your idea I see no other possibility than that you leave the company."

Diesel formally resigned from Linde's company, and on February 27, 1892, filed his patent application in Germany. On February 23, 1893, the German patent office granted Patent No. 67207 to Rudolf Diesel titled "Process for Producing Motive Power from the Combustion of Fuels."

Then the hardest work began.

Compared to other engines, Diesel's would be more complex, more expensive to build, and few engineers possessed the expertise required to construct the sophisticated design. But once built, his engine would deliver magic. The short-term pain of up-front design and manufacturing costs would deliver a long-term gain in performance and efficiency. In oil-scarce Europe, that was a worthy trade-off.

For Diesel, the initial cost of testing and development would be very high, and he needed money to put his patent into practice. The publication of Diesel's concepts, which he hoped would attract investment, created an uproar of both praise and scorn. Some of his critics claimed that the proposed engine was too fantastic to work. Impossible to square with this charge were the claims of other critics that Diesel's ideas were unoriginal and already in practice. Rival engineers and innovators who had been experimenting with competing engine concepts published scathing criticisms of Diesel's work.

Large manufacturing firms that were committed to the production of steam power, or the Otto cycle engine, dismissed Diesel's work as unimportant. Other experts published praise of the concepts outlined in the patent. What Diesel theorized to be possible with his engine was a frightening threat to the established modes of power of the day and the engineers who had designed them.

At this time, discussion of Diesel's ideas was limited to the European engineering community. His German patent didn't warrant even a memo inside Standard Oil, and certainly didn't rise to the attention of Wilhelm's military officers. But among the community of academics and thermal engineers, tempers flared. Through the din, Diesel found financial backing with the help of an old friend.

Years later, Rudolf reflected: "Publishing my brochure provoked violent criticism, on the average very unfavorable, if not utterly annihilating. . . . Only three voices were raised in my favor, but these carried much weight. I will give their names: Linde, Schröter, Zeuner. These men had a great deal of influence on the decision of the two firms Maschinenfabrik Augsburg and Friedrich Krupp, Essen to put this new idea to a practical test." (Many more than three voices were raised in Diesel's favor at this time, as his son Eugen notes in his biography. Rudolf was slightly hyperbolic when looking back on this period.)

Gustav Zeuner was a German physicist considered the founder of thermodynamics, and Moritz Schröter was one of Diesel's university professors in Munich.

While the public support of Linde, Schröter, and Zeuner was helpful, Diesel's own persistence won the day with Heinrich Buz. Diesel first wrote to Buz on March 7, 1892, asking M.A. to sponsor development of the engine. On April 2, Buz replied with a terse and disappointing letter. "We have carefully considered all aspects of the matter and come to the conclusion that the difficulties inherent in the realization of the project are so great that we cannot undertake the venture."

But the erstwhile refugee who had traveled alone from Paris to Augsburg with hardly more than the shirt on his back was now a thirty-four-year-old accomplished engineer who believed he had the best idea for power in the Industrial Age. He had worked alongside the brightest engineering minds in Germany and had been immersed in the science of his idea for more than a decade. He did not surrender to rejection. He knew the engineering community was already determining whether he would be an asset or a threat, and he knew how to make the choice clear for Buz. In a way, Diesel's message to Buz was similar to Rockefeller's to competing oil refineries: Join me or I'll defeat you.

The manufacture of steam engines was one of the main product lines for Buz's Maschinenfabrik Augsburg at that time. On April 9, Diesel wrote to Buz that should his concept prove correct, his engine would entirely displace the market for steam engines. He suggested that it would be better for Buz to be the disruptor than the disrupted.

Diesel was hardly in the power position Rockefeller had enjoyed. His independent pursuit of the engine from his makeshift lab in Berlin had nearly bankrupted him and his family. He needed financial support or his cause would stall. Without waiting for a response, Diesel sent a barrage of additional correspondence to Buz, further outlining the promising opportunity.

On April 20, Buz's office sent a letter to Diesel in Berlin with the answer Diesel wanted. "Your 3 esteemed [letters] of [April] 6, 9 and 13 instant to the undersigned could not be answered till today because he was away for a time on a trip. Per your new statements, we are willing to undertake, under certain conditions, the completion of an experimental machine which must be of such construction to avoid all possible development complications."

Buz, the "Bismarck of German Industry," was now behind him. Diesel's family remained in Berlin while he moved back to Augsburg. Buz had committed a walled-off section of the M.A. plant to Diesel's development team. Friedrich Krupp, the German industrialist, joined as a sponsor and agreed to pay Diesel 30,000 marks as an annual salary in return for the rights to manufacture and market the engine when (and if) Diesel developed a successful model.

Nine months later, in January 1894, Diesel completed the construction of his first test engine. He and his senior assistant, Lucien Vogel, and their engineering team had assembled the specially cast metal fittings according to the Diesel design. They were ready for a trial run.

Rudolf opened the air valve to start the test motor. He had calculated that the pressure inside the cylinder would reach 645 psi (pounds per square inch).

For this first test, Diesel used gasoline, highly flammable even in normal conditions. Upon the first charge of gasoline to the cylinder the atmospheric pressure soared to 1,175 psi, far higher than he'd estimated, and a tremendous explosion turned the engine into a lethal bomb. The blast sent glass and metal parts flying and could have killed Rudolf and Vogel. The two men, closely observing the engine operation, hit the deck at the sound of the deafening blast and suffered nothing more serious than temporary ringing in their ears.

Though the engine didn't run, Diesel had proved the core principle of his patent and his pitch to Buz. The explosion was evidence that the fundamental concept worked. He had not used any kind of spark or fire for ignition. Compression alone had fired the engine. He had taken the old bicycle-pump-shaped cigar lighter and turned the simple design into the cylinder and piston of an engine: the heart of the Diesel motor. Now he needed to expand on this success to make a working motor. The immediate challenge was to control the colossal burst at the engine's ignition. As a part of meeting this challenge, Diesel shifted his testing to use the viscous heavier fuels (such as heavy oils and coal tar), which happened to be both far less expensive and far more stable.

Diesel wrote of what he found to be a success: "The engine never succeeded in running, not even one revolution, because at the first injection of fuel . . . there occurred a terrible explosion . . . nearly killing the Author. But the Author knew then just what he wanted to know . . . it was proved possible to compress pure air so high that the fuel injected into it ignited and burned." He and Vogel continued trials of the first test engine from January to April 1894.

By April, the walls around the engine were thoroughly pock-marked from engine parts and other shrapnel flying off the machine. As Heinrich Buz happily observed, "The practical application of the process is proven in this imperfect machine."

From this proof of concept, it was a long and arduous climb to a commercial engine. Diesel acknowledged that he still took steps backward in order to jump forward. But he knew now that he was on the right path.

———

Diesel struggled to find the solutions to the obstacles presented in the first test engine. Through the spring and summer of 1894, he ran a succession of experiments on an ignition system that met with mixed results. He corresponded frequently with Robert Bosch,* a German inventor and pioneer in electrical ignition systems for combustion engines. Bosch had founded a successful engineering and technology company in 1886 and was well regarded in Germany. The two bandied ideas back and forth, but without a breakthrough.

During these months of work, Rudolf had once again been invited to live in the Augsburg home of Christoph Barnickel and his wife, Emma. He was comfortable, and among family, but it wasn't home. From Berlin, Martha wrote to Rudolf: "My heart pounds when I think of your work and the difficult, difficult time of anticipation . . . that I am anxious and await your news, Dearest, you know, but I remain nicely content until you have time to be with your wife."

Diesel wrote back right away: "I hope that you, sweet wife, will remain true in your help and not give up. When you believe in me and my device I have the strength to work, otherwise not . . ."

———

* Robert Bosch later became an asset of British Intelligence, providing information to Group Captain Malcolm Christie, a member of Britain's "Z" intelligence organization focused on the German threat during WWII.

Rudolf may have needed Martha for emotional support, but he needed Krupp and Buz for money. During the summer of 1894, Krupp discussed pulling out of the venture. Diesel knew if Krupp and Buz withdrew their support, the entire project would come to an end. On September 18, 1894, Diesel anxiously wrote to bolster his two sponsors. "Courage, just for a little while longer, and then I hope everything will be alright."

On October 3, 1894, Diesel scrapped the plan for the electrical ignition system he'd been designing for the second test engine, and he later wrote, "This was the worst time of the entire development period, and it took every bit of confidence the people involved had in the scientific truth to prevent us from abandoning the whole thing then and there."

The irony of this brief tangent with Bosch in the development period is that Diesel didn't need an external ignition system at all. The heat generated from the highly compressed air eliminated the need for any spark to the fuel, he just needed to find a way to manage the first explosion. Diesel went on to write in the October letter, "Unfortunately, I have not reached the goal this time either, but I hasten to add that this does not discourage me. On the contrary, I feel much closer than ever before. Faithful to my principle of 'I will', I am going ahead, slowly but surely."

Buz was steadfastly in Diesel's corner. Together they kept Krupp on board.

———————

In November 1894, Diesel completed the design for a new test engine that he showed to his sponsors. He had found a way to control the initial explosive start to the engine without using external ignition. After an eight-hour meeting, Diesel, Buz, and Krupp decided to halt general testing and begin the construction of a second test engine based on the new design. Diesel completed the build in March 1895, and the initial testing period ran from April to July. Buz and Diesel were very pleased with the results.

On July 3, 1895, Rudolf wrote to Martha, still living in Berlin with the three children while he dedicated himself fully to his work, "My motor still makes great progress. I am now so far beyond what all can presently accomplish that I can say I am first and foremost in this area of the technology of engine design, the first on our small globe."

Throughout testing, Diesel and his assistants made constant adjustments to the motor, each tweak earning a small increment of performance improvement. Parts of the motor continued to fail, and occasionally fly dangerously across the room, but mostly these failures were due to substandard metal casting. The sourcing of the component parts was yet another obstacle to overcome, but Diesel and his Augsburg team were rapidly raising the level of expertise.

Rudolf knew that success and prosperity were within his grasp. He approached Buz with a proposal of a personal kind. Rudolf wanted his family closer to him and the Augsburg laboratory. Berlin was too far, though he also felt that Augsburg was too small and lacked the big-city trappings both he and Martha enjoyed. He decided that nearby Munich was the perfect spot for his wife and children, and a quick train ride away for visits with them. Buz agreed to pay the full expenses of moving the Diesel family into a comfortable Munich home.

Rudolf had written to Martha on November 2, 1895, "In Munich one has the beautiful, easily accessible surrounding environment, a cosmopolitan atmosphere, museums, wonderful art exhibitions, theater, the intellectual excitement of a large city in which art and science flourish. One has the possibility of intercourse with intellectually significant people. In Augsburg—nothing, nothing, nothing."

During the years of feverish work on engine development in Augsburg while Martha and the children were in Berlin, Rudolf had grown distant from the family. Martha had jokingly taken to calling the engine Rudolf's "mistress."

The family moved into a home in Munich in late 1895, just in time for the holiday season, and Rudolf came to be with them for an extended stay. Rudolf remarked that Martha, now thirty-five, looked more beautiful than on the day they met. Eugen, at six years old, was reading his first books. Hedy, at ten, was tall for her age and a bundle of energy who could take over a room. Rudolf Jr., a year older than Hedy, was determined to raise rabbits. When Rudolf arrived in Munich he built an array of rabbit hutches for his eldest child, and soon the family tended an exploding population of the boy's pets.

Then Rudolf designed a playroom for his children with a complete set of child-sized furniture, hand-carved and painted. In the adjoining room he designed a Chinese shadow theater for the family, and he built the silhouettes by hand.

At the time of this visit, it was Martha who came up with the proper name for her husband's "mistress." Rudolf had toyed with several possibilities. Prior to 1895, the engine had no official name. In contracts, Rudolf referred to the engine as "Rational Heat Engine on the Diesel Patent." He had considered calling it the Delta Engine, Delta being the mathematical symbol for change. Later he considered the name Excelsior Engine, *excelsior* then a popularly used word in the names of hotels and newspapers to indicate high quality. Then, with his usual flare for the romantic, Rudolf settled for a time on the name Excalibur. He liked the idea that a magical device could dispel ills and, in the hands of benevolent leaders, rescue man. An engine of near-mythic serviceability deserved such a name.

Finally, in late 1895, Martha said to him, "Just call it a Diesel engine."

"Yes," he replied. "I guess you are right about that."

After spending some time in the embrace of his family, and with a name for his engine, Diesel returned to Augsburg in January 1896 having restored his connection to his family and replenished his energy. He was now ready for the homestretch.

Heinrich Buz was still a believer, but the world had doubts about this new compact engine without a coal-fired boiler that promised astounding efficiency and power. The doubters included even the other engineers working nearby on the more established, conventional business lines within Buz's Augsburg plant.

Diesel struggled to hire the engineering talent he needed. At the end of 1895, he was searching for an engineering assistant and decided to look for a candidate outside the Maschinenfabrik Augsburg plant. He found a young engineer named Imanuel Lauster.

Lauster later explained the reason Diesel had to look outside the Augsburg factory for his assistant: "Little by little I came to realize that the entire group in the factory would offer only slight confidence in the Diesel business. This had to be the reason why there was no interest from the available personnel at M.A. for the new position as Diesel's assistant; no one was willing to give up his secure position compared with the uncertain Diesel business."

But when Diesel returned feeling reenergized in January 1896, he had completed the design for the third and final test engine—the engine he believed would be a commercial success. Lauster, only twenty-three at the time of his hire, would be Diesel's right hand in building it. Diesel felt confident enough, given the success of the second test engine and the enhancements that he planned for the third, that the Augsburg plant could begin inviting outside experts into the lab to observe his progress.

Based on the merits of Diesel's latest design, he and Buz wrote to Krupp on January 23 that the time had come to show the engine to the outside world:

> It has been confirmed that [the Diesel engine] is significantly superior to every other petroleum engine. . . . We suggest that licenses be offered to able firms that already build similar engines . . . such firms should be invited to examine the engine without obligation. . . . When the advantages of the engine are recognized, it will not be difficult to negotiate agreements.

Working with Buz in the Augsburg plant, Diesel had delivered his first test engine in January 1894, and the second in March 1895. In January 1896, Diesel earned an enthusiastic green light from Buz and Krupp, and with the steady hand of Lauster, Diesel completed the build for his third test engine in October 1896.

From October through the end of the year, Diesel and Lauster ran the engine every day during daylight hours, stopping the engine in the evening and starting it up the next morning. They tested the engine for use in factories and water plants, each hour making adjustments to the piston, the cylinder, valves for fuel injection, air intake, and exhaust. Throughout these months of robust testing, there were no additions to the artwork of scars across the laboratory walls.

On December 31, 1896, Diesel and Lauster ran the engine with all parts corrected and optimized according to Diesel's design. The operation was smooth and excellent. Diesel felt success was assured and he was ready to put the engine to a formal, and public, test.

On February 17, 1897, Diesel's engine purred to life.

Rudolf's benefactor, Heinrich Buz, had waited four years for this moment. Repeated setbacks had delayed the market acceptance test of the engine. But now the moment was finally here. Rudolf had done it.

Professor Moritz Schröter conducted the performance test. The engine itself, A-frame in shape, was of the vertical design meant for stationary use and stood nearly ten feet high.

As a smiling Schröter stood by the engine, he turned to see his former engineering student, Rudolf Diesel, one month shy of his thirty-ninth birthday, about to become a historic figure in the age of power. Shoulder to shoulder with the confident and composed Diesel stood his young assistant Lauster, also confident though less composed.

The laboratory was more crowded than ever before. The engineering heads of the other Augsburg divisions came to witness the event. Engineers from the neighboring firm Deutz and from Mirrlees, a well-regarded Scottish engineering firm, wanted an early look at the engine that had long been stirring up rumors in the community of motor designers. The normally cavernous space got stuffy with the crowd of onlookers. An untimely burst from Diesel's 1894 test engine might have killed half of them, but there was no need to worry about Diesel's latest machine.

All looked to Schröter as he turned the air pressure valve to start the machine, which immediately sprung to life, then held a steady hum of quiet work, the exhaust almost invisible and odorless. These near absences of sound and smog made a stunning effect. Schröter let the machine run and began his inspection of the fuel consumed and the resulting work of the motor. The onlookers kept quiet, as if they had placed a bet on a spinning roulette wheel, until the engine burned off the specified amount of fuel. All awaited Schröter's calculations.

The university professor verified his numbers, then looked up with a new and wider smile. He verified 26.2 percent thermal efficiency. The fuel efficiency of the Diesel engine far surpassed that of every other mode of power. This was the birth of the Diesel engine and marked a new age of industry.

———————

Diesel's primary goal had always been engine efficiency. His approach of using constant high compression in the cylinder to burn the fuel efficiently led to other benefits, such as the sparkless ignition, the immediate readiness for work without the required time to boil volumes of water and raise steam, and the ability to burn alternative, heavy fuels that were stable and inexpensive. At the outset, these subsidiary benefits were happy accidents for Diesel in his singular quest for engine efficiency. But these benefits, when put into commercial practice, would deliver significant advantages over all prior engines.

Additionally, because of the heavier parts in the Diesel engine and the advanced metallurgy required to withstand high compression, the Diesel engine could deliver more power, or torque (which is different from speed), than the Otto cycle internal combustion engine. Torque is what delivers the sensation of acceleration that pulls a passenger backward into the car seat and is what can handle a heavy load. As an analogy, imagine two riders of exercise cycles. One rider is very skinny and quick (this is the Otto gasoline engine—perhaps a one-horsepower engine of a Benz motor bike), and the other rider is a three-hundred-pound NFL player with legs like sequoias (this is the Diesel engine).

With no resistance on the exercise bike, the skinny rider can make rotations (piston cycles) very quickly and move at high speeds. But with resistance cranked up, the skinny rider can no longer make a rotation and stalls, while under the same conditions the sequoia-legged rider (Diesel) can comfortably spin the pedals.

In 1897, it was unthinkable that the compact internal combustion engine delivered by Otto with its lightweight parts could drive a ship or train or provide power for a large manufacturing plant. These jobs had always been the domain of the steam engine. But Diesel power held the promise of bridging the worlds of the compact design of internal combustion with the massive output of power required for ships and large industry. Diesel had the potential to scale to the massive tasks that only steam power could address, while also maintaining the compact design and sleek benefits of internal combustion—not to mention additional advantages that neither steam nor Otto offered: sparkless ignition, the ability to use stable and inexpensive liquid fuels, and near-invisible exhaust.

———

Four months later, on June 16, 1897, Diesel and Schröter presented the results of the February test to the assembled members of the Association of German Engineers in Kassel, Germany.

The meeting created a sensation, both positive and negative.

To the negative, Diesel spent considerable energy answering public criticism and (successfully) defending legal challenges to his patent. But the prevailing sentiments were overwhelmingly positive.

Eugen wrote, "They had been laughing Diesel to scorn while he was working away in his laboratory at one thing or another without success, but now that he was successful, they crawled out of hiding and made a bid for the honor and financial rewards that were Diesel's due."

Powerful firms with deep pockets each had ideas for the application of the marvelous mode of power. These ideas were quite different from Diesel's. In his personal files, Rudolf kept the handwritten list he had made ten years earlier while living in Paris, in which he identified the intended uses for his motor. His vision had always been to place his motor inside workshops that looked much like his father's had looked—artisans engaged in leatherwork, weaving, woodworking, printing, or other small businesses. Only a few months after his presentation in Kassel, this list would seem quaint.

This was the moment Diesel's engineering and social visions for the motor began to fracture. When he signed the licensing agreements, which was a matter of course, he gave up control over how his machine would be used.

There was always a certain tension between Diesel and his partners Buz and Krupp, just as there is a tension between any entrepreneur and venture investor. The relationship is generally aligned, but not perfectly. Diesel was the scientist and social theorist, while Buz and Krupp were investors. By 1897, it was time for the investors to make their money, and naturally the large industrial interests had far more money to spend on new technology. The large firms that came forward with substantial payments for the rights to Diesel's engine were not interested in Rudolf's handwritten list of intended uses.

Diesel had made perhaps the greatest technological advance of the era, but only in a laboratory. Maturing the engine from a singular success in the lab to repeatable successes in the complexities of the real world was yet another Herculean challenge, one that, when met, would attract the attentions of the wealthiest and most powerful men on earth. Men like John D. Rockefeller and Kaiser Wilhelm II.

PART II

—

DIESEL
PROLIFERATION

1897–1910

CHAPTER 10

Lord Kelvin Goes First

I N THE AUGSBURG LAB, Diesel had proved his theories correct and had surpassed the efficiencies previously thought possible in the field of engineering. Commercial interest in the Diesel technology was intense. There was no beating of the bushes required on Diesel's part. The leading industrialists sought him out.

Diesel and Buz were already familiar with the common licensing practice of the era, having worked with Linde's refrigeration business. A firm from each nation could acquire the right to manufacture and market engines according to the Diesel patent within that designated national territory.*

Maschinenfabrik Augsburg and Krupp had acquired licenses for Germany and Austria during the early production period of the mid-

---

* This licensing system ensured that there was no more than one Diesel engine manufacturer in each national territory during the life of the patent. However, from the perspective of the customer, one could purchase from anywhere. For example, a customer in Denmark could purchase a Diesel engine from a manufacturer in Germany, Russia, Italy, etc., or from a compatriot manufacturer in Denmark if the Danish manufacturer made suitable engines.

1890s while the engine was still in its trial phase. The first Diesel license outside Germany went to the Scottish engineering firm Mirrlees, Watson & Yaryan. The company's cofounder, Sir Renny Watson, had been following reports of Diesel's work and wanted an early look at the new wonder motor, before the public unveiling. Shrewdly, Buz invited him in. Watson and several of his colleagues had been among the guests in the Augsburg lab in February 1897 to watch Schröter perform the engine tests that were later announced in Kassel.

Rudolf knew Mirrlees had a strong reputation and liked them as a partner. After Sir Renny witnessed the performance test, he was convinced the Diesel engine had an important future and invited Rudolf to London where they could negotiate a license for the exclusive rights in Great Britain.

After several days hunkered down in London wrangling over legal terms for the license, Diesel found his talks with the Scots to be exasperating. He wrote to Martha on March 16, 1897, that just when they "are almost in agreement then come the lawyers to give the perfect wording . . . The fatal result with it is that they fear about the worth of the patent and, as with Krupp, I must fight my way through the entire struggle once again. Evenings I fall in bed like I am dead and wonder how will I have enough strength to begin again on the next morning."

To end this impasse, both Diesel and the representatives of Mirrlees agreed to travel to Glasgow to ask William Thomson to review the patent and evaluate the engine design. In 1892, Thomson had been the first British scientist to be ennobled for his achievements, and was thereafter known as Lord Kelvin, First Baron Kelvin. His work had determined the temperature of absolute zero as -273.15 degrees Celsius, and absolute temperatures are stated in units of kelvin (K) to this day in his honor.

In 1897, Lord Kelvin was at the height of his fame and considered to be the world's foremost expert on thermodynamics. He met with Diesel on March 17 to discuss the details of the engine. Almost two weeks later, Lord Kelvin issued his report to Mirrlees. Not only was the report a ringing endorsement of Diesel's ideas, but the astute Kelvin was early to recognize an aspect of the engine that others would soon see as a key military differentiator: the "cold start."*

Lord Kelvin wrote in his report:

> *Diesel's process of heating the air, simply by compression, to a temperature far above the igniting point of the fuel . . . supersedes all use of flame or hot chamber for ignition, even when the engine, cold in every part, is started for its first stroke . . . This capability for instant starting from cold . . . is a very valuable item of superiority over any gas or oil or other interior-combustion engine previously made.*

This was exactly what Mirrlees needed to hear.

Diesel executed a license agreement with the Scottish firm on March 26, 1897. For the exclusive rights to manufacture the Diesel engine in the British Isles, Mirrlees paid Diesel 80,000 marks immediately, another 20,000 in three years (the total is the equivalent of $875,000 in today's dollars), and a 25 percent royalty on all sales.†

This was just the beginning. At this time, two nations in particular were growing at a rate to attract the nervous attention of the traditional powers of Western and Central Europe. America and Russia had vast lands, large and growing populations, and abundant natural

---

* The "cold start" capability of the Diesel engine was an enormous military advantage for both surface ships and submarine vessels that needed to deploy rapidly. Vessels with other modes of power required a lengthy, and strategically costly, period to warm the engines or "raise steam" before leaving port to engage the enemy.

† Diesel made his first visit to the Mirrlees factory the following year, in July 1898. Somewhat disappointed, he wrote to Martha of his engine in the Scottish factory: "How it looks in its gloomy, dirty corner covered with dirt and neglected like a Cinderella." However, he also noted that the engine was running well. Betraying an aspect of his character that earned him a reputation for arrogance among some, he went on to tell her that the engineers were eager and "good people . . . but they are not motor-people" and he feared they would get the engine off to a slow start in Britain.

resources that were the envy of the world. Each seemed primed to reap the benefits of Diesel's engine.

The type of industrialists who stepped forward for the Diesel patent tended to be men who were bold, ambitious, enterprising, and, frequently, self-made. These men also tended to become lifelong friends of Rudolf Diesel. Adolphus Busch, the beer magnate, was one of the wealthiest men in America by the end of the nineteenth century. Breweries were among the many businesses that had thrived during and after the Civil War, and Busch's factories required enormous amounts of power to pump water for the brewing process and to refrigerate the resulting beer.

Born in Hesse, Germany, as the twenty-first of twenty-two children, Busch emigrated to America in 1857 at age eighteen. He and three brothers traveled to St. Louis, Missouri, where there was already a large German immigrant population, and the demand for beer was accordingly high. The city was a natural fit for brewing, given the water supply from the Mississippi River and the many surrounding caves for cold storage in the days before Linde's refrigeration machines.

In 1859, Adolphus's father died, leaving behind enough money for Adolphus and a brother to open a brewing supply business. One of their clients was the successful local brewer Eberhard Anheuser, who also happened to have two lovely daughters. The Busch boys married in.

After serving six months in the Union Army in 1861, Adolphus returned to St. Louis where he joined his father-in-law's brewing business. In 1879, the company name was changed to Anheuser-Busch and Adolphus was close to achieving his vision of making its product, Budweiser, the country's preeminent national beer, which had become popular far beyond just the German population.

Busch was a natural entrepreneur who continuously expanded his empire in new directions, and he shrewdly adopted technical innovations that gave him an edge over competitors in the brewing business. He implemented pasteurization in 1878 so that he could keep the beer fresh longer and reach markets across the country. To expand distribution, he launched the brewing industry's first fleet of refrigerated freight cars. He bought into new businesses that supported his brewing empire, including bottling factories, ice-manufacturing plants, coal mines, and a refrigeration company.

Busch was exactly the kind of bold innovator in need of an industrial power source who would pair well with Rudolf Diesel.

———

Busch never lost touch with his German roots. Each year the charismatic millionaire made a lengthy visit to his homeland to visit friends and numerous relations. On one such trip word reached Busch of a stunning new power source built in Augsburg at the plant of the famous Heinrich Buz, designed by a young engineer named Diesel.

Adolphus Busch's right-hand man, particularly for engineering matters, was Colonel E. D. Meier, a fellow German and veteran of the Civil War.* Busch dispatched Meier to Augsburg in September 1897, where he spent weeks thoroughly testing the engine, reviewing the Diesel patents and new designs as well as interviewing numerous engineers and experts, including Buz and Diesel.

On October 4, Meier delivered an encyclopedic report to Busch with a detailed technical analysis of the engine and several pages that were an assessment of Diesel himself.

Of Diesel the man he wrote admiringly:

> *Since the publication of his lecture of June 16, 1897, he has been fairly overwhelmed with praise and congratulations by the leading experts in Europe. Perhaps no better gauge of the strong common sense and real greatness of the man can be found than the fact that all this praise and adulation has not turned his head in the least. He remains the simple, earnest, conscientious student that he was before his great invention. . . .*

———

* Meier was a prominent railway engineer and was later elected to the presidency of the American Society of Mechanical Engineers in 1911.

> *He considers his present success only as an incentive and a stepping-*
> *stone to further work and progress.*

Meier also noted that "As an engineer he is of course more theoretical than practical, but has now at his command some of the best practical talent of Germany."

Meier wrote in his report that the Diesel engine was "the greatest advance ever made in dynamic engineering," that it would entirely replace steam power, and soon the "probability of [Diesel motors] ultimately replacing the machinery of war ships."

Meier stated in conclusion, "I believe the purchase of the Diesel Patents for America is as promising an investment as the purchase of any patent claim could be."

———

Rudolf received a cordial invitation to join the St. Louis beer magnate in the resort town of Baden-Baden, Germany. Busch had reserved an entire floor of the best hotel in town for his entourage of near fifty friends, relatives, and business associates.

When the somewhat reserved Diesel arrived, he was amused to see the excited hotel staff catering to the whims of the jovial Busch, who strolled around the hotel with jacket pockets stuffed with American-minted $5 and $10 gold pieces, tossing them to eager staff who held a door, refilled an ice bucket, fetched a drink, or performed the most minor of services for the gregarious man from "Zaint Louee."

Perhaps this display emboldened Rudolf. When the time came to discuss business, Adolphus inquired as to the "anticipated fee" for the American license. Rudolf boldly set the price at 1 million marks (almost $9 million today).

With no hesitation and no apparent surprise, Busch nodded his agreement, wrote out a check, and had the contract drawn up for signature. Busch had read Meier's report, he knew Diesel had built the engine of the future, and he was already envisioning uses for the engine far beyond pumping water in his breweries and powering refrigeration.

On October 9, 1897, Adolphus Busch and Rudolf Diesel signed the agreement granting Busch the exclusive rights to manufacture and market Diesel engines in the United States and Canada.

Upon hearing the news of this financial windfall, Martha wrote to Rudolf, "It all seems to be some sort of Fata Morgana. It is difficult to get used to the idea of being rich."

On the other side of the world, there was a clear candidate for Diesel power: the Nobel family. While dynamite, guns, and oil are today not typically associated with the Nobel name, the money Alfred Nobel bequeathed in his last will and testament to establish the Nobel Prize came from these sources. Alfred was the youngest of three brothers who owned Branobel ("Brothers Nobel"). With wells in Baku near the Caspian Sea, Branobel was one of the three dominant oil producers in the world at the turn of the century, along with Standard Oil and the Rothschild's Caspian-Black Sea Oil Industry & Trade Company. Alfred Nobel's name lives on in the legacy of his prizes, but he was not the richest nor the most successful of the brothers.

The vast Nobel empire had all the characteristics of an ideal partner for Diesel: elite engineering expertise, a bold entrepreneurial spirit, deep financial resources, and a strong reputation, especially in its home market of Russia.

Like Busch's brewing empire, the Nobel empire began with humble roots. The patriarch, Immanuel Nobel, a self-taught engineer, emigrated from Sweden to Russia in 1837, where he founded a munitions factory in Saint Petersburg and built undersea mines that he sold in quantity to the navy of Tsar Nicholas I for use in the Crimean War (1853–56). The mines were successful, and Immanuel garnered some wealth and fame.

Russia lost the Crimean War in 1856 and under the rule of the new tsar, Alexander II, the monarchy did not honor past debts nor future sales contracts with Immanuel. His firm floundered and he returned to Sweden nearly impoverished, but he had managed to give his eldest three sons the formal education he lacked. These three brothers—Robert (b. 1829), Ludvig (b. 1831), and Alfred (b. 1833)—made the Nobel name world-famous.

Alfred returned with his parents to Sweden, where he devoted his efforts to the study of explosives. He experimented with combinations of powdered stabilizers and the volatile explosive nitroglycerin to create dynamite. He earned the patent in 1867, and the world immediately applied this useful and stable explosive wrapped in the shape of sticks to mining, construction, and weapons of war.*

Robert and Ludvig, the older brothers, stayed behind in Russia. There Ludvig took charge of the munitions factory and established Maschinenfabrik Ludvig Nobel in Saint Petersburg, where he built munitions as well as marine steam engines. Ludvig's brilliant engineering mind and hard work led to impressive growth for the firm.

But the truly massive growth came through serendipity.

Ludvig held a purchase order from the tsar for one hundred thousand breech-loading rifles. He needed more wood for the stocks of the rifles, so he dispatched his adventurous older brother, Robert, to the forested regions of the Caucasus in southern Russia, famous for walnut trees that grew eighty-feet high.

As Robert approached the Caucasus, he passed through Baku, an ancient city that since the Bronze Age has had a reputation as the "Land of Fire" due to pools of petroleum bubbling to the surface and seeping natural gas that burned continuously. In the present age of kerosene-fueled illumination, these phenomena that were previously a nuisance, or in the distant past had inspired pagan worship and the construction of temples, now had a modern economic purpose. Rob-

---

* When Ludwig Nobel died in April 1888, French newspapers incorrectly reported the death of Alfred, who was in fact alive and well. Alfred then read his own obituary, which was a scathing critique of his life and work. The obituary named Alfred a "merchant of death" and declared that his invention, dynamite, "killed more people faster than ever before." Alfred was so disturbed at this potential posthumous reputation that he later changed his last will and testament to bequeath his entire fortune to a new foundation that would award a series of prizes to "those who, during the preceding year, shall have conferred the greatest benefit on mankind."

ert's focus shifted from trees to oil. He immediately wrote to his brother and convinced Ludvig to purchase tracts of land in the Baku region. This began the Nobel oil empire in 1873. By 1876, the Nobels were the leading oil refiner in Russia.*

When Ludvig died in 1888, leadership of Branobel passed to his eldest son, Emanuel. Emanuel's ascension came with the full support of his uncle Alfred, who was living in France and still an active advisor and shareholder in the firm.

Emanuel was in the mold of his father—a bold technical innovator and savvy businessman. He was also one of the richest men in Europe. When word reached him of the wondrous new Diesel engine, he was quick to embrace what the technology could mean for his oil pumps, his engine-manufacturing plants, and his fleet of ships.

———

Rudolf Diesel met Emanuel Nobel in Berlin's Hotel Bristol on February 14, 1898. The next day Emanuel agreed to terms with Diesel and on February 16, Nobel incorporated the Russian Diesel Motor Company based in Nuremberg, Germany. Diesel received stock in the company worth 200,000 marks (20 percent of the company) and 600,000 marks in cash. In connection with this agreement, on April 9 Emanuel confirmed the exclusive rights to the Russian market for his manufacturing plant in Saint Petersburg.

Emanuel oversaw the first Diesel engine built in Russia in 1899. The following year he built three 100-horsepower engines for his oil-pumping operations in Baku. The year after, he built fifty-two engines

———

* In 1878, Ludvig Nobel launched the *Zoroaster*, the world's first oil tanker, which was designed by him and built in his foundry. Nobel built a pipeline from his refineries directly to his ship in port. With steel tanks strategically placed in the hull, the 180-foot ship could carry 240 gross tons of oil to markets across the Caspian Sea and along the River Volga, while competitors still transported oil in leaky wooden barrels pulled by horse-drawn wagons and loaded onto the decks of ships. The Nobels soon built a fleet of tankers as well as pioneered steel cisterns to transport oil across the railroads. Rockefeller was caught flat-footed by Nobel's advances in distribution, and by the turn of the century, Nobel's oil production exceeded that of Standard Oil.

of 150-horsepower each to power the oil pipelines running from the rapidly growing Baku region. To Diesel's surprise, Russia was off to the quickest start with his new motor.*

Many in the engineering community now recognized that the Diesel engine had the potential to fundamentally change power in the modern era. Firms from every industrialized country in the world eagerly sought a license from Diesel. Following the same distribution model as Linde, he rapidly proliferated Diesel technology. In just over a year, Rudolf executed more than twenty licensing agreements that covered Europe and North America.

These licensing deals represented a change in course for the Diesel engine that perhaps felt like a subtle shift to Rudolf at the time. He was now in bed with big business because it was big business that could pay the hefty licensing fees. These massive corporations were not tinkerers and dreamers who wanted to find a way to manufacture a tiny engine for the dentists, jewelry makers, and artisans like Theodor Diesel. These firms were already in the business of building engines of massive scale, huge engines that served the centralized economies of modern industry and, increasingly in this period of hyper nationalism, engines that served the military.

But for Rudolf, in the last years of the nineteenth century, this shift in direction was not so apparent. Though his engine had the potential to scale up to deliver much greater horsepower, it had not yet done so and delivered only a fraction of the power of the steam engine. Rudolf still had so much to figure out with his technology, and the grueling work of advancing the capabilities of his engine kept him from considering what the consequences of his success could mean.

Rudolf had yet to take the core engine from a single implementation in the laboratory environment to mass production. Beyond that, he

---

* By 1910, Russia had more Diesel power than any other nation in the world, with the exception of Germany.

also had to apply the engine to disparate industrial uses ranging from stationary engines that pump water, grind wheat, or generate electricity to mobile uses of the engine for transportation of ships and trains.

Despite these hurdles, the largest firms from nations around the globe recognized the transformative implications of Diesel power. In Denmark, the famous ship and steam engine builder Burmeister & Wain, based in Copenhagen, acquired the Diesel license for the country, and on December 20, 1897, paid Diesel 60,000 marks as well as guaranteed a 10 percent royalty on future sales by the company.

For France, Frédéric Dyckhoff, an old friend and confidant of Rudolf's, formed the holding company Société Française des Moteurs R. Diesel on April 15, 1897, to acquire the patent rights. Rudolf attended the signing in Bar-le-Duc and received 1,200,000 francs in company stock.

The French were among the first to apply the horizontal design of the engine (as opposed to the vertical design for stationary use) for marine propulsion on small canal boats. The French engineers also made some of the earliest efforts at a design for a reversible engine.

The momentum of Diesel dealmaking continued to swirl through Europe. It was in the national interest not to be left behind. In Sweden, Marcus Wallenberg, president of the Stockholm Enskilda Bank, and Oscar Lamm, an engineering tycoon, formed the Swedish holding company Aktiebolaget Diesels Motorer to purchase the license, and on January 25, 1898, paid Diesel 50,000 kronor in stock, 50,000 kronor in cash, and future payments of a 10 percent royalty.

For Italy, Fiat took the license. In addition to automobile fame, in the early twentieth century the company built well-regarded submarine engines. Japan also embraced the technology early in the new century, and eventually South America became one of the most highly "Dieselized" parts of the world.

———

In each of the Diesel licensing agreements at the close of the century, Rudolf contractually required his partners to share in the engine improvements and new patents. He envisioned an internationally cooperative network of engineers with a central and shared body of knowledge.

Each application of the engine was a new fork in the road for engineering design that required up-front effort for long-term benefit. Diesel intended for partners to share in their achievements to accelerate the benefit among the whole Diesel community.

Busch's expert, E. D. Meier, applauded Rudolf's requirement of his license partners to contribute to a shared knowledge base: "The broad minded and liberal policy inaugurated by Mr. Diesel in making all licensees agree to interchange experience and inventions, insures a rapid development in every field now commanded by the steam engine."

At first, Diesel's intention seemed to be embraced throughout the network of licensees, who viewed the required collaboration as a benefit. But as the world began to recognize the significance of his engine, in particular its military application, the sharing of new developments was tempered by the nationalism of the age. At the dawn of the new century, this nationalism was reaching fever pitch throughout Europe.

The more generous, internationally networked approach of scientists that Diesel envisioned soon gave way to the proprietary, militaristic approach of independent and paranoid nations.

CHAPTER 11

A Hiccup Before
the Grand Prize

"PERHAPS I—ONE SMALL MAN—will succeed in doing what all the governments together have failed to do: throw out the Rockefellers— that would be amusing!" Rudolf wrote these words to Martha on February 15, 1898, after a year of stunning licensing success for his superior engine that could burn fuels not derived from petroleum. Diesel's technology was the talk of engineering circles, and dozens of the most powerful firms in the world were committing substantial resources to bring the new engine to market. Companies that built the competing steam or Otto cycle engines were on notice. Producers of coal, natural gas, and petroleum that fed these types of engines were on notice too. But Diesel still had to replicate his laboratory success in the outside world.

Behind the closed doors of Diesel's new manufacturing partners, new teams of engineers were having trouble following in Diesel's foot- steps. E. D. Meier's cautionary afterthought in his report to Adolphus Busch that Diesel was more "theoretical" than "practical" seemed to have merit. Rudolf's presentation in Kassel had shown the world only that Diesel technology was possible, not inevitable.

The engine, now licensed to hands other than those of its creator, was not fully realized. Perhaps the engine needed more time in Augsburg under Rudolf's care. But business was business, and sponsors, especially the impatient Krupp, demanded a return on their investment. The engine had already earned Rudolf a fortune from the initial licenses. Now four Diesel engines built by international licensees would go on display at the much-anticipated 1898 Munich Power and Works Machine Exhibition. But Rudolf and the engineers of his new licensee partners knew the engines built for the exhibition were not ready.

More than Rudolf's reputation was at stake. Not only did he face the possibility of public humiliation in Munich but he also faced what would be the scorn and vengeance of the powerful industrialists who had trusted him with their reputations and money. He had accepted their millions on the premise that he had delivered the engine of the future. If he subjected these partners to embarrassment, the result would be far worse than merely having to start over. He likely would never be given another chance in his profession. His future as an engineer was at stake.

A panicked Rudolf knew that none of the engines built by his partners and brought to Munich was as robust as the evaluation engine he'd built in Augsburg. But Rudolf and his partners were caught in a river of press and high expectations. The partners, who had shelled out large sums for patent rights, had immediate sales and marketing objectives already teed up behind a successful showing at the exhibition. The momentum of predetermined plans carried the moment. Diesel prepared to walk a very public tightrope.

———————

The exhibition opened in June 1898 and the press billed it as the technical event of the year. Rudolf attended with his wife and three children, reconnecting with family during what ought to have been a moment of glory after long years building, then selling, his engine.

Hedy, thirteen, had grown to be a pretty young woman with facial features that resembled her father's. Rudolf Jr. and Eugen, fourteen and nine, both slender and growing tall like their six-foot-one father, had features more like their mother. Hedy was a happy teen and socially adept. Rudolf Jr. was sullen and withdrawn, and his own siblings described him as being this way throughout his life. Eugen was a father-worshiper and at this early age was determined to follow him into the engineering profession.

The most thrilling exhibit for the younger family members was a massive slide that launched passengers into the Isar River. Customers dressed in bathing attire, which then was as all-covering as evening dress, entered a wheeled cart that was pulled to the top of the slide by a power winch and then released so that the cart plummeted at breathtaking speed down the ramp and into the river with a soaking splash.

Photography was another thrill at the fair that Diesel, as an ardent fan of the medium, especially enjoyed. One booth featured an "automatic photo-machine." Customers deposited a coin, faced the magic box and a bright flash of light. In a few minutes, a small metal plate with the imprinted picture dropped into the "bath" beneath the box.

The exhibition included automobiles from Daimler and Benz that sputtered and spread fumes around the fairgrounds to the delight or disdain of onlookers and the clear consternation of the many horses.

For engineering aficionados, Diesel was the star. His four licensing partners had constructed a massive and costly display booth for the engines called Pavillion Diesel. A tall exhaust pipe stretched high through the roof of the large brown wooden structure. This pipe served mainly to highlight just how hard it was to see the barely visible exhaust. Diesel noted with pride the stunned faces of the crowd when contrasting the exhaust of the new wonder motor with the thick and sooty black smoke of the neighboring steam engines on display.

But problems arose from the start. The four manufacturing partners each presented the engine they had built in some haste to be ready in time for the exhibition. Krupp brought a thirty-five-horsepower engine, only the second Diesel motor its factory had ever built. During the first hours of the opening day, a part of the motor burned out. The engine didn't run most of that day.

Augsburg delivered a thirty-horsepower engine, but as Diesel's assistant engineer at the time, Paul Meyer, said: "At about ten minutes from the time of starting, even before it had reached operating temperature, there would be such a frightful detonation that no one stayed around it. It went into operation in the earliest morning hours so as not to frighten the visitors." Diesel later discovered that only a small modification to the engine fixed the problem—the type of issue easily caught and addressed in a lab.

The Deutz and Nurnberg plants each delivered a twenty-horsepower engine that had a set of problems too. Rudolf tossed aside the top hat and tailored suit, and for the duration of the fair returned to the work clothes of his laboratory and student days. Through sleepless nights he sweated and toiled alongside engineers from the four partner companies to make emergency fixes to the demonstration engines. He took risks and made shortcut modifications in the desperate hope that the motors could run during the daylight hours of the exhibition. The strain and lack of sleep began to take a toll and he suffered severe headaches.

Though his theoretical concepts were pure, this was complex and nascent technology. Not just any engineer could execute on the blueprint. Diesel's frenzied nocturnal efforts behind the scenes rescued the day, however. At least for the moment. As a matter of publicity, the exhibition was a great success. The English periodical *The Engineer* wrote on November 4, 1898, "The four engines at Munich ran very quietly, with no noise and scarcely any smell. The noiselessness of the exhaust was also commented on . . ."

Diesel had demonstrated his theory to the public to the benefit of his fame, but the hard truth was that the engine was not yet ready for the commercial market. As with many complex inventions, the engine needed more time with its creator in a laboratory before delivery to lesser-trained hands. But as the engine already existed outside the confines of Augsburg, Diesel needed to quickly close the gap between laboratory and commercial viability, as each public event represented possible ruin.

Diesel confided to one of his collaborators, Ludwig Noé, at the time of the exhibition that he was experiencing headaches, insomnia, and shaky nerves. Noé wrote that Diesel claimed "the development of his engine caused him great worry; he had many enemies and it was hard to defend himself because of his health. In addition, his engine was not yet ready for sale, various parts had to be fundamentally altered before one could view the Diesel engine as foolproof . . . On the way to the train station, Herr Diesel repeated again and again that his nerves were shot, and he had to go immediately to the mountains."

Diesel's licensees, who had paid handsomely, became increasingly aware of the unready state of the engine. E. D. Meier, as firm an ally as Diesel could have, wrote to Rudolf in frustrated terms:

> *There can be no doubt that great inventions require much of a strictly commercial nature to make them grandly successful, but it is after all an injustice to the commercial manager to start him on his work too soon. . . . The large sums of money paid for licenses can only be deemed to have been fairly earned when so much of them as necessary has been actually applied to the development of a motor which is a commercial success. The motor we bought was a mechanical success only.*

Diesel was already exhausted from his globe-trotting efforts to proliferate the technology. He was now taxed beyond his limits by the need to engage with his disparate network of licensees to problem-solve a range of engine troubles that should have been worked out prior, in the central lab of his Augsburg plant. The technology had spread far and wide, but the fact remained that only Diesel himself could truly do the job.

As Meier noted, Diesel's theory was sound. It was just hard for anyone else to achieve the reality. One engine customer at the time put it, "Everything went quite well as long as a mechanic from Augsburg and an engineering school professor were permanently on hand."

This was entirely the case with respect to the period 1898–1900, and to a large extent remained the case for certain marine and rail applications of the engine for another decade. Through the onset of the Great War, the Diesel engine worked best in the hands of talented engineers who had trained closely with, and who had the benefit of the ongoing participation of, Diesel.

Rudolf tried to reduce his load of increasingly noisy complaints from his partners by training a handful of promising engineers in the care and repair of the engine. He termed these men that he trained and employed his "first-aiders" and assigned them by territory. Karl Dietrich worked France and Germany; Ludwig Noé in Sweden, Denmark, and Hungary; Hans Erney in Great Britain and Belgium; and Anton Bottcher in Switzerland and the United States.

———————

Rudolf wanted to be a full-time scientist again, not run a commercial enterprise. On July 16, 1898, he wrote to Buz that he wished to put the business aspects of the engine aside so that he could devote himself again to the "one real goal of my life, the technical perfection of my engine."

In the same month he wrote to his friend and partner Berthold Bing of his plan to achieve this aim by removing the burden of business affairs related to the engine and placing them in a new company in which he maintained majority ownership.

On September 17, 1898, Rudolf founded the General Society for Diesel Engines in Augsburg, which united the many threads of his international business. The new company took over all of Diesel's stocks, royalties, and rights to patents as well as licenses both present and future. Diesel earned a cash payment of 3,500,000 marks (approximately $30 million today) and was the majority stock owner of the new company with minority owners Buz, Krupp, Nobel, Busch, Wallenberg, and Bing.

This transition greatly simplified Diesel's affairs and allowed him to focus on the commercial readiness of the engine core as well as pursue applications of the horizontal design for marine, rail, and automotive use.

But by the time he'd established the company, Diesel's nerves were shot and his health too frail to continue his present pace of work. His doctors prescribed a period of strict rest. In the fall of 1898, Diesel traveled to Merano, a resort community in the mountainous Tyrol region of northern Italy near the Alps. He remained there until April 1899.*

Diesel's engine hung on the edge of worldwide adoption, but an adverse wind could blow it back to obscurity, a mere museum piece alongside Cugnot's steam car and other technical marvels that might have been.

As the twentieth century dawned, Europe was in the mood to celebrate. The desire to capture the noteworthiness of the occasion was perhaps best reflected in the 1900 World's Fair in Paris, for which nothing was spared to make it the grandest fair in history.

This was the fifth such Parisian fair since 1855. Rudolf had attended as a child in 1867 to witness the triumph of the Otto engine, then in 1889 to witness the Eiffel Tower and exhibit Linde's ice machine.† In 1900, Diesel returned for a triumph of his own.

The fair opened on April 14, 1900. Over the course of its run through November 12, a staggering fifty million people attended, more than ten times the number that attended the well-publicized initial fair of 1855.

The strong presence of the upstart Americans was apparent. By 1900, industrial production out of the New World had surpassed that of Great Britain, which had led the world since the start of the Industrial Age. America accounted for 6,564 exhibits at the fair (up from only 703 exhibits at the 1867 fair), which represented nearly 10 percent of all participants and was second only to the host nation.

In the immediate wake of the Munich exhibition eighteen months prior, Rudolf had solved a series of reliability issues that his partners

-----

* The ever-clubbable Adolphus Busch took the opportunity to rib his friend and partner in a letter he wrote in early 1899 to the executives of Diesel's new company joking that he was unsure whether Rudolf's illness was from overexertion or from having too much money, and if the latter, he would be glad to relieve Rudolf of some of the 1,000,000 marks he had paid for the American license.

† Paris also hosted in 1878 when Diesel was a student in Germany.

had experienced. He also had ample time to prepare for the Exposition Universelle of 1900, to make his engine closer to "foolproof," and for the event in Paris he worked directly with his French partner to build the demonstration engine.

Diesel set up in the Palace of Industry, located on the esplanade between les Invalides and the Alexandre III Bridge. Next to Diesel inside the same pavilion, the young Austrian Ferdinand Porsche presented his first electric car, the Lohner-Porsche Mixte Hybrid 630. But the Grand Prix, the highest honor bestowed on any exhibit, went to the Diesel engine. An eighty-horsepower engine built by Frédéric Dyckhoff in Bar-le-Duc dazzled the spectators and judges.

The fair was a landmark occasion for the Diesel engine under the brightest spotlight of the international stage, and the engine performance was remarkable for two reasons. The first was obvious to onlookers—the smooth operation of the compact and fuel-efficient motor that looked and sounded a cut above the rest. The crowds nodded approvingly at the scant noise and air pollution.

The second reason was invisible to the ticketholders strolling by the Diesel booth, because the remarkable feature was held neatly in a tank and taken automatically by the engine during operation. The original characteristic was the nature of the engine's fuel. What the casual observer did not know, but the judges certainly did, was that this wonder motor that performed so impressively ran entirely on peanut oil.*

The high compression, and resulting high temperatures, in the cylinder efficiently burned viscous peanut oil that was so safe and innocuous at room temperature that it seemed incongruous with engine

---

* The peanut belongs to the broader category of nuts called arachide, plants widely cultivated in tropical regions, many of which were the colonial possessions of France, England, and Germany. The Diesel engine therefore made these prized territories a possible source of fuel. Rudolf Diesel frequently used the term "arachide" in his notes and speeches when referring to the nuts he used for oil. In direct collaboration with Diesel, Dyckhoff's designs were among the first to recognize the importance of stable engine fuels and greater fuel efficiency for marine use. Dyckhoff began a singular focus on engines for surface and submarine vessels, delivering successful models on the heels of the fair.

combustion. The implication of a leading combustion engine running on a readily available fuel not derived from petroleum or coal was certainly attention-grabbing, but not so geopolitically stunning as it seems today. In 1900, most people weren't thinking about gasoline and engines. Petroleum generally wasn't refined to make gasoline for engines at all, but to make kerosene for illumination. At this time there were scarcely any cars on the road, nor even roads built for cars, and it would be still another sixteen years before gasoline production finally surpassed kerosene production. The main mode of power was still the coal-fired steam engine, and though the geopolitics of global oil reserves as they related to engines would advance suddenly, in 1900 they were hardly understood.

But very soon after the event in Paris, the engine specialists, the captains of industry, and the leaders of nations without a domestic supply of fossil fuels would be paying attention to Diesel and the potential applications of his new technology. Conversely, the petroleum trusts that were looking to the internal combustion engine as a growing market began to recognize Diesel technology as a new threat.

The year 1900* was an inflection point for the Diesel engine. Five years earlier, prior to Diesel first presenting his engine to the public in Kassel, there were 18,070 internal combustion engines in Germany. These were mostly small Otto-design engines burning gaseous fuels, and with an average of four horsepower. In the same year in Germany there were 58,500 steam engines with an average of forty-six horsepower.

---

* During the run of the fair, on July 2, 1900, Rudolf accepted an invitation to join his friend Ferdinand Graf ("Count") von Zeppelin at Lake Konstanz near the northern Alps for the trial run of *Luftschiff Zeppelin 1*, his first rigid dirigible. The 420-foot airship took off with a crew of five men and two lightweight Otto-cycle Daimler engines powering the propellers for a semi-controlled five-mile loop. Graf von Zeppelin asked Rudolf if he could build a Diesel engine for an airship—at a time when the lightest Diesel in operation weighed six hundred pounds. Rudolf thought it was possible. Thirty-five years later, the *Hindenburg* (also known as *LZ-129*, a designation that tracked the number of dirigibles) made its first flight powered by four 1,190-horsepower Daimler-Benz engines, which gave the ship a maximum airspeed of eighty-four miles per hour. The engines were Diesels (and unrelated to the *Hindenburg* fire). If still alive, Rudolf would have been seventy-seven at the time of the *Hindenburg*'s maiden voyage.

This is in stark contrast to the paltry 77 Diesel engines in Germany by 1899, two years after Kassel. Eighteen months later, in June 1901, there were still only 138 Diesel engines in Germany, all stationary, averaging thirty-five horsepower.

But things had already begun to turn around. These engines were meeting the lofty expectations of Rudolf's partners. Diesel had returned from his rest, and a level of expertise that could reasonably approach that of the creator had spread to a handful of engineers. Over the next twelve months, by June 1902, the number of Diesel engines in Germany nearly tripled. Diesel was delivering on his promise.

CHAPTER 12

The Trappings of Success

Enormous sums of money had poured in over the first year of sales. No longer was Diesel the anxious and austere young scientist tethered to the laboratory, toiling away under the looming threat of bankruptcy and with the constant task of assuaging his deep-pocketed business partners. Diesel now had deep pockets of his own.

Wonderful new possibilities opened before him. After years spent holding his family at a distance for long stretches while he focused on his leviathan of the compression engine, he yearned to reunite with his beloved Martha and his children in a new and permanent home. And he didn't have to rely on the generosity of Buz to make it happen.

As he collected millions of marks from the first Diesel licensing deals, Rudolf and Martha began to look around Munich for a nice piece of land where they could build a home. They found a site on Maria-Theresia-Strasse, an avenue already lined with the mansions of Munich's elite that overlooked a park of lush grass and trees and sloped gently down to the waters of the Isar River. The Diesels bought the empty lot for 50,000 marks in early 1898 (about $400,000 today).

Rudolf had confided to his close friend Graf von Zeppelin that he "intended to build a modest home on a suitable site." That is not what happened.

Martha and Rudolf began a very expensive and time-consuming period of construction and decoration that lasted several years. Rudolf hired the renowned architect Max Littmann, who had recently completed the Munich Hofbräuhaus, and Diesel personally participated in all important design aspects. The result was widely regarded as the most beautiful and extravagant home in Munich.

There was a vast two-story entrance hall paneled in oak with a winding staircase that featured a banister carved from a single massive oak log. There was a palatial living room that adjoined a Louis XV–style "salon," an immense kitchen, a multitude of bathrooms, and every principal room had its own fireplace with a marble mantelpiece.

Rugs throughout the home were imported from Asia, the vaulted ceiling of the entrance hall was hand-carved and painted. The interior decoration, mostly overseen by Martha, included hand-carved French furniture, ivory-covered walls, oil paintings,* sculptures, and other decorative items.

The earth excavated for the massive foundation provided the soil to grade the formal gardens that surrounded the house. The cavity for the foundation and cellar was so large that Rudolf Jr. and Eugen lowered in bicycles and raced around the empty pit before the construction began.

After two full years of construction, the family took up residence in 1901. The total cost of the land, construction, and furnishings exceeded 900,000 marks, and came with the ongoing expense of a large household staff. Local newspapers hailed the mansion, called Villa Diesel, as the most splendid home in all Munich.

---

* The artwork included the painting by contemporary Belgian artist Franz Courtens of an evening scene by the estuary of the Scheldt River, the place of Diesel's disappearance in 1913.

Perhaps inspired by the fact that his childhood home had also served as Theodor's workshop, Rudolf designed a suite of rooms on the second floor to be a study and workshop of his own so that he could be closer to his family. As at 38 rue Notre-Dame de Nazareth, this arrangement came at the price of the smell of engine lubricants permeating the air in parts of the home. Sketches of locomotives, automobiles, ships and submarines, and the corresponding engine blueprints were tacked onto the walls, papering the suite of rooms with Rudolf's work.

Diesel could now serve both a passion for his engine and a passion for his family under one, very large, roof. Hedy wrote of happy times at the mansion in her unpublished memoirs. The children had a governess, and they took music, dancing, and art lessons. The family hosted large parties and balls, and held season tickets to the opera and theater. They received prominent foreign visitors such as Jakob Sulzer and Adolphus Busch, as well as members of Germany's high society, such as the families of Carl von Linde, Oskar von Miller, the aristocratic Graf von Zeppelin, and the actor Ernst von Possart.

Hedy attended a posh Swiss finishing school from 1901 to 1902, and after debuting in Munich society was briefly engaged to the cousin of future Nazi leader Hermann Göring.

Though she recalled her older brother, Rudolf Jr., as "melancholic," she remembered her own years in the mansion as having been full of joy.

Eugen, the youngest, remembered an evening when Rudolf sat at the grand piano in the Louis XV salon to play "The Prayer of Elisabeth" from *Tannhäuser*. "We all gathered to listen to Father. His playing brought tears to all our eyes."

Biographers of Rudolf Diesel have contended that the extravagance of the Munich mansion was irrational and "un-Diesel-like." But there is a lens through which the new home is wholly consistent with the man and his values. For Diesel, art and beauty were more than ornamental, they served a purpose. He believed as the ancient Greeks believed— that art can raise the aspirations of humankind.

As a youth, Diesel was attracted to and inspired by great works of art and music. His aim as an adult was to create environs for himself that would stimulate him to reach his full potential.

Perhaps even more than this, Villa Diesel was designed to bring him and his work closer to his family. During the Christmas of 1895 when Rudolf's family had moved to be closer to him thanks to the generosity of Heinrich Buz, Rudolf had built for his children a Chinese shadow theater and a dollhouse with furniture that he crafted by hand. Now he could build them a true home that put a vast distance between what his children's experience would be and what his own precarious childhood experience had been.

He could toil away in his workspace just steps from his wife and children, who could wander in for impromptu visits. The mansion was also a gift to Martha, who enjoyed her exalted social status as the wife of a prominent inventor. Martha had become more active in Munich society, hosting famous guests and accepting many of the invitations the couple received.

Rather than being un-Diesel-like, perhaps the extravagance of the home was both a scaffolding for his remaining ambitions and a slight overcompensation by a devoted husband and family man after a decade of all-consuming work.

———

Diesel found there was still more to make up for, more that he needed to nourish within himself after the years of singular and tireless focus on his engine. He had always felt that he had a responsibility not only to his invention but also to the social application of the invention. The need for such stewardship was never so apparent as at the turn of the century.

Economic centralization to urban areas driven by the forces of the Industrial Age caused rural economies to shrivel. But as people moved to cities for work and opportunity, they typically encountered conditions just as brutal as the hunger and hopelessness they'd left behind, effectively trading one horror for another. Rudolf and others of the period referred to this collective dislocation as the "Social Problem."

Diesel's intent with his engine had always been to help resuscitate rural economies, to make them a viable place for industrial opportunity. In the years 1902–3, Rudolf began to write a thesis for a societal architecture that would solve the problems of the modern era and rid the new century of the ghastly working conditions that had haunted Rudolf since his brief stay in London as a boy.

As the intense strain of his initial entry to market relented somewhat after his success in Paris, he was free to apply energy to this broader social ambition. In the new century, Diesel was a celebrity and a wealthy man. He was not only welcomed but sought after by those in the highest echelon of society. He was now seen as a national intellectual treasure. Yet throughout his life he identified more with the artisan class, more with the masses who toiled in the factories than with the few who owned them and claimed the profits.

His life was a journey that involved a period of sustained membership at each rung in society, from the very bottom to the top, not with the relaxed sense of temporary enrollment, but with the dread of permanence. His experience living at each rung informed his thoughts on the ladder of society, some of which he shared in a letter to his son Eugen, who was preparing to start work in Winterthur as a lowly factory apprentice:

> *You will learn more there about the truth of life and social relations than in our circles which have absolutely no idea of such things and regard every worker as a kind of robber . . . I regard it as good fortune when a young man has the opportunity to get a glimpse into all social classes and recognizes that the lower rungs are better than the higher.*

The people who impressed Diesel, who became his intimates, were never the frivolous bons vivants, but the serious men of industry and science: Nobel, Zeppelin, Sulzer, Linde, Schröter, the self-made Adolphus Busch, George Carels, Ivar Knudsen, and increasingly Charles Parsons, the English inventor of the steam turbine.*

Over the years that Rudolf climbed the ladder of success, his logical engineering mind began to develop a blueprint to organize society in a more efficient, productive, and humane way. As with his engine in a laboratory, he conducted experiments with his workforce. For his household staff and the factory workers in Augsburg, Rudolf put in place what he called the "human honor system," which was his effort at fair treatment and a kinder, less rigid workplace environment. He gave the employees more autonomy in their duties, sensing that more freedom and happiness would result in higher productivity.

The results of this effort were less than spectacular. Diesel's heart was in the right place, but he proved an ineffective manager. Not one to throw in the towel, he tried a social experiment in shared ownership that made an interesting contrast to the employment practices of other business leaders of the era. In both his home and his factory, he placed a large mason jar on a table and encouraged the household staff and the factory workers to place a penny in the jar each day. Rudolf contributed as well, saying that the funds would be "in readiness for the day when a share of the ownership would accrue to each one present."

Diesel's efforts toward enlightened ownership were forward-looking, but many of his colleagues weren't quite ready for his vision. His business partners and investors noticed that foremen in the factory "charged him with excessive leniency—pampering the hired help. Although [Diesel] steadfastly denied the charge, he did, however, begin

---

* The steam turbine, invented by Parsons in 1884, powered the massive battleships and other great ships of the day. The steam turbine was an *external* combustion engine that still required boilers, however, it did not have the design of a piston and crankshaft that made power strokes to rotate a wheel (which is called a reciprocating engine). Rather, the steam turbine used blades, like the blades of a fan but in a more sophisticated design, which rotated directly as a result of the steam pressure. Note that as a characteristic of all external combustion engines, the fuel never touched the blades (or the piston in the case of a reciprocating engine), only the steam heated by the fuel.

to notice with increasing resentment that workmen, including assistant engineers, were taking advantage of the laxity of discipline."

Diesel stepped away from a direct management role in the factory. Though strict and exacting of himself, he left the discipline of others to the foremen, and focused on his core competencies. But his efforts to improve the organizational hierarchies of the workplace were indicative of Diesel's gentle nature.

———

Diesel held a deeply considered and modern balance of beliefs. He accepted militarism as "insurance against wars" though he believed "no less devotedly that mankind can live in peace." He openly favored what he called an "international capitalistic system" as the best way to advance societies. And though he valued this form of competition, he rejected the theory of Social Darwinism that had emerged in the 1870s and become popular by the turn of the century. Social Darwinists applied the same biological concepts of natural selection to societies and nations, believing that the strong nations should grow stronger and vanquish the weak, that it is not only natural for a superior race to extend its influence across the earth but it is a duty, that war is thus a noble endeavor. Diesel held an opposing view, respecting the "inherent dignity" and "oneness of man," and he spurned the idea "that one nation or race of men differs basically from another."

———

In 1902, with his business affairs in order for the moment, Diesel began writing a treatise on a social solution for the Industrial Age. Ever the romantic, he selected November 24, 1903, his twentieth wedding anniversary, to publish *Solidarismus*.* He explained that "Solidarism is the understanding that the well-being of the individual is identical to

———

* Diesel deliberately did not use the German *solidaritat* (solidarity), which refers to communal bonds, but *solidarismus* (solidarism), which refers to organized, conscious love of humanity.

that of the community. If the community should intervene to help the individual, the individual must understand that he needed to work and sacrifice for the community."

The cover art of the book is a large *S* at the center of a six-pointed star. Diesel explained that the six rays represented the six main tenets of solidarism: veracity, justice, brotherhood, peace, compassion, and—the main tenet—love.

He presented his solution exactly as an engineer might. Of the book Rudolf wrote, "You have seen that nothing in *Solidarismus* is doctrine, theory, arbitrariness or self-deception. Everything is developed and calculated strictly logically and numerically from life and facts. Everything . . . is practically achievable."

These words are an uncanny reflection of the letter he had written to Linde on February 11, 1892, regarding his expectations for the Diesel engine. "The results are not a conjecture or hope, they can be proven mathematically to the point that no doubt can exist that they are achievable." Diesel designed both his engine and his social thesis using scientific, evidentiary methods.

Diesel's pursuit of social theory was not uncommon among his peers. Many engineers and scientists of the age frequently moonlighted as social theorists. These highly trained thinkers were inevitably concerned with the connection between their scientific achievements and the resulting effects on society once industry applied the achievements.* Diesel believed that he and his colleagues were not only the ones to build the technologies to enable a more productive and equitable world but also the ones logically to develop the social construct to fit the advancing world.

---

* Diesel believed in the concept of a natural religion. He felt that the religious drive inside man is born of the fear of the unchangeable laws of nature. He argued that gods are the personification of these natural laws that govern men, and that the Christian religion had simply attributed all the powers of nature to one god rather than to many personified gods. Diesel believed that solidarism could be viewed as the "transformation of Christian personal morality into the social, economic sphere." Diesel felt his social construct would shift the emphasis from happiness in the hereafter to happiness in this life.

The impulse for inventors to broaden their scope from science to society continues in full force today. Innovators and entrepreneurs such as Bill Gates and Warren Buffett who made fortunes in industry then apply their acquired power to new endeavors with social benefit, such as to rid the earth of diseases, to preserve the environment through the removal of carbon from the atmosphere, to launch humankind into space. But these ambitions are comparative molehills next to Diesel's mountainous ambition to solve the "Social Problem," which has confounded man since the dawn of civilization.

Rudolf wrote to Martha of his treatise, "The engineer is entering a new era, in which he will gradually grasp the decisive influence in the state away from the lawyers."

Solidarismus was set for an initial print run of ten thousand copies in 1903. Diesel was thrilled at his latest achievement, believing that his treatise, even more than his engine, would better the world.

Pablo Picasso wrote hundreds of poems. Sycophantic fans of the artist gave high praise to his poetry. Late in his life, Picasso predicted that despite his achievements as a painter, the world would remember him primarily as a great poet. Diesel suffered from a similar delusion.

After his book's publication, Rudolf said, "That I have invented the Diesel engine is well and good, but my chief accomplishment is to have solved the social problem." Diesel soon became aware of his naïveté.

Sales of *Solidarismus* were poor—only a few hundred copies sold. Diesel was terribly disappointed. Public attention for the book quickly evaporated. As one reviewer wrote, *Solidarismus* was "like so many of its predecessors, a printed utopia, a beautiful dream."

CHAPTER 13

A Study of the Sleeping Giant

Rudolf boarded the SS *Kaiser Wilhelm II*, the glittering German passenger liner, in the summer of 1904. At more than seven hundred feet long and more than nineteen thousand tons, this high-speed transatlantic ship offered unprecedented levels of luxury for first-class passengers and a startling contrast in austerity for those in steerage. But all passengers, including Diesel, enjoyed her unmatched speed. In 1904, she held the Blue Riband, the accolade awarded to the ship making the fastest eastbound crossing.

Diesel, swallowing his disappointment with the reception of *Solidarismus*, headed for New York, eager to visit with his partner Busch, and to form his own opinions of the increasingly powerful young nation.

Ever the student and scientist, he kept a diary, yet it was no ordinary person's chronicle of events and impressions. Diesel recorded nearly two hundred densely filled pages with his thoughts on America, meticulously indexed by category of observation, including the arts, education, the economy, the people, the cities, railroads, ships, hotels, and the exhibition in St. Louis.

The insightful and often highly amusing observations recorded in his diary begin during the Atlantic crossing. In the pages, Rudolf kept detailed charts of the ship's longitudinal and latitudinal coordinates throughout the voyage (both eastbound and westbound), monitored the daily coal consumption of the engines, noted the size of the crew and number of man-hours required of the engine stokers, and calculated the ship speed. (For the opposite leg of the trip the much smaller steamer *Praetoria* had a median speed of 11.89 knots and completed the trip in eleven days, ten hours, and twenty-one minutes. The *Kaiser Wilhelm II* averaged 23.5 knots, completing the trip in half the time.)

At the same time, he took equal pleasure in his reflections on fellow passengers. Because of the period's greater ease of ocean passage, a rising trend in America was to travel to the Old World to work, study, vacation and, possibly, to find a spouse. Entertained by the behavior of the many Americans aboard, Diesel noted, "All the single ladies who have studied at some German university—medicine, pathology, languages—and who consider themselves very learned are grasping for originality. All the flirting at all the corners, the many games on deck."

Storms and rough seas took a toll on many of the passengers, especially the children. "Moving family scenes on the in-between decks, especially during sea-sickness, whole families gathered around one pillow. Children like on an anthill—men, women and children lying all over the deck—preferring to be completely drenched [in the storm] rather than crawl back inside." But as the storms passed and the seas calmed, the journey became high-spirited. "Happy games and melancholic national songs when the weather is fine, especially at night. . . . Flying fishes, whales, cloud formations and coloration more beautiful than in the mountains."

These diary entries—one of cold, mechanical observation and the other of warm, human whimsy—were bound together as sequential pages. The juxtaposed entries show Diesel's natural comfort moving between the sciences and the arts, embodying his belief in the connectedness of the two disciplines. Rudolf was the rare individual to hold the qualities of a practical man and the qualities of a dreamer in one person, giving scrutiny not only to the question *How?* but also to *Why?*

Once in New York Harbor, Diesel moved from the docks through the throngs of immigrants and the crush of locals looking to hire cheap labor. He was first awestruck by the beautiful bridges of the city. The Brooklyn Bridge, a celebrated feat of engineering, had opened twenty-one years before in 1883. It had been the longest suspension bridge in the world until just months before Diesel's arrival when the Williamsburg Bridge, also in New York City, opened in late December 1903 and claimed the title.

From his port of disembarkation, he visited Toronto, Philadelphia, Pittsburgh, Washington, D.C., then went on to Chicago and St. Louis and as far west as San Francisco. His astute and thorough record is one of the most revealing accounts of American life at the turn of the century, and shows him to be variously amused, stunned, appalled, and admiring of the things and people he encountered along the way.

Diesel observed a quality in Americans that he called the "utility principle," noting that "nothing superfluous is tolerated."

He respected this tendency in many matters, as one might expect from an engineer focused on efficiencies. But when Diesel observed that the American adherence to utility extended to the arts, travel, and leisure, he found it less admirable. He felt an all-consuming industrial obsession to be out of balance. Diesel's life and work were an attempt to bridge the arts and sciences, and he began to suspect that America in the boom times of 1904 undernourished the connection between the two. He wrote, "One can say [of America] that the main focus is on saving time and money, since there are hardly any other considerations. Just as we [in Europe] visit museums and galleries, one visits in America factories and industrial establishments."

He noted that at many of the industrial plants he visited there were "running balconies for the visitors, without disturbing the workers." People wanted to see the factories up close. In the New World, industry *was* the gallery, the active museum. Diesel noted approvingly, "There are big dining halls for the workers, splendidly set tables (lunch for women is free, for men it is ten cents), a big theater and lecture hall for free use of the workers which is also used by schools and clubs." Impressed with American hygiene, even among the working class, he logged in his notes a perk absent in Europe: "Wonderful baths and showers, and the management approval of bathing during the working hours, 1 hour per week."

Sharp contrasts with the Old World leapt out everywhere he looked. His most unpleasant surprise came with the first heavy rainfall on these young American cities and towns, which revealed the still-inadequate urban planning for drainage and sewage. During his stay in New York and San Francisco, Rudolf observed "whole parts of the city underwater for days" and the "total inability to pass through the standing water." Nor would anyone want to attempt to pass through what he described as an "ocean of feces."

Of the cities he visited as he made his way west by rail, he wrote, "One city after the other has incredibly savage conditions in the business centers. The cobblestone is miserable, not maintained, almost impossible to navigate with a cart . . . telephone wires and other wires dangle from crooked, crude poles or trees which makes an incredibly repulsive picture. Streets are hardly cleaned at all . . . they serve as workspace and storage space for residents, dirt and paper are everywhere."

In a departure from the stone and brick construction of homes in Paris, London, and Berlin, Diesel noted that wood from the abundant forests was the dominant material used in American construction. Through a European lens, the ubiquitous use of wood was startling. The rapid route to infrastructure taken by Americans led Diesel to observe that "the main characteristic of the American is the fear of fire."

He noted that the hotels throughout his continental journey conducted weekly fire drills and provided in each room "smooth ropes to climb out of the window in case of fire." Iron fire escapes covered the facades of hotels and even the most beautiful homes.

In city after city, he saw that, "Everywhere you have iron staircases all built outside the houses, ladders, water mains, alarm signals, water hydrants on the street, and still there are constantly fires everywhere you look. In Chicago a theater burned down while we were there, in Toronto a whole neighborhood burned in April. Traveling by rail, you see burned houses everywhere. No surprise if you build with wood and boards."

Of the rapidly built towns of the turn-of-the-century American West he wrote, "The horrendous wooden architecture of San Francisco (and many other cities), an imitation of classical style. Fabrication of Corinthian and Doric columns, thousands of whole architectural forms made out of wood, cypress, ordered from a catalogue and nailed from the outside on the wooden boards of houses. Almost all houses are wooden boxes, with the exception of the most wealthy residences, the businesses and public buildings."

In the American mindset for quick and easy beginnings, Diesel would soon recognize an obstacle for his engine. While the Diesel engine delivered greater performance, its construction required greater time, expense, and superior materials. The more rudimentary Otto-cycle engines were cheaper and quick to build, but required frequent ongoing maintenance, were smoky, and often caused hazardous fires.

Pollution had been a source of concern for Diesel as far back as his London days, and he saw from an American skyscraper that "almost every house has an enormous smoking chimney and a thick pipe for steam. The mixture of black smoke and white steam clouds is quite typical for the American city and covers it in an indescribable coat of smoke and fog."

He was happy to find that the Auditorium Hotel in Chicago housed vertical steam engines that delivered five thousand horsepower linked directly to "dynamos and pumps" that operated the lighting, elevators, washing machines, electric ironing machines, "humongous fire sprinklers" and powered running water to guestrooms on the top floors.

Amid the rapid, often haphazard, development of its infrastructure, Diesel recognized the unique potential of the United States. As a methodical engineer, he peppered his diary with dismay at the lack of planning in the American rush to seize the opportunities that had come to the nation through the combination of virgin territory, preposterously abundant resources, and near-total lack of regulation. He also knew from experience that the disorderliness he witnessed was the natural fits and starts of a massive undertaking in its first phases. He saw opportunity, greater than any in Europe.

––––––––––

Rudolf's observations of the people who inhabited these cities sound like the amused quips of a visitor to an exotic zoo. Each town he visited had a hotel and many saloons "with fierce looking clientele."

Observing the typical American hustle in the quest for the next buck, he noted another difference between America and Europe. "The hotel lobbies are like the hallways of the stock exchange, like public squares, there are a lot of vending booths; newspapers, cigars, souvenirs etc., then there is the barber shop, the bar, the shoe polisher, the soda shop and the pharmacy."

A certain roughness extended even to those whose appearance didn't suggest it. When he entered a bank, on the wall to the right was a poster with sketches of two fearsome men, wanted for robbery and murder. The refined and impeccably dressed German visitor walked farther inside the bank. Behind a counter sat the teller, a sweet-looking older lady. On the table beside this gentle-looking soul, within easy reach, were two loaded revolvers that she was prepared to use. Back home the traditional-mannered Diesel would have been taken aback even to see a woman riding a horse with a man's saddle. That grannies with pistols could be a commonplace scene in the American frontier was truly an alien experience.

Rudolf walked from the bank to the street where there were no sidewalks, and the way would have been impassable but for the wooden boards thrown down over the deep puddles of mud. He made his way to the train where, as was the custom in America, the conductors were armed to the teeth.

As the train moved from the city to the wilderness of Oregon and Washington, he witnessed raging "colossal" forest fires that clouded the skies for hundreds of miles and filled his nostrils with the odor of smoke. He despaired at the "waste" and "terrible devastation" of the forests.

However, he found that the construction of the rail lines was excellent. The train cars ran more quietly than in Europe and he noticed "the tracks are joined very tightly, and the railroad ties are at least twice closer together [than in Europe]."

But again, he noted the American prioritization of function over European form. There is romance in the European rail system worthy of a vacation. Not so in America. "The wagons don't have any suspension. Men, women and children all sleep in one wagon, as many as three in one bed. The toilets are cramped due to an excess of luggage and the many suitcases squeezed in tight spaces. The Pullman buffet cart is a single man with a petrol stove who serves only canned food, just like we have on mountain huts." And perhaps his chief grievance: "No alcoholic beverages!"

The stations were not designed for comfort but were only a place to stop, functional in the barest sense. "The train stations are dreadful, made of rough-cut boards and iron with rust as thick as your finger. There is no signal of departure, no announcement of the station. There are no sidewalks or underground access, so the public climbs over the tracks as it pleases and nobody even cares. Everyone urinates everywhere: passengers, officers, luggage carriers, etc. It is such chaos."

Moving from the train station into the town centers he observed, "On the streets, elbows are pushed in your ribs. Everywhere people spit, enormous amounts of smoking, chewing of tobacco, the foyers of hotels look like dirty bars and the men hang themselves in doorways. Feet are placed on tables, even in the presence of ladies."

———

In convivial disbelief that has extended to Europeans of the twenty-first century, he watched the Americans eat. "Food: as many courses as you like, huge quantities, therefore the tendency to consume a lot of food in arbitrary combinations. Ice cream is served with every meal, and in-between as a snack. Often, ice cream twice with one meal, in the middle and at the end."

With a more concerned tone, he noted the unhealthy canned foods that were commonplace fare for most Americans and blamed this on the culture of mass production and the monopolists. He felt that powerful financiers could vertically integrate industries to control markets, then hold the American consumers prisoner to a limited choice of products. Feeling subjected to the will of monopolistic forces he wrote, "Terrible hotels in Yellowstone, for days on end only canned food, ruthless exploitation by the food manufacturers who have founded the hotel corporations. Morgan's [J.P. Morgan] prunes are in every Yellowstone hotel just because Morgan [as a shareholder of the hotels] bought a whole shipload of prunes. Those canned foods he could not sell the year before are now being delivered to the hotels."* Morgan's business practice was objectionable on its own, but the taste and health concerns were equally concerning. "Half of America lives off canned goods!" wrote Diesel, adding, "It truly is a poisoning of the people by the monopolists . . . even the French fries are sold in ready-made cartons."

Embedded in each town was "a more or less well stocked hardware store" and Diesel surmised the shop owner to be "the future millionaire of the town." He observed many "primitive shops" in these smaller towns that "sell a bit of everything as it becomes available." He was amused at the American penchant for artifacts of the Old World, noting that some of these primitive shops sold "very old shelf huggers [something put aside, abandoned] of other countries, especially Germany, sometimes for enormous prices."

He recognized that here was the bad with the good, the elevation of function at the expense of form. America had the singular forward focus of a shark, which Diesel acknowledged was a recipe for success. But this came at the price of the simple joys and everyday luxuries relished in Europe. Rudolf, equally facile with quantitative and qualitative expression, understood the trade-off.

---

* Rudolf also noted that American art museums were poor compared to Europe, and that the best-quality art in America was in private collections. However, he had great admiration for the patronage and the contents of American libraries, noting that "the Boston library contains 350 newspapers in all languages, 1500 periodicals, and in 1903 made 1.5 million loans to the city."

Theodor Diesel's business card showing the address of his workshop and the Diesel family home in Paris at the time of Rudolf's birth.

Rudolf Diesel, age twelve, 1870.

Rudolf Diesel upon completing his studies in Munich, 1880.

Martha Flasche photographed in 1883, the year she married Rudolf Diesel.

5

The Gallery of Machines, which housed an eighty-horsepower Diesel engine
built by Frédéric Dyckhoff, at the Paris Exposition Universelle of 1900.

6

7

A first edition of Rudolf Diesel's treatise,
Solidarismus, published in 1903.

Rudolf Diesel (left), Heinrich Buz (center), and
Moritz Schröter at the public unveiling of the Diesel
engine in Kassel, Germany, June 1897.

Rudolf Diesel hiking in the Italian resort village Madonna di Campiglio
with his children: Rudolf Jr., Hedy, and Eugen, 1899.

A playful Rudolf Diesel
with daughter, Hedy, and the
family dog, 1900.

A view of the interior of Villa Diesel in Munich, Germany.

Exterior view of Villa Diesel.

Carl von Linde (1842–1934), a pioneer of refrigeration. Linde was a mentor to and early employer of Rudolf Diesel. He continued to support Diesel publicly and financially.

Heinrich von Buz (1833–1918) led Maschinenfabrik Augsburg from 1864–1913. Buz gave crucial support to the development of the Diesel engine, and also developed the first refrigeration machine for Linde.

Sir Charles Algernon Parsons (1854–1931), best known for his invention of the steam turbine in 1884. He exhibited his turbine-powered yacht, *Turbinia*, at Queen Victoria's Diamond Jubilee in 1897. He and Diesel became close friends.

Adolphus Busch (1839–1913), brewing tycoon and pioneer of Diesel power in America. In 1913, Busch tried to hire Chester Nimitz to work for his Diesel business, but Nimitz turned him down.

First Lord of the Admiralty Winston Churchill meets Danish shipping magnate
Hans Niels Andersen, founder of the East Asiatic Company and owner of the Diesel-
powered *Selandia*, March 1, 1912. The two men were attending the arrival of the
Selandia at the West India Docks of London on her maiden voyage. Churchill called
the ship "the most perfect maritime masterpiece of the century."

Kaiser Wilhlem II (center with hat) with Hans Niels Andersen (left)
and members of the German Imperial Navy aboard the *Fionia*, sister ship
to the *Selandia*, during the Kiel Regatta, June 25, 1912.

John D. Rockefeller (1839–1937), cofounder of Standard Oil and the richest man in the world.

Kaiser Wilhelm II (1859–1941) ruled the German Empire from June 15, 1888, until his abdication and exile on November 9, 1918.

Admiral John "Jackie" Fisher (1841–1920), a legend in the Royal Navy, returned to service as First Sea Lord in 1914 under Winston Churchill. Fisher was early to recognize the value of submarines.

Grand Admiral Alfred von Tirpitz (1849–1930) authored Risk Theory, the German Empire's strategy to develop a world-class navy that could threaten Britain's mastery of the seas. Tirpitz advocated for unrestricted submarine warfare during the Great War.

Titans of innovation, Rudolf Diesel and Thomas Edison in New Jersey, May 1912.

Poster for the 1913 exposition in Ghent where Rudolf Diesel was last seen prior to the *Dresden* crossing.

SS *Dresden*: A British passenger ship built in 1896, owned and operated by the Great Eastern Railway. Rudolf Diesel's hat and neatly folded coat were found by the rail of the promenade deck at the stern of the ship on the morning of September 30, 1913. The Royal Navy requisitioned the ship in 1915 for the war effort and renamed her the HMS *Louvain*. On January 21, 1918, the ship was torpedoed and sunk in the Aegean Sea by a German U-boat.

Rudolf Diesel's enameled pillbox that was allegedly discovered on a floating corpse in the North Sea, then used as an identification aid by Rudolf's son Eugen. The pillbox is slightly smaller than the palm of your hand.

While Diesel found the American urban planning of 1904 to be crude and the residents of the urban centers to be distinctly zoo-like, the country's economy was a different matter. Diesel identified elements that Europe should copy, and others that it should avoid.

He wrote approvingly, "The high salary of the masses is the main explanation for the economic success of the United States." He felt Europe would benefit from imitating this tendency to pay higher wages. Then, in a seemingly inconsistent declaration, he identified the trade unions as the main source of inefficiency in the American economy.

Rudolf wanted companies to pay high wages because it was the good and sensible thing to do. But he specifically wanted the high wages driven by the employer's common sense, rather than by a trade union that would then be in the position to force a raft of additional, insensible conditions. This merger of opposing philosophies in Diesel defies all description except utopian capitalist.

Witnessing the American prosperity, Diesel lamented that "the European worker has only the minimum to live, he cannot save anything or only very little. The American worker has much more than the minimum, he can save a lot and most of them do."

Then he aimed his hottest ire at the trade unions. As a businessman and engineer who strove to leap the hurdles of inefficiency in manufacturing, he felt sympathy for his American counterparts who were tied in knots by some of the unreasonable conditions of unions. In particular, he noted the challenges faced by his friend Adolphus Busch. "All brewery workers in St. Louis are unionized. Busch, for example, cannot choose his own workers, he has to take the ones the Union keeps sending him. Each dismissal is investigated by the Union. If it is decided that the dismissal was not justified, Busch has to hire him back, otherwise he will not get another worker."

Even worse, from the perspective of the inventor, was that "better and newer machines are boycotted by the trade unions. Certain machines that would save time in shoe production cannot be installed.

Busch is not allowed to have his bottles blown by compressed air, he <u>has to</u> have them blown by hand. The national printing press in Washington has gorgeous machines to print money, but they <u>have to</u> print them by hand and leave the machine idle" (Diesel's emphasis).

For a man like Diesel, who looked to gain increments of efficiency large and small at every turn, this inability to embrace new technology was sacrilegious.

Yet Diesel's devotion to efficiency was not absolute. He was equally committed to quality. Mechanized production should replace manual production only if the resulting product was of the same or better quality. In the wild growth of the American economy he noted, with some humor, three examples of the unfortunate application of mechanized production. He wrote that America had "wonderful bakeries with mills, but no edible bread; wonderful pie companies, but the pies are disgusting; wonderful furniture factories, but the furniture they produce is atrocious."

He also had a laugh at the marketing schemes blazed on posterboards at nearly every retail shop:

In almost all stores, even the very good ones, there are two prices, such as:

Worth: $5
Sales Price: $3

And the public falls for that scam.

More than anything else, Diesel saw in America her raw, untapped, and massive potential. He came to love the open possibilities for roads and railways to bind together the abundance of resources and the energized population, which seemed to accept no preordained limits. It was a nation fit for a man like Diesel, whose passion was to stamp out inefficiency, flip disadvantage to advantage, and, in his hoped-for vision, change the social fabric to match his "beautiful dream." America would continue to occupy his thoughts for the rest of his life.

CHAPTER 14

"The Old House"
Fights for Its Life

WHILE RUDOLF TOURED American cities from New York to San Francisco, America's largest company faced an existential crisis that forced a desperate overhaul of its products and approach to the marketplace.

Though Rockefeller also owned several coal mines, throughout the latter part of the nineteenth century he had generated his wealth primarily by refining crude oil to make kerosene for illumination. Having dispatched whale fat and vegetable oils as alternative illumination fuels, his petroleum-derived product was dominant, and his firm, now more than thirty years in operation, had earned the venerable nickname "the Old House."

His method in achieving monopoly had been to control costs and eliminate reliance on outside vendors through vertical integration of his company. Not only did he own the mines and oil wells but he also owned the refineries, manufactured his own barrels, laid his own pipeline network, and purchased railroads. His retail operation included horse-drawn wagons with the Standard Oil logo to deliver kerosene to rural neighborhoods. He owned every stage of the business, from the raw minerals in the ground to final retail delivery to the homes of his customers throughout the world.

Among his largest costs, and the most difficult to manipulate given the advent of unions, was labor. To fight the unions, Rockefeller did what many of the other major trusts (sugar, tobacco, steel) did. He hired the Pinkerton National Detective Agency. These heavily armed and trained detectives whose corporate logo was the menacing and ever-watchful "lidless eye" performed multiple tasks for Rockefeller including espionage, sabotage, and worse.

Pinkerton's work could be cruel and decisive. Andrew Carnegie and Henry Frick had famously employed the Pinkerton Agency to bust up a strike of the Amalgamated Association of Iron and Steel Workers at the Carnegie Steel Company in Homestead, Pennsylvania, in July 1892. When the union failed to reach a collective bargaining agreement with Frick, he locked the union workers out of the plant and installed barbed wire, sniper towers, and searchlights. Frick hired three hundred private security detectives from Pinkerton, armed with Winchester rifles, to escort replacement workers through the picket lines of the striking union workers. The result was a bloodbath with casualties suffered on both sides in the conflict, and a short-term business success for Carnegie Steel on the disputed issues. Through the late nineteenth and early twentieth centuries, Pinkerton won additional business of this type. The majority of Pinkerton's revenue through these decades came from clients who paid for union-busting rather than traditional detective work.

In conjunction with Pinkerton, Rockefeller designed an intricate system of intelligence and payoffs. Detectives bribed railroad employees as well as the bookkeepers of competing refineries. Some detectives posed as miners, taking jobs in Rockefeller's own coal mines alongside the unionized labor in order to exert influence and spy. These detectives were known only by a number (predating James Bond by several decades). For example, in 1903 A. H. Crane, known in the Pinkerton offices only as Operative No. 5, penetrated the hierarchy of the Mill & Smeltermen's Union in Colorado City and was appointed to lead the union's "strike committee" even as he was submitting near-daily reports of union activity back to Pinkerton. His activities eventually aroused suspicion from coworkers who followed him, discovered clear evidence of his betrayal, and then beat him nearly to death.

The corporate logo of the Pinkerton National Detective Agency showing the lidless eye and the promise "We Never Sleep."

Rockefeller was prepared to meet any threat to Standard Oil with force. The contrast between Diesel's masonry coin jar for shared employee ownership with Standard Oil's sniper towers, bribery, and espionage is almost laughable in its proportion. As Diesel made clear in the 1904 journal of his American trip, he did not support labor unions, but he held equal disdain for monopolies, especially ones made by unlawful practices. Diesel believed in a natural economic order whereby labor is paid a fair wage. He disliked both monopolies and labor unions because each exerts artificial pressure on the natural order, and as each works to counteract the other, the system can fall into chaos.

But Rockefeller was no utopian dreamer theorizing about the natural order of things. With his advantageous cost controls and the massive scale and resources of the company to absorb periods of financial loss in order to sell product below cost, Standard Oil engaged in predatory pricing tactics. In the way that Standard Oil had dumped low-priced kerosene on the Chinese market to undercut competition from vegetable oils for illumination, Rockefeller selected isolated competitive markets where he would reduce prices temporarily and kill off competition.

While vegetable oils could provide fuel for illumination, as well as fuel for Diesel's new engine, there were enormous infrastructure costs associated with developing the agriculture and refinery operations to produce the oil. Rockefeller was strategic in supplying his petroleum-based oil to certain markets at an attractive cost to undermine the incentive to develop vegetable-based oils on a large scale.

From 1902 to 1904 Ida Tarbell published a nineteen-part series on the practices of Standard Oil for *McClure's Magazine* in which she observed that once Rockefeller had killed his competition through predatory pricing, "the price of [Rockefeller's] oil has always gone back with a jerk to the point where it was when the cutting began, and frequently higher."

As part of his predatory pricing schemes, Rockefeller often created fake companies, such as Eureka, Eagle, and Dixie Oil Works, to sell low-priced oil so that it wouldn't be under the Standard Oil brand. When the trend toward natural gas illumination began, Rockefeller, as the owner of the wells and mines that produced natural gas, was well positioned to continue his domination.

But by the end of the nineteenth century there was a new market entrant for illumination. In 1879, Thomas Edison filed a patent for the incandescent light bulb. In that year, he created a bulb that glowed for one hundred hours, and the market for artificial illumination, until then provided mainly by kerosene, natural gas, or candles (if anything at all—most rural and urban areas were dark and quiet after sundown), entered a period of enormous change. Edison took on Rockefeller's kerosene lighting, touting the "soft radiance" of electric lights as "singularly powerful and even . . . perfectly steady." Electric lights were soon installed along Boston's sidewalks and in Philadelphia's

Wanamaker department store, and famously in the New York City offices of J. P. Morgan on September 4, 1882. Rockefeller fought back in typical fashion. Among other illegal efforts, he gave his emissary G. A. Shelby $15,000 in cash and $10,000 in gas stock with which to buy Detroit politicians who were deciding on the future of the city's municipal lighting.

By 1885, there were still only 250,000 electric light bulbs in use in America. But with an inferior product like kerosene, even Rockefeller couldn't hold back the tide of electric illumination. By 1902, the number of bulbs in use had risen to eighteen million. Standard Oil was defeated.

Rockefeller might have been ruined except that nearly simultaneously with the collapse of the kerosene illumination market, a lifeline appeared: the internal combustion engine and, in particular, the automobile. Gasoline, a by-product of the refining process once thought to be of insignificant value, could be the savior of the world's largest industrial trust.

Automobiles were initially thought to be noxious, noisy, and so slow that onlookers were prompted to yell "Get a horse!"* But soon after the turn of the century, improvements to the automobile brought the horseless carriage into vogue. With desperate anticipation, Rockefeller looked to the automotive market to take off. Yet it was not so simple as that.

As Rudolf Diesel passed through New York City in 1904, the urban population was served by a fleet of one thousand New York City taxis. Yet none of these automobiles burned gasoline. As vegetable oils offered an alternative fuel for illumination, the electric car offered an alternative to the gasoline-powered car and threatened to yank away the lifeline to Standard Oil.

However, unlike a light fixture, the one thousand NYC taxis, called

---

* In May 1899 Jacob German, a New York City taxi driver, received the first-ever speeding violation in America for traveling twelve mph in an eight-mph zone. He was pulled over by a policeman on a bicycle. This predates the advent of the speeding ticket in 1904, and Jacob German had to spend the night in jail.

Electrobats, purchased by William Whitney's Electric Vehicle Company (the same Whitney of philanthropic, horse-racing, and art-collecting fame), were mobile and required a battery. Early batteries were lead acid, powering three-horsepower motors with a range of fifty miles. Whitney installed battery-charging stations in his taxi warehouse and at strategic locations around the city, including on Broadway in Midtown Manhattan. As the American rural road system was hardly built by that time, the fifty-mile range (a multiple less than gas, depending on the size of the fuel tank) for an urban car was acceptable.

But the battery technology proved problematic almost immediately. The lead-acid batteries and the upgraded nickel-iron batteries developed by Thomas Edison were a frequent maintenance headache, took hours to recharge, and after short periods of use would leak corrosive acid that was destructive to the vehicle.

Henry Ford, a former employee of Edison Illuminating Company in Detroit, now encountered his old boss in the automotive market as Edison tried to tackle the battery problem. Once again, Edison aimed to capture a market that was presently served by Rockefeller's petroleum. There was a brief reunion and collaboration between Edison and Ford that might have posed a crippling threat to the gasoline automobile. The two men worked together to build prototypes of an electric vehicle called the Edison-Ford, but this vehicle never reached commercial viability, largely due to a mysterious fire at Edison's laboratory in West Orange, New Jersey. The fire at the Edison plant and laboratory made national headlines and led to speculation that the oil trusts were behind the incident.

———

The massive blaze that consumed eleven modern concrete structures that were supposed to be "fireproof" was economically devastating. The *Anderson Intelligencer* reported, "The fire covered almost a square mile of ground causing a property loss of $7 million [$261 million adjusted to 2022], all of which except $3 million of insurance Mr. Edison will have to bear." Arson was never proved, although it was clear that

Pinkerton (and similar agencies such as Baldwin-Felts) was acting as the paramilitary wing of Big Business, and because Rockefeller had been villainized as the very public face of American oil trusts, the court of public opinion was ready to convict.

But public sentiment was of little use to Edison and Ford in the matter. Ford abandoned his pursuit of electric vehicles soon after the fire, and ultimately swung the market fully to the combustion engine by delivering a reliable gasoline-powered car for $500, a fraction of the cost of the more expensive electric cars that cost anywhere from $1,500 to $4,000. With the advent of the electric starter for gasoline-powered cars, eliminating the need for the hand crank, the electric car fell by the wayside. Rockefeller could step back from the abyss.

That is, until Rudolf Diesel revealed an entirely new internal combustion engine that posed fresh danger to Rockefeller because of its capacity to burn a range of fuels. Diesel's engine gave Rockefeller a reason to call again on the lidless eye of Pinkerton.

Thomas Edison next to a Bailey & Company electric car with installed batteries designed by Edison, September 1910.

CHAPTER 15

The Kaiser Adopts "Risk Theory"

IN JUNE 1897, two seemingly unrelated events occurred. Kaiser Wilhelm II attended his grandmother Queen Victoria's Diamond Jubilee, and Rudolf Diesel unveiled his engine in Kassel. In the decade that followed, Kaiser Wilhelm would come to see Diesel as essential to achieving his imperial ambitions for Germany. Wilhelm deemed it equally essential that no other nation have access to Diesel's genius.

The paths of the two men began to converge on June 26, 1897, when Wilhelm visited England to celebrate the sixtieth anniversary of his grandmother's reign and to take part in the Fleet Review. On that day, German naval weakness was on display for all the world to see. Not just Wilhelm's uncle Bertie, but the sovereigns of Russia, France, and Italy noted with a smirk the dilapidated German fleet. By contrast, the fearsome Royal Navy sailed fifteen first-class battleships in parade (and boasted fourteen more in commission that did not show at the jubilee), each with the latest technology, hulls, and armaments made entirely of steel. Massive twelve-inch guns with a greater range than earlier models were mounted in rotating turrets encircled by armor.

Germany sheepishly paraded thirteen "old ironclad" battleships, which resembled large sailing frigates with three masts, iron plates mounted over a wooden hull, and outdated guns with limited maneuverability. Germany managed only four of the first-class battleships while Russia, France, and Italy each had ten. Even America had six.

The German fleet seemed a mere trifle, easily sent to the bottom. Wilhelm vowed immediate and dramatic improvements, no matter the cost. But he needed a champion, someone to take up the mantle of this cause. In Alfred von Tirpitz, Wilhelm found his internal ally and a new leader for the German navy.

At the age of sixteen, Tirpitz had joined the Prussian navy in 1865, prior to German unification. At this time, Prussia barely had a navy to speak of, so much so that during the Franco-Prussian War the outmatched Prussian navy spent the duration of the war at anchor. Tirpitz spent his early career developing technology and naval tactics for torpedoes. With a quick mind, gruff manner, and family connections, he rose quickly through the ranks of the German navy and soon earned a near-mythic reputation among the sailors, including the report that his favorite drink was foam skimmed from the waves of the North Sea.

Like Wilhelm, Tirpitz was a disciple of Alfred Thayer Mahan and his book *The Influence of Sea Power upon History*, which confirmed the necessity, since ancient times, of a dominant navy for a successful civilization. Both Tirpitz and Wilhelm believed that Germany needed overseas colonies with natural resources to fuel growth, that Britain was the impediment to acquiring them, and that therefore Britain was the true enemy of Germany. Tirpitz argued that the best strategy was to build capital ships (meaning large warships, typically the battleships and battlecruisers* that were the pride of all navies), despite their limited operational range. He aimed to concentrate the German naval

---

* Battlecruisers were very similar in size and design to battleships. However, having slightly less armor, smaller guns, and larger engines, the sleeker battlecruiser could attain greater speed.

force in the nearby North Sea between Germany and Great Britain. He argued that building the smaller cruisers, which had the range to reach the far corners of the globe where colonies might be, was the wrong imperial strategy because the real obstacle to imperial power was not resistance in the potential colonies. The obstacle was the mighty British fleet that controlled the sea lanes Germany needed for its imperial design.

The admiral, with Wilhelm's support, lobbied for a set of measures called the Fleet Acts, a commitment by the government to pay for new ships over multiple years, codified by law so that there would be no annual wrangling over budgets. These laws, once passed by the Reichstag, set Germany on the Tirpitz Plan.

Tirpitz knew that Britain would recognize the threat of this committed naval expansion. His plan, which introduced "risk theory," analyzed the possibility that the Royal Navy would strike preemptively to destroy the growing German fleet before it reached the strength needed to challenge Britain on the seas. Tirpitz called the period of vulnerability the "Danger Zone." He concluded that if Germany built ships according to the Fleet Acts, then Germany would emerge from the Danger Zone in 1905 with a fleet strong enough to challenge the Royal Navy. The German fleet wouldn't be stronger than the Royal Navy but would be strong enough that the British would choose to avoid confrontation.

Tirpitz believed that an actual naval battle, after clearing the Danger Zone, was unlikely. His new fleet would be a diplomatic ace in the hole without having to fire a gun. Though the Royal Navy would still be the strongest navy in the world, a fleet of German battleships in the North Sea would pose a near-crippling threat, such that a battle would weaken the Royal Navy to the point that the navy of a third nation could finish off the British. The threat of this potential damage would alter British foreign policy to be more permissive of German imperialism.

Tirpitz and Wilhelm went to work on the German parliament, trying to win the votes in the Reichstag for the expenditure in the Fleet Acts. To gain support, they needed to raise the specter of a hostile

Great Britain. Ironically, their effort came just as Great Britain was opening the door for a closer relationship with Germany.

———————

Great Britain was fully aware of the proposed German naval laws. The news was especially unwelcome as the Liberal faction of Parliament was hoping for decreases in Britain's military spending estimates, but even the Liberals recognized that a wide margin of superior naval power meant life or death for the British Isles. If Germany spent one gold piece on ships, Great Britain would spend two. (As it later worked out, Britain was determined to maintain a ratio of 1.6 superiority.*)

Compounding the stress from the German threat were two other problems. Russia was expanding its interests in China, which rubbed up against Great Britain's Far East territories, and France was competing with British interests in Egypt. Even more alarming were the warming relations of the "Dual Alliance" between France and Russia, both traditional enemies of the British.

Joseph Chamberlain, Secretary of State for the Colonies and among the more pro-German statesmen in England, took the bold step of reaching out to Germany to dangle an alliance. But from Wilhelm's perspective, this olive branch came at exactly the wrong time. He and Tirpitz were busy painting Britain as a dangerous threat so that he could pass his naval budget. Treaty discussions with Chamberlain would sink his prized fleet before he'd even built it.

Wilhelm rejected Chamberlain, though he was privately delighted the English had come hat in hand. The kaiser felt the present rejection would bring greater benefits down the line. The longer he pushed off talks with the British (certainly long enough to pass the Fleet Acts through the Reichstag), and the more he forced Britain to take the

———————

* Great Britain adhered to the "Two-Power Standard" codified by law in the Naval Defense Act of 1889 mandating that Britain maintain naval power equal to the next two most powerful navies combined. Throughout the nineteenth century, Britain judged these to be the navies of Russia and France. Wilhelm's focus on German naval strength later changed this calculation.

initiative in treaty discussions, the better the terms he'd be able to command. Despite his intentional delay, however, Wilhelm assumed that the island nation still led by his grandmother would eventually be his official ally, even as he made negative public remarks about it. He simply felt a greater kinship with the British than he did with the French or Russians.

Chamberlain advised the German ambassador that if he could not reach terms with Germany, then he would move on and broach treaty terms with either France or Russia. Wilhelm underestimated the urgency of Britain's new desire for security. Upon reading his ambassador's report of Chamberlain's threat to ally with another power, Wilhelm wrote in the margin "Impossible!"

———————

By the turn of the century, the global situation worsened for Great Britain. There was a new and embarrassing catastrophe, this one coming from six thousand miles away in South Africa. Britain dramatically shifted policy toward the long-neglected territory due to the discovery of a massive vein of gold near Witwatersrand. Britain wanted greater control, which soon led to war with the two Dutch settlements, the South African Republic (Transvaal) and the Orange Free State, collectively the Boers.

Britain quickly suffered humiliating defeats at the hands of the Boers, who were wealthy enough through mining to afford the latest in German rifle technology and a horse for each soldier. The frontiersmen sharpshooters, highly skilled with their rifles and deadly effective from a range the British had not anticipated, outclassed the poorly trained English recruits.

Parliament approved massive reinforcements and the British overseas force swelled to more than 400,000 troops, while the opposing Boer Commandos and auxiliary troops totaled about 60,000. It was a play for quantity over quality. Often employing barbaric tactics, including concentration camps to starve out the guerrilla campaign of the enemy, the British eventually overwhelmed the Boers. Opinion of the international community turned strongly against the British. The German people, sympathetic to the Dutch Boers, were especially outraged and condemned Britain's pattern of exploiting colonies for financial gain.

On June 20, 1900, with the German public feeling a new anti-British ardor, Wilhelm pushed through his second Naval Law, a massive increase in expenditure for ships specifically designed to target Great Britain. Germany leapfrogged over France and Russia to become the primary seaborne threat to the Royal Navy.

On November 15, 1901, Lord Selborne, First Lord of the Admiralty, informed Prime Minister Salisbury and the British cabinet of his view that German naval policy was clearly meant to aid the acquisition of German possessions overseas, and that should Britain ever find themselves at war with either France or Russia then Germany would be in a "commanding position."

Months later Selborne went on to write, "The more the composition of the new German fleet is examined, the clearer it becomes that it is designed for a possible conflict with the British fleet."

Britain had to act. The official end of "Splendid Isolation" came on January 30, 1902, with what might have seemed the most unlikely of allies. Britain signed a five-year defensive alliance with Japan. The design of the partnership was to thwart Russian expansion in the Far East. If Britain found herself in conflict with the Dual Alliance of France and Russia, then Japan could distract the enemy from the rear.

Wilhelm, increasingly confident in his military power, continued to stall diplomatic talks with Great Britain. Maintaining the specter of Great Britain as his enemy, without making an actual enemy of them, served his purposes with the Reichstag. He hoped to build his fleet and come out the other side of Tirpitz's Danger Zone. As his fleet of battleships grew at a frightening pace, he finally went too far for the British. In 1903, Great Britain opened diplomatic talks with their centuries-old rival, France.

Great Britain and France had multiple neighboring colonial interests around the world that were a source of friction, but in most cases the issues were minor. As an example, in Newfoundland, French fishermen had rights to dry fish on the British-controlled shores. When the French began to catch lobsters for tinning on the shores, the Newfoundlanders objected on the grounds that lobsters were technically not fish. Violence erupted. A frustrated Lord Salisbury groaned, "I am in despair over this grotesque lobster difficulty."

France and Britain set aside these sorts of small frictions and were willing to come to the table, motivated by the fear that Wilhelm intended to roll up Europe in the way that his grandfather had rolled up the confederation of thirty-nine German states in 1871. Britain and France each had interests in Morocco and Egypt. In the face of the German threat, France relinquished rights in Egypt and Great Britain cleared the way for France in Morocco. Conflict resolved. On April 8, 1904, they signed the Entente Cordiale (Cordial Agreement). France was no longer isolated while Germany was growing increasingly so. In a swoop, this agreement obliterated what had been Bismarck's chief tenet of foreign policy: to isolate France.

Wilhelm was so successful in convincing the Reichstag and the German people that Britain was their enemy that, as a matter of course, Parliament and the British people became convinced that Germany was the enemy of Great Britain. Even though the British had feared invasion by the French since long before Napoléon, Wilhelm had now substituted himself for this traditional enemy of Britain. Popular penny novels of the time were a clear reflection of this change.

Through the late 1800s, these British spy novels had typically featured French antagonists. When a channel tunnel to connect France and England was first proposed in 1882, a flurry of novels had flown off shelves with titles like *Battle of the Channel Tunnel* or *Surprise of the Channel Tunnel* or the more blunt *England in Danger*. Each was a variation on the same plot: a party of French agents with rifles hidden in their luggage would penetrate London, with battalions of the French army following behind by the new underwater train. Hysterical Londoners violently protested outside the offices of the Channel Tunnel Company to stop construction.*

But after Wilhelm's posturing, by the turn of the century the English public had a new fear. Spy novels such as William Le Queux's *The Invasion of 1910* (1906) and Erskine Childers's *The Riddle of the Sands* (1903) focused on the threat of German invasion from across the North Sea.

Both Childers and Le Queux had done intelligence work and maintained high-level contacts within the British intelligence community. Le Queux remarked that it was his national duty to leverage his access to classified information and to "present the facts in the form of fiction." In 1909, Le Queux published *Spies of the Kaiser*. In this work of patriotic fiction, he claimed there were presently five thousand German agents secretly operating within the borders of Great Britain, primarily focused on the naval arms race. The novel was an instant bestseller. The true number of German agents was far fewer, but Germany did have a robust intelligence network operating inside Britain prior to the war. British naval intelligence, led by Mansfield Smith-Cumming (known as "C"), was less developed but growing more sophisticated, motivated partly by the hysteria these novels created.

———

The British public may have felt a frisson of fear when reading these tales of German invasion, but the truth was that Britain controlled the vital North Sea and the oceans beyond. Britain was the master of the seas because Britain was the global leader in building capital ships. Britain's shipyards possessed unparalleled expertise in achieving a shorter time to completion for larger ships that traveled at faster speeds and that were mounted with bigger guns. But as the rival German fleet grew, and as the German merchant fleet began to include vessels capable of speeds even greater than the aging British merchant fleet, Par-

---

* Digging of the tunnel began more than one hundred years later in 1987. The Channel Tunnel officially opened on May 6, 1994.

liament felt a new urgency. In 1904, the Admiralty began the design of a new class of battleship to increase Britain's margin of naval superiority by a quantum leap.

What made the HMS *Dreadnought* nearly unsinkable didn't have to do with its armor. She was the most feared ship of her day because of the technological achievement that combined the biggest guns with the fastest ship. Her main armament consisted of ten twelve-inch guns, each capable of firing an 850-pound shell a distance of ten thousand yards (5.6 miles) with accuracy. The maximum range of her guns was twenty thousand yards. The ten guns fired simultaneously delivered more than four tons of steel and high explosive at the enemy.

The difference of an inch diameter in the barrel size of a cannon has a multiplicative effect on the power of the gun. The 9.2-inch guns, common on the pre-dreadnought battleships, had an effective range of less than four thousand yards and carried a much smaller payload. These earlier guns were relative peashooters and meant that enemy ships were well within the *Dreadnought*'s range while she remained far outside the range of enemy fire.

To survive, the enemy battleships with the smaller 9.2-inch guns would somehow need to get deep inside the range of the *Dreadnought*'s guns. But the Admiralty ensured that this was impossible. Her massive steam turbines delivered a top speed of twenty-one knots (twenty-four mph), faster than any capital ship on the oceans. The *Dreadnought* could therefore dictate the range of combat. Given her superior speed, she could sink enemy ships without exposure to enemy fire. It was an unfair fight.

The benefit for Great Britain was that the *Dreadnought* rendered all previous battleships obsolete. However, by the implied corollary, this was also a pitfall for Great Britain. Everyone now needed dreadnoughts, and Britain's naval margin was suddenly down to a single ship. The naval arms race was taken up with renewed fervor.

Because of Germany's limited coastal access, the enormous size of the *Dreadnought* gave the Admiralty an additional advantage in shipyard construction over Germany: time. The fast, big-gun battleship, commissioned December 1906, was 527 feet in length and weighed more than twenty thousand tons. Critically, the draft (depth of water required) of this new castle-at-sea was nearly thirty feet. As Tirpitz knew, this was too deep for the Kiel Canal, the route used by the German fleet to travel between the North Sea and the Baltic.

Germany faced a near-paralyzing decision. Many of the German admirals didn't value the big ships enough to alter existing construction plans. But Tirpitz understood the significant role the bigger ships would play, and that Germany needed to acquire ships to match Britain's new seaborne monster. He halted construction at the German yards, and at the expense of millions of marks and more than a year of effort, he dredged the Kiel Canal to fit dreadnought-class ships of his own.

———

While advances in naval technology were a factor in Germany's budget and policy decisions, so was Wilhelm's behavior. Starting in 1906, Wilhelm ran a gauntlet of personal and diplomatic troubles that reflected his aggressive and unpredictable nature, weakening his standing even within his own government. With diminished influence, Wilhelm was unable to continue to win the Reichstag support needed to keep up with Great Britain in the dreadnought race. This change in strategic direction for the German fleet coincided with an opportunity that made Rudolf Diesel indispensable to the desperate kaiser.

In May 1906, a personal scandal for Wilhelm began to brew. Dangerous rumors circulated in Berlin. By October 1907, there was a full-blown crisis inside the palace walls.

Homosexuality in Germany was a criminal offense. With regard to professional and social standing, the mere accusation of homosexuality could be deadly.

Count Philipp von Eulenburg was tall and handsome, with large eyes and a trim beard. He had shunned a military life and embarked on a diplomatic career. In this capacity, when thirty-nine, he met the twenty-seven-year-old future kaiser, and they became fast friends.

"Phili," as Wilhelm called him, was a piano-playing, ballad-singing, storytelling joy to be with, and Wilhelm remarked that "[Phili] was like a flood of sunshine on the routine of life."

Friedrich von Holstein served as head of the Foreign Office and shouldered much of the blame for the recent failed diplomacy in Morocco. The wounded diplomat suspected Eulenburg of working further to harm his reputation with Wilhelm. In response, he unveiled a state police list of suspected homosexuals dating from the 1880s that included Eulenburg. Holstein demanded an official investigation, and the questions soon led to a number of other men within Wilhelm's inner circle, all suspected of homosexuality.

In October 1907, Wilhelm suffered a nervous breakdown (his first of three in the prewar period). In December, he wrote to a friend, "It has been a very difficult year which has caused me an infinite amount of worry. A trusted group of friends was suddenly broken up through . . . insolence, slander and lying. To have to see the names of one's friends dragged through all the gutters of Europe without being able or entitled to help is terrible."*

———

Meanwhile, Wilhelm's blind obsession with naval power continued to reset European diplomacy. From the time of Bismarck, Germany had enjoyed its Triple Alliance with Austria and Italy, while the other great powers were hostile to one another. France was isolated, Britain and Russia despised each other, a hatred reinforced through the years by Queen Victoria's personal distaste for the Russians.

When Russia and France formed the Dual Alliance, Germany felt no real threat to its war machine. Still confident, when Britain decided to abandon splendid isolation at the turn of the century and made overtures to Germany, Wilhelm had the chance to make a combina-

---

* The Eulenburg trial dragged on for years, then was abandoned when the court determined Eulenberg was not fit to stand trial. He lived in seclusion until his death in 1921.

tion that would ensure continental supremacy. But he rebuffed Chamberlain, which led to Britain's formal diplomatic agreements with Japan and France.

What Wilhelm had determined was "Impossible!" happened. On August 31, 1907, ministers from London and Saint Petersburg signed the Anglo-Russian Entente. The hostility between Britain and Russia had been a cornerstone of Bismarck's strategy. Wilhelm's reckless spending race against the Royal Navy brought these two powers—one to Germany's east, the other to its west—together. Germany came to see Austria as its only sure ally.

On the heels of the Anglo-Russian Entente, in October 1908, Wilhelm gave an interview to the English newspaper the *Daily Telegraph*. His remarks outraged nearly every government in Europe and Asia. The subject of the interview was Anglo-German relations.

Executives at the newspaper who were sympathetic to Wilhelm, along with the kaiser's advisors and Wilhelm himself, felt that if the British public only knew how much Wilhelm truly adored them, then relations between the two great powers would improve. But in the lengthy piece, Wilhelm's complicated and frustrated feelings about Britain came to the fore, exacerbated by several factual misstatements he made that offended Britain, Russia, France, and Japan in particular.

Regarding Great Britain, he groaned that he found British suspicions of German ambitions to be "a personal insult." He complained that the undeserved hostile attitude among the English for Germans made his peaceful efforts more difficult because the majority of Germans had come to dislike the English.

He then claimed that eight years prior during the Boer War, France and Russia had proposed a coalition with Germany such that the three powers together would then crush Britain for all time, but that Wilhelm refused. France and Russia, outraged upon reading this salacious claim in the *Daily Telegraph*, denied Wilhelm's story as absurd.

Regarding Britain's anxiety about the German fleet, Wilhelm stated that the true purpose was not conflict with the Royal Navy, but only to protect far-reaching colonial interests, particularly in the Far East. He pointed out the rising power of Japan, and that Germany must be "prepared for eventualities" to the east. This of course put Japan on alert, wondering what eventualities he might mean.

Britain, on the other hand, knew this was a feint. The German fleet had almost no presence in the Pacific. All her might was centered in the North Sea, right at Britain's doorstep.

The fallout from the *Daily Telegraph* interview was swift. Even the German public and the Reichstag were furious with the kaiser. From England, Lord Edward Grey remarked, "The German Emperor is like a battleship with steam up and screws going, but with no rudder, and he will run into something one day and cause a catastrophe."

––––––

While Grey's remark was prophetic, he missed a defining element of Wilhelm's character. Wilhelm did have a rudder. He knew exactly what he was aiming for: to place an enlarged German High Seas Fleet in the North Sea. In his fixation, he assumed that all, particularly the Royal Navy, would clear a path for him. As Churchill later reflected upon the German foreign policy of the time, Wilhelm had a Napoleonic ambition for territory yet hoped to achieve it without firing a shot.

Great Britain was a wealthy nation that enjoyed relatively minimal requirements for a standing army.* As such, Parliament could commit enormous resources to the expensive dreadnoughts. This capital flowed into the long-established infrastructure of British shipbuilding that efficiently produced a fleet of warships to outstrip the other navies of the world.

Wilhelm faced a very different set of circumstances. He now found himself in a continental squeeze between France and Russia, who had

––––––

* Germany had almost no concern over the British army. Late in Bismarck's career, a biographer asked him if he had contemplated the possibility of the British army traveling to the continent to aid the French during the Franco-Prussian War. Bismarck quipped, to the delight of his generals, "Yes, and if they did I should most certainly have rung the bell to send for the police."

grown increasingly close while at the same time increasingly hostile to Germany. It was critical for Wilhelm to maintain Europe's strongest army. With this financial burden, he could no longer afford to play catch-up with Britain in the dreadnought race. Yet the North Sea and German influence over the world's oceans was still his great ambition. He couldn't concede the race.

Then his admirals showed him another way to control the seas. Not with capital ships on the surface, but with deadly stealth weapons that cruised while submerged beneath the surface. As events unfolded throughout the first decade of the twentieth century, this change in strategic direction for the German fleet made Rudolf Diesel a vital part of military planning.

CHAPTER 16

A Place Among the Armaments of Nations

WINSTON CHURCHILL WAS among those in Britain who were most wary of the kaiser. The aspiring politician had already seen action in Cuba, India, and South Africa as both a war correspondent and soldier by the time he ran for office in 1900. At the young age of twenty-five, and just as the forty-two-year-old Diesel won the Paris World's Fair Grand Prix, Winston Churchill secured victory to become a Member of Parliament.

Churchill was a known technophile though he was mindful of the dangers of technical advancement in an unpeaceful world. He wrote of the new century, "War really began to enter into its kingdom as the potential destroyer of the human race." Churchill further observed that, "The achievements of science in the nineteenth and twentieth centuries were not necessarily to the happiness, virtue, or glory of mankind. Thus the 'Supreme Issue' facing mankind is the choice between moving forward into a paradise of earthly delights and plunging into a senseless hell . . . It is our right and duty to choose—and to choose well."

———————

At the same time, across the North Sea in Munich, Rudolf Diesel wrestled with the very same paradox. Diesel's belief system made room for the recognition that having a strong military capability was a useful tool in politics. He had grown up around wars, he'd seen that weakness invited attack. Possessing a strong military could achieve safety and peace.

Even so, Diesel became increasingly concerned with the kaiser's policies. He feared that obsessive militarism, as displayed by his kaiser, was not only a provocation to other nations but also came at the expense of the elements of a nation that truly matter, namely the arts, the sciences, and the overall betterment of the quality of life.

Wilhelm eagerly supported the growth of technology and innovation, but invariably for military advantage, and Diesel believed that if Wilhelm only reaped technology for military applications, he would eventually strangle the sciences. As Eugen Diesel later wrote of prewar Germany, "And since victory by arms became the sole ideal of national endeavor, the vital forces [science and industry] by which the army had attained its pre-eminence began to lose their power."

———————

In February 1901, Churchill took his seat in the House of Commons. In his very first speech, he cut across the grain of his Conservative party, and his words drew wide attention in the press. Churchill's main point was to criticize additional military spending for the army. He felt all additional spending must be directed toward the navy. Churchill believed that the Royal Navy needed new ships of war and new technology, and supported Britain's eventual push for dreadnoughts. Yet amid the battleship-obsessed powers of Europe, Churchill was beginning to understand the advantages of Diesel power.

With infectious courage, a keen wit, and a silver tongue, Churchill ascended the political ranks rapidly. He would soon assume charge of the entire Royal Navy and be the counterweight to Tirpitz and the kaiser, with Rudolf Diesel at the fulcrum.

Kaiser Wilhelm II and Winston Churchill observe German army maneuvers, 1906.

The commercial application of Diesel technology for the seas began in Russia. Emanuel Nobel was the first to put the Diesel engine in front of a ship's propeller. Nobel mounted three engines of 120-horsepower each to the triple screw oil tanker *Vandal* in January 1903. The ship was 244.5 feet long, with a beam of 31 feet, 9 inches, and a draft of only 6 feet. Inside the cargo tanks, the ship held 820 metric tons of lamp oil, bound for foreign markets.

When the ice of the Russian waterways broke up in the spring of 1903, the *Vandal* entered service. The shallow draft vessel, capable of traversing Russia's network of rivers and canals, brought oil from Nobel's fields by the Caspian Sea over the nineteen-hundred-mile route to Saint Petersburg on the Baltic.

Nobel's embrace and shared vision for what the Diesel engine meant for international shipping was largely unheralded at the time and is dramatically underappreciated to this day.* But more than one hundred years ago, Nobel recognized that his tanker fleet under Diesel power could connect with foreign markets in a way that no other type of ship could do.

Diesel-powered ships didn't require room for teams of stokers or room for coal. The engine typically required no maintenance at all over periods of years and delivered far-greater speeds with fuel efficiency, so much so that transoceanic trips required no refueling stops. Diesel power was a game-changer for merchant marine fleets.

Nobel launched a nearly identical ship, the *Ssarmat*, the following summer in 1904. The *Ssarmat* ran with her original Diesel engines until 1923, a remarkable record for one of the very first marine Diesel engines. Comparable cargo ships under steam power typically returned to port every four months for "retubing" to replace pipes and valves that conducted the steam. Word of the *Vandal* and the *Ssarmat* spread. Engine builders and shipping companies in Europe and America took note of the competitive advantages enjoyed by Nobel's new fleet and made plans to follow suit.

With the benefit of a front-row seat to Diesel's triumph at the 1900 World's Fair, the French were close behind Nobel.

Rudolf's close friend Frédéric Dyckhoff focused on small marine Diesel motors with the aim to power the flat-bottom, shallow-draft barges that operated in the network of canals through northern France and Belgium.

Crossing the finish line only months after Nobel's *Vandal*, Dyckhoff launched the *Petit Pierre* in September 1903 in the Marne-Rhine

---

* The *Vandal* was the first step in modern globalization. Renowned scholar Vaclav Smil published his book *Prime Movers of Globalization: The History and Impact of Diesel Engines and Gas Turbines* in 2010. He identifies Diesel's engine (for shipping and rail) and Frank Whittle's gas turbine (for jet airplanes) as the two inventions responsible for the modern global economy. As of Smil's writing in 2010, Diesel engines, operating under the same basic principle as Rudolf's 1897 engine, powered 94 percent of shipping around the world.

Canal. A twenty-five-horsepower engine from the Paris factory of Sautter-Harle powered the barge. On her maiden voyage, the *Petit Pierre* traveled the seven miles between Bar-le-Duc and Commercy in two and a half hours (several times faster than barges pulled by horses), and Dyckhoff reported to Diesel that during the trip he had "breakfast on board" with his family.

Dyckhoff invited Rudolf to join him for a Diesel-powered trip along the canal. On October 25, 1903, Rudolf wrote to Martha that after the triumphant cruise on the barge, he and Dyckhoff were "celebrating the momentous event with an omelet and country wine."

The few ships that had installed Diesel power in the first years of the decade had all been commercial ones on the surface of the seas. This was about to change, in large part due to a forward-thinking British admiral.

Britain hadn't fought a significant naval battle since the days of wooden ships, and certain British admirals worried that the tactics and the equipment of the Royal Navy were not keeping pace with modern advances. The loudest and most respected of these admirals was John "Jackie" Fisher. His career began in the era of sailing frigates and spanned more than sixty years to his eventual retirement in 1915. In the years 1904–10, Fisher held the position First Sea Lord, the highest-ranking position in the Royal Navy.*

Fisher had a reputation as a reformer, an innovator, and a strategist. He had taken an early interest in the potential of submarine warfare when the rest of the Admiralty had remained mostly skeptical. Fellow admirals claimed that the submarine was "the weapon of the weaker power," that it was "unmanly, unethical," and even "un-English." The

---

* First Sea Lord is a military position that reports to the closely named First Lord of the Admiralty, which is a political position. In 1911, Churchill became First Lord of the Admiralty and upon the outbreak of war, brought Fisher back as his First Sea Lord in 1914, so Churchill, though he was nearly thirty-four years younger, was Fisher's boss during the war.

battleship admirals of the Royal Navy came to refer to submarines derisively as "Fisher's toys."

In secret, the Admiralty had begun pursuing a submarine program in 1899. Unknown even to most Members of Parliament, the Admiralty had ordered five *Holland*-class submarines through Vickers in Barrow-in-Furness under a license from the Electric Boat Company in Connecticut. These primitive submarines with petrol engines had reliability problems common to subs powered by the Otto-cycle engine. In a 1903 test run around the Isle of Wight, while not even submerged, four of the five submarines traveled less than five miles before breaking down. The test reinforced the opinion of the irrelevance of the submarine in the minds of most in the Admiralty.

Thorsten Nordenfelt—Swedish industrialist, arms dealer, and inventor of munitions and submarine designs—believed submarine technology would evolve to the point where it could be an offensive weapon, and writing in 1885 he defended the ethics of submarine warfare:

> There is nothing cruel or horrible in the idea of a submarine boat . . . what can be more cruel than the leaden bullet which kills at the distance of a mile when you can see neither the rifle nor the man who fires the bullet.
>
> The principal raison d'être of a submarine boat is the suddenness of its attack, and if the attack by torpedoes fired from a submarine boat is more effective than that fired from a surface boat, it should find its place among the armaments of nations.

The problem with submarines when Nordenfelt wrote these words was that submarines simply weren't any good yet. The technology, particularly the engine technology, did not exist to enable the submarine to be offensive. Submarine boats of the era could only submerge and hope the enemy ship came close enough to the home shores to present a target, while also hoping that fumes or fire from the submarine's engine didn't kill its own crew.

Fisher recognized that with a more reliable power source, the submarine would alter naval combat. He continued his efforts to develop submarine technology within the Admiralty, and in 1904, he aimed to win royal support for his advocacy of submarines. He invited the Prince and Princess of Wales to Portsmouth for a trial run. The prince (who six years later would become King George V) went to sea on a submarine that submerged within sight of the harbor, prompting the princess to say, "I shall be very disappointed if George doesn't come up again." Of course, the future king did resurface, and the event was a boost to Fisher.

————————

Engine and undersea technology were rising to the task. After the crowning success of the Diesel motor at the World's Fair in 1900, followed by Dyckhoff's promising development work on the *Petit Pierre*, the French Navy had also become very interested in the advantages of Diesel power. The French government requested Rudolf return to France in early 1902 to meet with Maxime Laubeuf, chief engineer of the French Navy.

Thirty-two years earlier Rudolf had fled Paris as a twelve-year-old boy with his family, at that time near penniless and with no place to sleep for the night. In 1902, he might have strolled by the broken-down home-workshop of his childhood where he had picked apart the family cuckoo clock, worn the placard that denounced him as a liar, been shackled to furniture by his father. And now, at forty-four, he was a lauded inventor, impeccably dressed in top hat and tailored suit, a fortune to his name, sought after by the world's leading industrialists, and requested to come to the aid of the French Navy, a part of the same military apparatus that forced his expulsion from France those years ago.

Laubeuf was so impressed with Diesel's presentation that in April 1902 he quickly left with a French delegation to visit Diesel at the Augsburg plant. On April 28, 1902, Laubeuf issued an internal report that announced the importance of adopting Diesel power:

The Diesel motor is entering the phase of current usage. According to our thinking, it will have a very great future, and presents very remarkable advantages over all other internal combustion motors existing at present. In particular, for the cruising submarine it is ideal for being the only recommended motor, along with its fuel, to be used.

The French Navy commissioned a Diesel engine based on the *Petit Pierre* design for their new submarine Z. The initial engine performed poorly and Dyckhoff quickly replaced it with a next-generation 190-horsepower engine.

Z launched with the new engine on March 28, 1904. It was the first-ever Diesel-powered submarine. The French quickly followed up with the launch of submarine Y (there is no documentation from the French Navy that explains why Z came before Y) as well as the submarines *Aigrette* and *Cigogne*, which had a different hull design from Z and Y. All used Diesel motors.[*]

While the Z was not in itself a successful boat, it succeeded as a proof of concept and rang the bell for a new era of warfare. Admiralties of many European nations became convinced of the great potential in the very near-term of the Diesel-powered submarine. A frenzy of development work began to advance this military application of the engine.

———————

The French recognized not only the benefit of Diesel power, but also, of course, the benefit of having it to themselves. In 1903, the French Navy had prohibited Dyckhoff from sharing engine design drawings with the General Society for Diesel Engines in Germany. This decision violated a basic tenet of the original license contract with Rudolf

———————

[*] France was the first of the major powers to commit entirely to Diesel power for its submarine fleet. By 1911, the French had commissioned sixty Diesel-powered submarines while Great Britain had only thirteen. Both Germany and the United States had zero Diesel submarines, and by 1911 both were desperate to catch up.

Diesel and led to suspicion and unease among the network of Diesel licensees.*

It was an early indication that the world powers recognized that Diesel's engine was too valuable to leave in the control of the hands of scientists. Nationalistic-minded governments would intervene in the proliferation of Diesel innovations. The sharing of knowledge and the lending of a hand up to foreign firms began to give way to more Darwinist tendencies.

———————

Until about 1906, most navies pursued Diesel exclusively for submarine programs and not for surface ships. Two reasons explain this. First, the exacting undersea requirements of the submarine effectively eliminated the possibility of any type of engine other than Diesel. Second, the power requirements for a submarine were fairly low, so the smaller Diesel engine (the largest yet achieved was still less than three hundred horsepower) was sufficient for a submarine. Larger surface ships required much greater power that the steam turbine delivered. (The battlecruiser HMS *Indefatigable*, designed in 1908, had two sets of Parsons steam turbines rated at forty-three thousand horsepower.)

Yet with advances in Diesel engine functionality and massive increases in attainable horsepower, Diesel was soon in contention to power certain warships on the surface as well. In this endeavor, Nobel in Russia was again among the leaders.

Persian pirates in the Caspian Sea had been wreaking havoc on Russian shipping. Port cities in the region were hives for wooden schooners and clunky steamships (except for Nobel's fleet of Diesel-powered tankers) that hauled cargoes of equipment and essential supplies in one direction, then

———————

* During the prewar years, engineering firms frequently filled Diesel engine orders for foreign navies. In 1909, Germany placed an order with the Italian firm Fiat for a Diesel that was later installed in *U-42*, the only foreign-made engine Germany ever purchased. Conversely, Sulzer filled a 1910 order from the Italian navy for four Diesel engines to power the submarines *Nautilus* and *Nereide*, later launched at the Venice navy yard in 1913. Japan also ordered four Sulzer engines in 1916. M.A.N., by far the leader in Diesel manufacturing, delivered engines to eight foreign navies (many were eventual belligerents) prior to the German navy launching its first submarine with a M.A.N. Diesel in 1913.

returned with oil and other natural resources to complete the round-trip.

Commercial vessels needed protection from pirates, and the Imperial Russian Navy saw the need for highly maneuverable, fast-moving gunboats with oil engines that could leave port quickly, without the usual time to raise steam.

By 1907, Nobel Brothers had developed just such an engine to do the job. It was the first *reversible* four-stroke* Diesel engine. The pilot of a ship could crank the handwheel from the positions AHEAD to STOP to ASTERN and bring the vessel from full ahead to full reverse in eight seconds. Though such a capability seems trivial today, in the steam era of 1907 it was awe-inspiring to see a ship with such maneuverability. By contrast, for the same maneuver, steam engines needed to reverse the flow of steam pressure to the gears using a separate "reversing" turbine, a process that could take up to ten times as long.

The Russian navy signed a contract with Nobel to supply two 490-horsepower reversing Diesels each for the Caspian Sea gunboats *Kars* and *Ardagan*. The *Kars* began sea trials in the Gulf of Finland in 1908. The Russian captain brought the new gunboat into the Neva River, the engines humming dependably. The captain began naval maneuvers, testing the limits of the ship's turning radius and acceleration capabilities. The crew enjoyed the spectacular absence of any soot raining down on them like a gray snowfall. In every past deployment, the smog released from the ship's funnel would slowly paint the deck, their clothing, hair, and skin. Now they enjoyed the clear breeze on their faces and an unimpaired view of the horizon.

The exhilarated captain's maneuvers took the *Kars* near the coastline, and he mistakenly sailed too close to a granite embankment with-

---

* In a four-stroke engine the piston makes four strokes to complete a power cycle: (i) **intake** of fuel and air from the intake valve as the piston drops from top to bottom dead center, (ii) **compression** of fuel and air in the cylinder as piston rises to top dead center, (iii) **combustion** in the cylinder, which forces the piston back to bottom dead center, and (iv) **exhaust** as the piston rises to top dead center to expel the spent fuel-air mixture through the exhaust valve.

out enough room to avoid a collision with the shore. The captain was used to driving ships under steam power, with no capability to reverse in time to avoid a collision. Realizing the predicament during the captain's hesitation, Dr. M. P. Seiliger, a civilian director of the Nobel company who was observing from the bridge, threw the handles of the engine room telegraphs to FULL ASTERN. The gunboat slowed, came to a shuddering stop, then surged backward away from the embankment. The sea trial demonstrated the terrific advantage of quick reverse engines in a dramatic (and unplanned) fashion.

The lesson of the *Kars* incident spread to admiralties and engine builders around the world. The Russian navy, having the proximate firsthand account, immediately boosted its Diesel business with Nobel.

The *Kars* was part of a broader rearmament by the Russian navy after the disastrous war against Japan in 1905. In addition to the terrible loss of all types of warships in combat, the submarine captains suffered regular fires and explosions from the gasoline engines that were simply not suited to the purpose of powering an underwater vessel.

On the back of the successes of the *Vandal*, the *Ssarmat*, and the *Kars*, combined with the salesmanship of Emanuel Nobel, the Russian navy placed a rush of Diesel engine orders with the Nobel company beginning in 1907, and mandated that all Diesel motors for military use be Russian-built.

Nobel was up to the challenge. Some of the most sophisticated prewar Diesel engine designs came from the Nobel plant over the next several years.*

As national militaries recognized the vital nature of Diesel, the technology spread. Innovators across industries and geographies learned of this safe, reliable, and efficient power source, then sought to adapt it to their

---

* Between the years 1911 and 1918, Nobel delivered fifty-seven submarine Diesel engines to the Russian navy. In 1918, amid the Russian Revolution, the Bolshevik threat forced Emanuel Nobel to flee Saint Petersburg. The Red Army took possession of all Nobel assets in Russia, including the Baku oil fields.

specific needs, each adaptation increasing the momentum of Diesel expansion. It was no accident that the more successful of the manufacturing firms maintained a close connection with Rudolf. While cooperation between firms mostly ceased, each could still tie back to the creator, reaping the benefits of maintaining a direct connection with Rudolf Diesel.

Sulzer Brothers of Winterthur, Switzerland, continued to nurture a personal relationship with Rudolf and remained a Diesel stalwart. Sulzer designed successful engines throughout these years, including the world's first direct reversible two-stroke engine (as opposed to the Russian four-stroke design, the Sulzer engine performed the intake and exhaust steps simultaneously so that only two piston strokes completed a power cycle), which won for its category in the 1906 Milan International Exhibition.

The Swedes, with a proud maritime tradition and powerful navy, supported their national firm A. B. Diesels Motorer, which built perhaps the most famous Diesel installation of the first decade. In 1910, A. B. Diesels Motorer repowered the *Fram*, an old wooden schooner originally launched in 1892 that was built with a hull designed to withstand the pressure of ice floes. The new Diesel motor was a part of the preparation for the ship to make a trek to the South Pole. Led by the renowned explorer Roald Amundsen, the *Fram* left Norway on August 10, 1910, and powered south. On December 14, 1911, Amundsen, accompanied by his four human companions and ninety-seven dogs, was the first person to set foot on the South Pole.* During the

---

* Robert Scott led a British expedition to the South Pole during the same period, and the world kept tabs on the race between the teams. Scott's team traveled on the steamship *Terra Nova*, which was dangerously overloaded when leaving New Zealand for Antarctica (much of the cargo was coal for fuel). Hit with rough seas, the crew was forced to throw sacks of coal overboard. Waves washing over the deck leaked down to the engine room and coal bunkers. The water mixed with coal dust to form a thick slurry that clogged the bilge pumps. During the violent storm, the only way to access the bilges and clear the coal sludge in order not to sink was to pierce a wood and iron bulkhead. The coal-fired engines proved nearly deadly and wasted valuable time. Scott's team arrived at the South Pole thirty-four days after Amundsen. Perhaps Diesel was the difference.

return trip, Amundsen sent a telegraph on March 13, 1912, from Tasmania to his sponsors, reporting "Dieselmotor excellent."

The Diesel engine had logged more than 2,800 hours of work with no engine troubles. No other type of engine in the world could come close to matching this phenomenal performance and reliability. It was yet another milestone moment in history during which the Diesel engine worked quietly in the background, largely unnoticed by the public.

But navies and industrialists around the world were paying closer attention to these events. No serious military power could be without a domestic Diesel firm. The new engine was a security imperative, and governments began to encourage national capability.

In America and Great Britain, there was much ground to make up with Diesel expertise. In Germany, however, the expertise was well established. The kaiser needed only to plug any leaks of knowledge that might flow across his borders.

———————

Ironically, while the greatest engineering expertise in Diesel technology always resided within Germany, and in particular within M.A.N., during the early years, adoption of Diesel marine in other countries exceeded adoption in Germany. A frustrated Rudolf had written to his partner Heinrich Buz in 1902, "If one has come that far in France, so hopefully will the authorities of our Fatherland then gain the same opinion of the importance of our engine."

The French Navy's embrace of Diesel technology, especially for the submarine, placed them leaps ahead of their German counterpart. Even the Swedes and Russians had made greater progress. To Rudolf, and to anyone paying attention, the facts were plain. The Diesel motor was already the far superior choice for surface marine applications of small and midsize ships, and was the *only* choice for submarine application. What could hold up the Germans who had the famed inventor himself living and working in the city of Augsburg?

The answer is twofold. First, the Otto gasoline engine was also of German design, and powerful, entrenched German firms, such as

Deutz (which was founded by Nicolaus Otto in 1864 and employed the soon-to-be famous engineers Gottlieb Daimler and Wilhelm Maybach), manufactured and marketed the lightweight Otto-cycle engine as well as steam engines. Deutz was wary of the costly process of overhauling its manufacturing plants to back a new venture. Business was simpler and more profitable if the Otto engine could remain on top. Deutz initially resisted Diesel proliferation. Additional demand for the Otto design came from early success in the automotive field, led by inventors such as Daimler and Benz, where the lighter-weight, simple design and lower cost of the gasoline-model engines of that era were a good fit.

Second, Kaiser Wilhelm II wasn't thinking much about submarines in 1902. He had adopted the Tirpitz Plan, which called for a near-exclusive emphasis on the colossal battleship, and Diesel power had not yet scaled to meet such a massive assignment. Prior to 1910, the typical marine Diesel engine was no more than several hundred horsepower and was installed in ships meant for work on canals, lakes, or regional work across seas. The transoceanic Diesel vessel had not arrived. Though engine manufacturers such as Sulzer in Switzerland, Burmeister & Wain in Denmark, and M.A.N. were experimenting with larger engine designs, there was no Diesel motor that could fit the requirements of a battleship at that time, other than to provide auxiliary power (electric power for the ship provided by an alternate source from the primary engines).

But as the end of the decade approached, the German navy realized it couldn't focus only on the battleship and ignore the submarine weapon any longer. After hearing of the successful performance of the French submarines *Circé* and *Calypso* in 1907, the German navy finally placed an order with M.A.N. in December 1908* for a single subma-

---

* Rudolf Diesel's main patents expired in February 1907 and November 1908, after which Deutz and other firms began to manufacture and market the Diesel engine, in large part due to the undeniable market success of M.A.N. By 1908, M.A.N. abandoned all manufacturing of steam engines to focus on Diesel.

rine Diesel engine of 850-horsepower, much more powerful than the 300-horsepower engines in the French subs.

M.A.N. completed successful testing of this engine in April 1910. On August 4, 1911, the German navy placed an order for seven more identical engines, which were completed over the period July 1912 to May 1913 and installed in the boats *U-19*, *U-20* (which later famously torpedoed the *Lusitania* in May 1915), *U-21*, and *U-22*. These first German Diesel submarines had a maximum surface speed of eighteen miles per hour and a range of 7,600 miles at that speed.*

The German home advantage in Diesel expertise, particularly with the exacting requirements of the submarine, was daunting. The engineers at M.A.N. were motor virtuosos. Though foreign manufacturing firms had made impressive achievements with Diesel motors, and foreign navies had purchased some early submarine Diesels manufactured by M.A.N., by 1911 Wilhelm wanted the experts who had trained by Diesel's side to work only for Germany.

The kaiser began 1911 with zero Diesel-class submarines but hoped that by turning M.A.N. loose and committing the efforts of these unparalleled engineers exclusively to the Imperial German Navy, he might catch up to the submarine fleets of his rivals France and Russia. He deemphasized the dreadnoughts and now envisioned a fleet of U-boats, boasting the most advanced Diesels the world had yet seen, boats with the operational capability to frighten ships of war back to their ports, to control the sea lanes for merchant shipping and troop transport, and to terrorize the oceans and the imaginations of the public.

Although Rudolf still lived and worked in Munich and Augsburg in 1911, his relationship with M.A.N. had been souring for years. As the kaiser had become more interested in Diesel power, Rudolf Diesel had become more wary of the kaiser.

---

* Though Krupp, Deutz, Daimler, and Benz were also contributors of Diesel engines to the German war machine, Rudolf's home manufacturing plant in Augsburg built more than half of the German submarine Diesel engines used in World War I.

CHAPTER 17

Dawn of the New Era

I N FEBRUARY 1907, Diesel's main patent expired, which meant that new firms could freely pursue the original Diesel designs. This was a boost mainly to large German-national firms like Deutz, which were able to attract skilled engineers who had already been trained in Diesel technology while working under the main patent at firms like M.A.N.*

Rudolf now had even less influence over the direction of his engine technology, and the startling advances in the application of Diesel power for military use had further removed the engine from his initial dreams for it. Faced with this new reality, he had to consider, if not an alternate dream, then a way to curb the nightmare. Though he had hoped for German adoption of Diesel power in his 1902 letters, by 1907 he no longer hoped for a union between his engine and the kaiser's men, and he began to work separately from M.A.N.

---

* A notable exception in which a prized German engineer left for a foreign firm is Diesel's brother-in-law, Hans Flasche (b. 1875). Emanuel Nobel recruited Flasche away from the Augsburg plant to Saint Petersburg, where he worked from 1901 until 1914, leaving upon the outbreak of the Great War due to his German heritage. Hans and Rudolf corresponded frequently regarding the advances at the Nobel plant.

A notable shift occurred in Rudolf's professional and personal activity. He began to break with his longtime German colleagues and firm up relationships outside Germany's borders. He became increasingly friendly with the English, particularly with Sir Charles Parsons, the inventor of the steam turbine engine, which was the leading technology for *external* combustion. The HMS *Dreadnought*, launched in 1906, was the first battleship to install the new technology. (Therefore, the *Dreadnought* carried both engines—Parsons steam turbines for propulsion and Diesels for auxiliary power.) The men developed a close friendship and mutual admiration, and as the inventors of the two leading forms of naval motive power, were two of the people most sought by navies around the world that were conducting an unprecedented arms race.

At the same time, the once familial relationship between Rudolf Diesel and the leadership at both M.A.N. and the General Society for Diesel Engines in Augsburg began to fracture. Rudolf's original allies were no longer in their leadership positions. Friedrich Krupp had died under mysterious circumstances a few years prior in the wake of a scandal regarding his homosexuality, and Buz was semiretired from M.A.N.

Diesel continued his innovative work refining and adapting his engine, but not in concert with his German associates. Somewhat liberated by the expiration of his patents, Rudolf began specialized work on different applications of his engine core. In particular, he designed engine models for automobile, rail, and marine use, all while M.A.N. was primarily busy filling orders for submarine Diesels of greater and greater power.

Then the unthinkable happened. In December 1906, Diesel had announced that he was preparing a patent for a new fuel injection process. M.A.N. and the General Society demanded to see details regarding the patent. When Diesel refused, both M.A.N. and the General Society filed a lawsuit against their partner in February 1907. It was an abhorrent turn of events for the creator and caused an irreparable fissure between Rudolf and his colleagues.

Exactly ten years prior, Rudolf and Schröter had conducted the successful engine performance tests of the first engine in the Augsburg lab, then stood for newspaper pictures with Buz and embarked on a highly lucrative enterprise that spread Diesel technology to the corners of the world. It was stunning now to see lawsuits between M.A.N. and the father of the pioneering work in Augsburg. This conflict between Diesel and M.A.N. reflected a divergence that was far more profound than a dispute over technical matters. The tone of the disagreement was philosophical in nature, one that could not be resolved with a business realignment or with money.

The lawsuits dragged on until 1909 when the courts rejected the M.A.N. claim. Separately, the General Society decided to drop its litigation as the member firms that made up the board of directors no longer saw the advantage of maintaining a collective organization to promote the technology. The Diesel firms around the world were going their separate, nationalistic ways and the original mandate of the General Society, which was to promote a shared and coordinated knowledge base to support Diesel technology, no longer held. The board initiated discussions to dissolve the General Society altogether.*

Diesel was bitter, but free to pursue his creations unencumbered. He turned his focus away from U-boats and other direct implements of war to different ambitions. One such goal was to develop a lightweight Diesel engine for the automobile—what he saw as a clear application of the future.

In 1908, just before Rudolf gave his daughter's hand in marriage to Arnold von Schmidt (an automotive engineer from an aristocratic German background), he designed what he called the "petite model" of the Diesel motor.† Rudolf delivered a lightweight, five-horsepower engine to power an automobile.

---

* The board of the General Society dissolved the company on February 27, 1911. The remaining rights and duties passed to M.A.N. and Krupp.

† Though few of the "Petite" ever sold, Rudolf's work laid the foundation for the future Diesel automotive industry. He was once again ahead of his time. Though he correctly prophesied the Diesel automobile, ultimately the small power source that Rudolf imagined would "revitalize the artisan class" and rural economies was never the Diesel motor. The small power source came primarily in the form of the electric motor pioneered by Nikola Tesla.

A lightweight Diesel engine would disrupt the ongoing struggle between gasoline and electric cars by offering the best aspects of each. A Diesel car burning alternative fuels would have greater power, reliability, and range than a gasoline car combined with the electric car's benefits of reduced smell and noise and the elimination of the hand crank. The "Petite" went on to win the Grand Prix at the Brussels International Exposition of 1910.

Further, he prioritized collaboration with international firms that could no longer rely on the aid of the experts in Augsburg. The nationalism and paranoia of the prewar period had stymied cooperative efforts for engine designs between the firms of potentially unfriendly nations. Simply put, M.A.N. wasn't sharing anymore.

However, Diesel's attitude had changed since his 1902 letter to Buz. Diesel was no longer worried about Germany getting left behind by other nations. He was worried about the other nations getting left behind by Germany. He worked closely with Sulzer on a motor for the railroads that would later bear fruit. He worked closely with Ivar Knudsen of Burmeister & Wain on plans for a large-scale Diesel engine that the men hoped could power large oceangoing merchant vessels.

On December 8, 1909, in a letter written by hand in English, Rudolf informed his friends E. D. Meier and Adolphus Busch in America of developments in Europe, and he encouraged haste with Busch's efforts on the engine.

As the first decade of the new century came to a close, Rudolf turned more of his attention to Britain. He consulted with the English firm Vickers at Barrow-in-Furness, which had been struggling mightily to make a workable submarine Diesel engine for the Royal Navy. Vickers had been an armaments supplier to the British military since 1888 and had a very cozy relationship with the Office of the Admiralty. The firm's shipyard built a range of vessels for the fleet, including battleships. After 1900, when the Admiralty became interested in submarines, Vickers emerged as the country's principal submarine Diesel engine builder, though it was far behind its rivals in Germany, France, and Russia.

There were urgent and increasingly dire communications between Vickers and the Admiralty during this period as letters later revealed. The contest for the North Sea and Germany's imperial design would now be fought differently. Submarines and surface warships powered by Diesel engines could play a deciding role, and it had become clear that an elite level of domestic expertise with Diesel technology was critical for Britain. As British engineers were cut off from M.A.N., Churchill would have to look elsewhere to acquire the expertise he needed to bring his fleet into the Diesel age.

PART III

MASTERPIECE

1910–1913

CHAPTER 18

Rudolf Diesel Breaks Ranks

RUDOLF'S RELATIONSHIP WITH M.A.N. was now frosty after the conclusion of the litigation between them in 1909. Most of the period between 1910 and 1912 Rudolf spent traveling to aid the development of Diesel technology in foreign firms. He maintained close relationships with his significant partners in each country and provided critical consultation as each worked to overcome technical obstacles.

In America, Adolphus Busch had gotten off to a frustrating start with his Diesel business. Busch had founded the Diesel Motor Company of America in New York City in 1898 after acquiring the license from Rudolf. Diesel and Buz had then provided engine design drawings that the Americans largely ignored. Busch, still employing E. D. Meier as lead engineer, felt that because the American market was saturated with inefficient but inexpensive engines combined with an abundance of all types of fuel, his company required a different approach.

However, Busch was unable to deliver a successful engine, and in 1901 he reorganized the firm as the American Diesel Engine Company (ADE) in New York. Again, Buz and Diesel encouraged Busch to copy the engine designs of M.A.N., and again Meier rejected the advice, writing to Rudolf on January 6, 1902, "Kindly explain to Mr Buz that he is in error in condemning everything we have done here. We have made mistakes, it is true, but no more than were made by various other parties in Germany and France. . . . it was only a recognition of difference in conditions, not the vanity of a designer, that induced us to depart from [Buz's] standard design." But the American company continued to struggle. In 1908, ADE sold only eight engines. Busch put the company into receivership later that year.

Rudolf was fond of Busch's gregarious style, admired his gallon capacity for malt beer, and envied his cunning and pluck for new business ventures. Prior to Busch putting ADE into receivership, Busch and Diesel had already begun secret talks to pursue the American market anew.

Not only did Adolphus need the Diesel motor for industrial use but he now had the US Navy urging him on to become a competent manufacturer of submarine engines. Busch knew he needed powerful outside help. Rudolf was presently in the midst of litigation with M.A.N., which the German government had prohibited from sharing expertise with anyone outside the country. The split between Rudolf Diesel and M.A.N. bifurcated the two leading sources of Diesel knowledge. Reading the landscape, Busch crafted an innovative and winning partnership.

On September 8, 1908, Busch and Diesel signed their second agreement, ten years after the first. Busch bought the remaining assets of ADE out of receivership for $110,000 to become its sole proprietor, then combined these in a new company with himself, Diesel, and the Sulzers as the principal stockholders. From back in Augsburg, the General Society for Diesel Engines again brought litigation, this time to halt the American-Swiss-Diesel merger. Rudolf's former colleagues-turned-antagonists sought to contain and control his expertise. Busch prevailed in the litigation but only after a significant delay. The official beginning of the Busch, Diesel, and Sulzer partnership was July 12, 1911, nearly three years after signing the agreement.

Busch established the headquarters of the new company, Busch-Sulzer Brothers Diesel Engine Company, in St. Louis. With Rudolf formally in the fold, Busch was finally on a track for success.

———————

Great Britain's Diesel program was in equally dire straits. Mirrlees Watson Co. Ltd had let its Diesel program languish. The dusty Diesel engine in its shop that Rudolf had observed to be like a neglected Cinderella continued to gather dust until 1903. By that time, the noted success of the Diesel marine motor, particularly in France and Russia, prompted the Royal Navy to encourage Mirrlees to have another look at its Diesel program. Charles Day, who had spent most of his career focused on gas and steam engines, picked up the abandoned Diesel efforts for the company.

Upon his new appointment, Day remarked, "I learned of the work done by [Mirrlees] on the Diesel engine, but was warned against having anything to do with it, as the engine had caused heavy losses and was considered dangerous."

Day had visited Rudolf Diesel at the Augsburg plant in October 1903. The talented English engineer spent hours on end in the presence of the creator, learning the details of the engine design. Rudolf's enthusiasm and genius made a convert of Day, who then returned to Glasgow with renewed confidence in the potential of Diesel technology. He began testing engines following the German designs through 1904.

Day's work was timely as the British Admiralty completed plans for the battleship *Dreadnought* in 1905. Though Parsons steam turbines propelled the ship, the Admiralty chose Diesel, rather than steam engines, for the auxiliary power, and awarded the contract to Mirrlees. While Mirrlees delivered satisfactory engines on schedule for the commissioning of the ship in late 1906, the engines were not perfect. A chief engineer on the *Dreadnought* reported that repeated troubles with the Diesel engines aboard led to a revised jingle that the engineering crew sang:

Up and down the voltage goes,
Pop goes the Diesel.

However, in general, the Royal Navy was satisfied with the benefits of the Diesel motor for the purpose of marine backup power, reporting in October 1908 that "every battleship and cruiser launched during the last few years carried at least one example." But the British engineers were still not meeting the exacting requirements of the submarine Diesel.

Vickers, Britain's largest armaments and shipbuilding firm, began building submarine Diesels in 1906 through a partnership with Carels Brothers, which had the Belgian Diesel license. After the expiration of the main Diesel patents in 1908, Vickers was free to pursue its own course. Still, by 1912 Great Britain had a wide gap in Diesel expertise to close. And despite Jackie Fisher's advocacy of the submarine as a critical weapon, he continued to face skeptics in the highest ranks. Sir Herbert Richmond, assistant director of naval operations for the Royal Navy, issued his report, *Outline of a Memorandum on Submarines*, in July 1914, the same month that Balkan hostilities sparked the Great War. In the report, Herbert wrote, "The submarine has the smallest value of any vessel for the direct attack upon trade. She does not carry a crew which is capable of taking charge of a prize, she cannot remove passengers and other persons if she wished to sink one." (Years after the Great War, Herbert returned to his memorandum and with humility penned an addendum in the margin: "I made a pretty bad guess there!")

But important for Fisher, he found in his new First Lord of the Admiralty a leader who was a true innovator. Winston Churchill was willing to take bold steps in the face of skeptics like Richmond. From 1911 onward, Great Britain and Churchill recognized the need for a Diesel strategy, not only for submarines but also larger Diesels for surface ships.

———

From Sulzer Brothers in Switzerland to Carels Brothers in Belgium, Burmeister & Wain in Denmark and Vickers in England, Rudolf Diesel traveled Europe and personally assisted these manufacturing firms. He developed close relationships with George Carels, who stood by him, quite literally, to the end, and Ivar Knudsen, technical director for Burmeister & Wain, of whom Diesel said, "[Knudsen is] the man who in the whole world has best understood my ideas and been able to improve on them as well."

But Augsburg was the cradle of the Diesel engine and still the leader. Because of this home advantage, Wilhelm II was in position rapidly to build a fearsome Diesel-powered U-boat fleet, and to block other nations from replicating the superior German-made Diesel engine designs of M.A.N., if not block the designs of Rudolf Diesel himself.

After years of feeling undervalued by the German navy, M.A.N. now felt the crack of the kaiser's whip. The submarine had suddenly become a prized ship of every navy, and therefore the Diesel became a prized engine. For this reason, M.A.N.'s resources for building Diesel marine engines were allocated almost exclusively to the delivery of larger and more reliable U-boat engines for the kaiser. Engines for the surface ships of naval and mercantile fleets were a lower priority.

M.A.N. strove to meet the evolving engine demands of the larger submarine designs, and the engineers in Augsburg began building reliable submarine Diesels of one thousand horsepower in support of Wilhelm's arms race. (Eventually, during the war, U-boats put to sea with engines of three thousand horsepower built by M.A.N.)

Wilhelm, desperate for his long-neglected submarine fleet to leap from last place to first, looked to augment the efforts of M.A.N. by calling on other national firms. Deutz, Benz, Daimler, and Körting Brothers had moved into the Diesel market after the 1908 expiration of the main patents. Wilhelm pressed these firms into naval service to develop Diesel submarine engines. By the conclusion of the war, Körting had built 115 Diesel submarine engines, Benz 72, Daimler 64, Krupp 69. The leader of course was M.A.N., which built an astonishing 512 engines for the fleet of U-boats.

M.A.N. Diesels were elite. During the war, Allied naval commanders observed the superior performance of the U-boats with awe. Admiral John Jellicoe, promoted to commander of the Grand Fleet of the Royal Navy at the outset of war, believed his naval base at Scapa Flow, far to the north in the Orkney Islands off the coast of Scotland, was a haven. From Land's End at the southernmost point of England to the northern tip of the Shetland Islands, the British Isles span more than seven hundred miles, and with this longitudinal expanse along the coast of Europe can control any approach from the west to the German coast. Jellicoe knew that no British submarine from as far north as Scapa Flow could reach the German port of Heligoland, and he therefore assumed that no German U-boat could reach Scapa Flow where the Grand Fleet rested at anchor. Even when *U-15* was sighted and rammed by a British cruiser near the Shetlands, no one at the Admiralty believed the U-boat could possibly have been coming from Germany, but rather that the Germans must have a secret base off the coast of Norway. Then, on September 1, 1914, as the Fourth Destroyer Flotilla along with twelve dreadnoughts and armored and light cruisers rested quietly at anchor with engines cold, a U-boat was sighted *inside* Scapa Flow, apparently having navigated the rocks, currents, and tides of the treacherous channel approach to the sheltered waters. In what came to be known at the First Battle of Scapa Flow, the fleet immediately raised steam to scatter, fired shells at the various periscope sightings, and barked commands to "prepare for torpedo attack" as propellers churned the waters. Jellicoe lost no ships in the incident, but he realized the U-boat threat was greater than anyone had previously imagined and determined to temporarily move the fleet farther west to a less strategic but safer position.

After the war, upon taking possession of the German submarines and inspecting the engines, the Allies were even more impressed. The captured M.A.N. submarine Diesel engines became the foundation of the US Navy engine development program through the 1920s and 1930s, yet America still struggled to match what M.A.N. had achieved by 1916. As late as 1927, Commander John H. Hoover wrote to the secretary of the navy, "Our attempts to copy the German submarine engines have not as yet, after six years work, resulted in performance and weight efficiency to that of the captured samples."

———————

While the engineers at M.A.N. toiled away at designs for submarine engines (and also experimented with "cathedral" Diesels large enough to power battleships), Rudolf Diesel was mostly outside Germany. Though it was not the custom of the day, Martha accompanied Rudolf on his business trips. Personal diaries reveal the two were still very much in love, enjoyed travel and spending time together. For Rudolf, any journey was always easier with Martha by his side. And by this time their youngest, Eugen, was already twenty-one and embarking on an engineering career of his own.

First they went to see the Nobels in Saint Petersburg in the spring of 1910. The Diesels traveled comfortably by train, and Emanuel Nobel received them in lavish style. Nobel's wealth was astounding and, though a hardworking and serious man, he loved to entertain with extravagant dinner parties and shower close friends with staggeringly expensive gifts, in particular Fabergé eggs that were also the favored gift of the tsar.

Rudolf examined the progress of his partners in Russia, where Martha's younger brother Hans still worked. The expertise of the Swedish-Russian Diesel operation was second only to those in Germany. Nobel's Diesel motors powered commercial shipping and were increasingly in demand from the Russian military. Nobel was more optimistic than ever about the future dominance of Diesel power around the world, and the important role that both he and Rudolf would play in achieving that dominance.

Diesel gave a number of lectures at technical universities during this trip, on occasion alongside Hugo Junkers, an engine and aircraft design pioneer, who was visiting with Nobel at the same time. In that year, Germany had awarded Junkers patent No. 253788 for an all-metal aircraft, and Junkers already had a test aircraft running a Diesel engine.*

Rudolf and Martha departed Saint Petersburg in high spirits. The Diesel motor was supreme in Russia, and with similar application of effort and skill, could become supreme in every market. Nobel encouraged Rudolf to spend time in America to assist in the adoption of the motor there. Rudolf's friend Busch had been pleading for a return trip from the inventor. Diesel resolved to lay the plans for a trip across the Atlantic, but there was more immediate work to do in Europe, and he'd already made other commitments. Busch would have to wait a bit longer.

———————

Rudolf next went to Turin, Italy, where he had the honor of presiding as the judge for the mechanical exhibits at the World's Fair of 1911. From Turin, Rudolf traveled to England. His friendship with Charles Parsons was stronger than ever, and he'd been approached by several potential business partners, including George Carels, offering to co-found a UK-based Diesel operation.

The stated purpose of Diesel's trip to England was to represent Germany at London's World Congress of Mechanical Engineers. The most renowned engineers and industrial leaders from around the globe attended the event. Diesel naturally had a place of honor, seated right beside Sir Charles Parsons during the banquet. Though Diesel was still not a headlining name to the general public, within engineering, industrial, and military circles, especially those in England and Germany, he was revered.

Rudolf was quiet, reserved, and with manners that made him seem more aloof in public than he was in private. To those who knew him only from a distance, Rudolf was another stiff and impeccably dressed German. But those who knew him well discovered, as his let-

———————

* Several of Junkers's aircraft saw service in the Great War. He continued designs with Diesel engines for flight and in March 1938 a Deutsche Lufthansa Do 18 E, under Diesel power, broke the long-distance flight record, covering the 5,250 miles from the English Channel to Caravelas, Brazil.

ters to Martha and his friends reveal, that he was an intimate communicator, just as at ease with discussing his emotions as he was with discussing thermodynamics. He was charming, even playful at times with peers. He wrote to his dear friend Parsons ahead of the London visit, "I will enjoy your monkeyshines," borrowing a popular American phrase of the time meaning mischievous behavior.

The event in London began with a grand banquet, courses of food and drinks, though Diesel ate and drank lightly. As the featured speaker, he then rose, paid a warm tribute to his friend Parsons, and in flawless English delivered a technical address on the topics of fuels and combustion engines. At the close of his speech the hall erupted in applause, the leaders of science and industry from around the world coming to their feet to praise the inventor.

From London, Rudolf returned to his Munich home. America was still in his thoughts. He declared to his engineering colleagues, "Nowhere in the world are the possibilities of the prime mover as great as in the United States of America."

Rudolf made arrangements with Adolphus Busch to visit the new St. Louis Diesel plant for a ground-breaking ceremony on April 7, 1912, to help promote the new Busch-Sulzer operation, and he agreed to give four public lectures at the Associated Engineering Societies of St. Louis (April 13), Cornell University in Ithaca, New York (April 18), the US Naval Academy in Annapolis, Maryland (April 26), and the American Society of Mechanical Engineers in New York City (April 30).

The White Star Line's *Titanic* was presently making a sensation around Europe. Rudolf and Martha hoped to join the maiden voyage, but the ship's departure date from London of April 10 was too late for them to get to the event with Busch in Missouri.

Instead, the Diesels confirmed earlier passage to America, planning to depart from London on March 26. They traveled to London several weeks prior to this as Rudolf had several speeches to give and other important work there before the Atlantic passage.

CHAPTER 19

The Admiralty Boards
the MS *Selandia*

T HE MONARCHS OF the major European powers had advance knowledge of the great occasion. Advisors to the king of Denmark informed him that the new ship built by Burmeister & Wain of Copenhagen would bring renewed stature to the elite seafaring heritage of the Danes. The crown prince, who would become King Christian X three month later, required no persuasion to accept B&W's invitation to join the first leg of the maiden voyage of the *Selandia*.

While M.A.N. had prioritized the submarine Diesel, Burmeister & Wain had committed to a different goal. If the rumors surrounding this miracle ship were true, it would revolutionize the merchant marine industry. Great Britain had dominated commercial shipping for a hundred years, boasting the world's largest and fastest merchant fleet of coal-fired steamships. But this domination was now threatened. Other countries were converting steamships to burn fuel oil in the furnaces rather than coal. The engines of these oil-burning ships were still external combustion steam turbines with furnace, boiler, and chimney apparatus releasing towers of smoke—they simply burned the petroleum-derived fuel oil drawn from a tank rather than coal shoveled into the furnace. But they were delivering advantages in range and efficiency that challenged Britain's primacy in commercial shipping. Naturally, the move from coal to a petroleum-based fuel for marine engines represented a massive potential boon to Rockefeller and his fellow oil magnates.

Once again, the Diesel engine endangered a possible lifeline to Rockefeller, who was desperate for new revenue to backfill his loss of the illumination market when the electric light bulb came into common use. Standard Oil eagerly anticipated that merchant and naval fleets would continue to convert their ships from burning coal to oil. This shift would create a surge in demand that would dwarf the small but growing market in petroleum for the automobile. Rockefeller's fear was that Diesel technology might succeed in scaling to the horsepower required for large ships and locomotives, and thus replace steam technology altogether. Though most commercial Diesel engines did burn a petroleum distillate (petrol-Diesel), Rudolf persistently advocated for vegetable- or coal-based fuels such as coal tar,* for which any country could build fuel-refining infrastructure. Burmeister & Wain's *Selandia* was an early realization of Rudolf's vision for his engine to power global shipping.

———————

On February 22, 1912, the *Selandia* left the port of Copenhagen. The owner, Hans Niels Andersen of the Danish East Asiatic Company, or-

———————

* Coal can be refined, or fractioned, through the application of high heat in the absence of oxygen. This process, called the coking process, produces coal gas, coke, and coal tar—each a useful fuel. Coal gas, also called town gas, is a flammable gaseous fuel delivered to the user by a network of pipes. Coke is a gray, hard, porous rock-like fuel commonly used in blacksmithing, and in the mid-twentieth century for home heating (especially common in Australia) as it burns more cleanly than coal. Coal tar is a thick, dark liquid that has been used as an industrial dye or to make paint. It can barely be poured when at room temperature, has an extremely high boiling point, is safe to store, and makes excellent fuel for the Diesel engine.

dered the hull painted a gleaming white to accent the complete absence of sooty black clouds. With no smokestacks at all, the elegant lines of the ship made her look like an angel passing through the water, despite her enormous size. She was 370 feet long, 53 feet wide, and her keel dipped 30 feet below the surface, when fully loaded with cargo. The ship ran two B&W reversible Diesels of 1,250 horsepower each, and two more Diesels for auxiliary power of 250 horsepower. As there was no need for holds of coal for fuel, nor a team of sweating men stoking the fiery furnaces, the ship had a remarkable cargo capacity of 7,200 tons.

When traveling at a moderate speed of eleven knots (12.6 mph) she could cruise for seventy-five days and cover more than twenty thousand miles without refueling (with petrol-Diesel at this time). Sea trials the month before had gone beautifully, and Andersen intended to put the ship into service on the Copenhagen-to-Bangkok run.

Joining the Danish crown prince and princess on the first leg were Andersen, Knudsen, and Admiral Andreas du Plessis de Richelieu of the Royal Danish Navy. As they got underway, in the sea lane just off Copenhagen, a smaller ship under the Swedish flag held a course to pass directly in front of the *Selandia*. If neither ship altered course, they would collide. Men on the bridge stared ahead nervously, and Andersen ordered his captain to blast the ship's horn to signal a warning. Blast after blast got no result from the seemingly wayward boat. The Swedish captain failed to respond to the blasts and held his course, though the *Selandia* held the right of way. A deadly crash was imminent. At the last moment the *Selandia* veered, and the Swedish captain, finally recognizing that the 370-foot vessel was nearly upon him, also maneuvered to safety.

Knudsen knew immediately why this near catastrophe had happened. The old Swedish captain had never seen such an alien ship as the *Selandia*. From the Swede's initial distance, he had assumed the *Selandia* was merely resting at sea and would remain so for some time. He hadn't adjusted his course until the panicked last moment. He had assumed the *Selandia* hadn't been moving at all, as Knudsen said, "because he saw no smoke."

After, though not because of, that harrowing experience, the royals disembarked at Elsinore, a port city in eastern Denmark. Then after a stop at Aalborg, another Danish coastal town, the *Selandia* continued to London's West India Docks, where the highest-ranking official of the Royal Navy was eager for her arrival.

The two engines of the first oceangoing Diesel ship were performing flawlessly. She entered the Thames and cruised toward London.

The *Selandia* churned upriver and by this time the officers, crew, and passengers of the ship were accustomed to the gaping stares of amazement and confusion that the ship caused. Several tugboats and tenders drove toward the massive ship, assuming she was disabled and dangerously adrift. Knudsen wrote of the run up the Thames: "The *Selandia* was often hailed by sympathetic skippers with offers of assistance, for none had ever before seen a great ship without a smokestack, and they thought it must be the victim of some mishap." Of course, the crew knew she was far from disabled. At that moment she could come about and make a round-trip to the Far East faster than any other merchant ship on the seas.

On February 27, 1912, the *Selandia* tied up at the West India Docks, and on March 1, Knudsen and Andersen escorted Churchill and his staff on an inspection of the ship. The new ship had no innovative weapons technology, nor any weapons at all. There was no special hull design, no breakthrough navigation equipment to study. What made the *Selandia* remarkable, what brought Churchill and his admirals to the docks that day, was the Diesel engines.

Knudsen proudly led the First Lord and his entourage to the engine room where Churchill studied the Diesels. Churchill had been thoroughly briefed ahead of time on the promises of what the ship could do. Even so, upon seeing the ship firsthand he was astounded.

The extraordinary performance of the *Selandia* had far-reaching implications for Churchill's ideas about the Royal Navy's mastery of the high seas, as well as the fuels required to sustain it. At the conclusion of his inspection, he turned to Knudsen and expressed unqualified praise. As Knudsen wrote of the exchange, Churchill "declared that Englishmen remembered the stamp which the Vikings had set upon England, and were thankful for the new lesson now taught the British Isles by Denmark."*

Churchill later reported to the Admiralty that the *Selandia* represented "an advance which will be epochal in the development of shipping. This new type of ship is the most perfect maritime masterpiece of the century."

Churchill also recognized the advantage of the Diesel engine over the steam turbine (whether fired by coal or converted to burn fuel oil) with regard to maintenance and readiness for combat. Admiral Jellicoe, who would serve as commander of the Grand Fleet during the Great War, was well aware that after four months at sea his ships with brand-new steam turbines developed leaks in the condensers and pipes that deliver the steam pressure. These leaks caused engine performance and ship speed to plummet, rendering the ships less effective until they returned to port for refitting with new tubing. Jellicoe estimated that wartime patrols and the resulting near-constant return to port for engine refitting would diminish his overall force by a third. Churchill knew Diesel engines required no such maintenance and were therefore a force multiplier.

———

At the time of the *Selandia*'s launch, the engineers of M.A.N. and Krupp were feverishly filling Diesel submarine contracts for the kaiser and doing so with no assistance from Diesel, who was in London. Diesel did

———

* After taking on cargo, the *Selandia* cruised to Antwerp accompanied by Albert, the 4th Earl Grey (the tea was named after his grandfather Charles, the 2nd Earl Grey), who sent a telegram from the ship to congratulate King Christian X on the great Danish achievement, as well as a telegram to King George V to update him on the success of the new ship. From Antwerp, the *Selandia* made the round-trip voyage to Bangkok. In her first twelve years of service, the *Selandia* cruised more than one million kilometers and required a mere ten days of service. The Danish East Asiatic Company never ordered another steamship.

The Diesel engines of the Selandia *while on the shop floor of Burmeister & Wain.*

not visit the *Selandia* on the same day as Churchill, since reports of that visit across the North Sea would likely have disturbed the kaiser. Rudolf instead visited the *Selandia* on a separate occasion. As Knudsen noted, it was only through close collaboration with the creator, Rudolf Diesel, that he was able to succeed with the *Selandia*.

Churchill understood that the era of the marine oil engine had arrived. Though Britain possessed an abundance of coal, the coal-fired warship was becoming a thing of the past. If he didn't modernize his fleet's engine technology, the dominance of the Royal Navy across the oceans of the world, which had been the springboard to empire, would end. The quandary for Britain was its lack of domestic oil supplies. Could Churchill acquire sufficient oil at a reasonable cost to power Britain's industry and navy in peacetime, and would he be able to acquire oil at all in times of war? For the present, Diesel technology had scaled to offer a solution for merchant fleets. Churchill wondered if there might soon be Diesel engines powerful enough to be a solution for large ships of war.

Transcripts of a special parliamentary subcommittee meeting on the Royal Navy on March 4, 1912 (three days after Churchill visited the *Selandia*), reveal that Churchill had long had his eye on the Diesel engine as his future power source to completely supplant steam power:

> Mr. BURGOYNE [member of House of Commons for Kensington North] *asked the First Lord of the Admiralty whether his attention has been called to the Danish vessel, "Selandia," now in London, driven by internal combustion engines,* * *and whether, in his view of the accepted efficacy of this method of propulsion, he will state what policy the Admiralty propose to pursue in the development of ships fitted with engines of this type?*
>
> Mr. CHURCHILL *I paid a very interesting visit, with other members of the Board of Admiralty, to the "Selandia" on Friday last. Important experiments were begun some time ago with a view to ascertaining the possibilities of the internal combustion engine as a method of propulsion in ships of the Royal Navy.*

On March 17, still fresh from his inspection of the *Selandia* two weeks before, the First Lord of the Admiralty, the man ultimately responsible for the future of the Royal Navy, delivered an important speech to Parliament:

> *To build any number of oil-burning ships meant basing our naval supremacy upon oil. But oil was not found in appreciable quantities in our islands. If we required it we must carry it by sea in peace or war from distant countries. We had, on the other hand, the finest supply of the best steam coal in the world, safe in our mines under*

---

* Note that the general knowledge of engines in 1912, even for key members of Parliament such as Burgoyne, was very limited. While Burgoyne could differentiate between the internal combustion engine and the external steam engines given the obvious visible differences, he failed to differentiate between the kerosene/gasoline internal combustion engine and Diesel. The word *Diesel* is never mentioned here, but Diesel technology made *all* the difference, and Churchill, unlike most of his colleagues, was well aware of that.

our land. To commit the Navy irrevocably to oil was indeed to "take arms against a sea of troubles." Yet, if the difficulties and risk could be surmounted, we should be able to raise the whole power and efficiency of the Navy to a definitely higher level; better ships, better crews, higher economies, more intense forms of war power. Mastery itself is the prize of the venture.*

Clearly his encounter with the *Selandia* had made an impact. Churchill had no choice but to raise his naval power to a "definitely higher level." That was the only prize that mattered. He wouldn't relegate the Royal Navy to a second-class power simply for lack of domestic oil. But how could he surmount the "difficulties and risk"? One path was to develop oil engines that didn't necessarily require petroleum-based oil for fuel. For this, the Diesel engine gave Churchill the answer he needed.

The two men were both in London giving speeches about the same critical subject at nearly the same time. On March 15, 1912, two days before Churchill's remarks to Parliament about Britain's precarious position regarding coal and oil, Rudolf Diesel read a paper to the Institution of Mechanical Engineers in London with the tantalizing title "The Diesel Oil Engine and Its Industrial Importance, Particularly for Great Britain."

Diesel was speaking directly to the quandary that he knew Churchill, the Royal Navy, and the British merchant fleet faced. Even the title of Diesel's paper, which advertised assistance to the British, was stunning, coming from a German inventor during the height of tensions in the naval arms race between Germany and England.

The opening of the paper recounted some of the history of the Diesel engine and its superior performance over steam engines and other types of oil engines. Rudolf mentioned that since 1899, versions

---

* The final line of Churchill's remarks containing the word *prize* is the origin of the title for Daniel Yergin's 1990 Pulitzer Prize–winning book *The Prize: The Epic Quest for Oil, Money & Power*, which examines the history of the petroleum industry. What has been misunderstood about Churchill's famous line ever since he said it is that the prize of mastery was as much about the Diesel engine as about petroleum.

of the Diesel engine could run on coal tar, and even on nut and vegetable oils with no modification to the basic motor.

Diesel deliberately avoided any discussion of military applications
during his speech in London, keeping to the peaceful uses of his motor.
However, he titled the final section of the paper, "Special Importance
of the Diesel Engine for Great Britain." To begin, he noted three facts:

(1) Great Britain is an exclusively coal-producing country
(2) Great Britain has the largest Colonial Empire in the world; and
(3) Great Britain is the greatest shipping nation in the world.

Regarding point one, Diesel argued that England had the greatest
interest of all nations to abandon steam power for the more efficient
Diesel engine in order to "effect enormous savings in her most valuable treasure—coal—and thus defer the exhaustion of her stock." Diesel advocated that England should pursue energy independence
through the use of Diesel power burning coal tar as its fuel, pointing
out that Germany already had the capacity to have fuel independence
should it fully embrace the Diesel motor. Rudolf calculated that Germany had sufficient annual coal tar production to power 1.75 million
horsepower running three hundred days per year at ten hours per day.
In a footnote to the paper, Rudolf wrote of Germany, "In case of war
and cutting off the supply of foreign fuel, the quantity [of coal tar]
would be entirely sufficient for running the whole fleet, war and mercantile, and for providing in the meantime the power for the inland
industry. The Author has not the figures for England, but he assumes
they are of similar significance."

Regarding point two, he argued that the Diesel engine would become the preeminent motor of all colonies because the cost of shipping
mountains of coal out to the colonies to provide them with power was
not feasible. As the colonial power source, the Diesel motor would
require a fraction of the fuel cargo, and the coal tar would be safer and
easier to ship. Liquid fuels would be even easier to distribute than the
traditional coal if a network of pipes was built locally in the colony.

And an engine that used vegetable or nut oils would spur the colonial agrarian economies to a point that a colony could derive power completely from its own resources, possibly even making the colony a net exporter of fuel back to Great Britain.

With the third and final point, Diesel fired a helpful warning shot across the bow of the British. He said that the marine Diesel engine had now proved superior for large merchant ships and that "Great Britain, as the greatest shipping nation in the world, will derive the greatest advantage from it." Only in his final paragraph did Diesel make brief mention of a military use for Diesel power. In a single line, he shared the news that at the very moment "a warship with a very large Diesel engine was in construction." Known to Diesel and few others in March 1912 (Fisher and British newspapers would gather more details by August), this was a definite reference to the experimental "cathedral" Diesel engines at the M.A.N. factory that Wilhelm intended for the *Kaiser*-class battleship the SMS *Prinzregent Luitpold*. (See the Addendum for the brief story of this secret operation at M.A.N.)

As Churchill worked to win the budget that he needed to modernize his navy, this warning from Diesel was of the greatest assistance.*

----

* After the initial *Selandia* voyage, Knudsen published an article titled "Smokeless Marine." All accounts of World War I naval combat reference the strategic implications and perils of the revealing funnel smoke. At the outset of war, several outmoded kerosene-burning submarines were in service. When traveling on the surface, these subs released a tower of black smoke visible on the horizon, a ridiculous condition for an ostensibly stealth weapon. These kerosene burners were quickly destroyed by enemy shells or rammed directly by warships, or else held back from offensive positions to preserve the lives of skilled submarine crewmen. Similarly, at the famous Battle of the Falkland Islands in December 1914, German armored cruisers attempted a sneak attack on the British South Atlantic port, not realizing the superior strength of the British squadron that was at rest, engines cold while coaling. An English lookout spotted rising black plumes over the mountains that otherwise concealed the approaching German warships. His warning gave the British time to man their guns and start to raise steam. The Germans, having lost the element of surprise and suddenly learning they were outmatched, turned and fled. The fearsome dreadnoughts *Invincible* and *Inflexible* steamed from port (because the British ships needed first to raise steam, they left port two hours later!), the British captain struggling to see the fleeing enemy due to the clouds of smoke from his own engines (though he eventually caught and destroyed the German ships). Diesels would change all this.

Rudolf Diesel was now out in the open as a crucial figure in the escalating arms race between Kaiser Wilhelm II and Winston Churchill. Like Churchill, Wilhelm kept a close watch on disruptive technologies that could affect the balance of military power, and he had his eye on another ship preparing for her maiden voyage.

Burmeister & Wain completed the *Fionia*, sister ship to the *Selandia*, on June 20, 1912. She had the same capacity and performance, and identical reversing 1,250-horsepower Diesel engines. Andersen, the owner of both ships, decided to show off the *Fionia* at the famous Kiel Regatta, the largest sailing event in the world, held annually in the German port city on the Baltic Sea.

On June 23, the *Fionia* made her maiden run to the gathering of yachtsmen and marine experts at Kiel. On the first day, she was christened with a new name, *Christian X*, in honor of the Danish king.

The following day, Kaiser Wilhelm II announced he wished to see the ship and "came on board at the head of a large staff of admirals and technical experts to inspect the whole installation." This was just three months after Churchill had done the very same in London with the identical ship built by Knudsen and Diesel.

From the ship Wilhelm sent a telegram to the king of Denmark, "I am on board the *Fionia* and hasten to send you my congratulations on the remarkable work of the Danish technologists. The ship indicates an entirely new chapter in shipbuilding which deserves admiration." The kaiser was holding his cards close to the vest. He well knew that by June 1912 his engineers at M.A.N. had already accomplished a test marine Diesel design with a multiple of the power of the Danish engines. The engineers at M.A.N. were still superior.

But Burmeister & Wain, in collaboration with Rudolf Diesel, had made a significant advance for commercial shipping. This new type of mercantile ship had raised the bar for commerce in a way that even Germany had not yet done. As the first of its kind, the *Selandia* would forever more be known in maritime circles as "the ship that changed the world."

With the *Christian X* back in port at Kiel, on June 24, Albert Ballin, general director of the Hamburg America Line, boarded the ship to meet with her owner. Ballin purchased the ship from Andersen on the spot, to the satisfaction of his emperor. The ship passed to German hands.

CHAPTER 20

Secrets of the First Lord

THOUGH PERHAPS NOT a man for all seasons, Churchill was certainly the best man for this one. Britain's continuing mastery of the seas rested on the shoulders of Winston Churchill, and he made the submarine a critical priority. Despite many of Churchill's admirals affirming the pre-eminence of the dreadnoughts, First Sea Lord Jackie Fisher recognized that the Diesel submarine represented a clear and present danger. And like the Swedish arms dealer Thorsten Nordenfelt, Fisher had no moral objection to the submarine weapon. He wrote in an Admiralty memo, "There is nothing else the submarine can do except sink her captives . . . The essence of war is violence and moderation in war is imbecility." Fortunately for Fisher, his boss was as much a realist as he was and committed to pursuing a Diesel submarine program for the Admiralty.[*]

---

[*] Churchill also deserves credit for pioneering the battle tank in World War I. When the British army failed to take up design plans for the project, Churchill overstepped the bounds of the navy to form the Landship Committee in February 1915 to develop an armored vehicle for the war. Engineers worked in secret. In typical English fashion, even men providing security for the plant didn't know what the project was and were told that the materials arriving were for the construction of water tanks. "Tank" became a code name for the operation, then was adopted as the name of the armored vehicle itself. Churchill, always convinced of the superiority of Diesel motors, tasked Mirrlees with developing a Diesel for the battle tank, though none was completed until after the war.

What could the colossal dreadnought battleships do from above the surface against these new stealth weapons circling beneath them? Churchill first publicly acknowledged this frightening and radical shift in naval priorities in his March 26, 1913, speech to Parliament: "The strength of navies cannot be reckoned only in 'Dreadnoughts,' and the day may come when it may not be reckoned in 'Dreadnoughts' at all." He later went on to say to the House of Commons, and specifically for the ears of the battleship-obsessed detractors of Fisher, "The whole system of naval architecture and the methods of computing naval strength are brought under review by the ever growing power, radius, and sea-worthiness of the submarine."

The *Dreadnought*, which literally means "fear nothing," finally had something to fear.

With Churchill's advocacy and unparalleled powers of persuasion, the Admiralty began a strategic shift. In a letter to the London *Times* on June 5, 1914, Admiral Sir Percy Scott wrote, "Now that submarines have come in, battleships are of no use either for defensive or offensive purposes, and, consequently, building any more in 1914 will be a misuse of money subscribed by the citizens for the defense of the Empire."*

A like-minded Churchill urgently wrote at the outset of the war to the secretary of the Admiralty with the requirement for more submarines. "It is indispensable that the whole possible plant for submarine construction should be kept at the fullest possible pressure day and night."

While maintaining a desperate push for submarine technology, Churchill still had to solve his immediate fuel quandary. England's military and

---

* This was a bit of an overstatement. In 1944, Great Britain launched the HMS *Vanguard* and the United States launched the USS *Missouri*, the last of the battleships. The United States decommissioned the *Missouri* on February 26, 1955, later recommissioning and refitting the 887-foot ship nicknamed "Mighty Mo" for action in the Gulf War. On January 29, 1991, in support of Operation Desert Storm, the USS *Missouri* fired her guns for the first time since 1953. She was decommissioned a final time in March 1992. Largely due to vulnerabilities to air and submarine attack, today the battleship is an obsolete class of ship.

commercial advantage required rapid adoption of the oil engine. As Rudolf Diesel had proved, the decline of steam power did not necessarily equate to the decline of coal as a fuel to power industry and war. Churchill shrewdly worked two strategies in parallel to safeguard the British Empire. One was to acquire his own supply of fuel oil, which was the fuel he lacked for the engines he had (the Parsons steam turbine). The other was to acquire Diesel engine expertise, which was the kind of engine he lacked for the fuel he had. (England had the capacity, after building the refinery infrastructure, for sufficient coal tar production.)

———————

Churchill was aware that British geologists had been prospecting in the oil-rich regions of the Middle East for more than a decade. William Knox D'Arcy had obtained the exclusive rights to prospect for oil in Persia (modern Iran) from Shah Mozzafar al-Din in 1901 in what is called the D'Arcy Concession. In the first years, D'Arcy's work turned up almost nothing, and after suffering major financial losses with no profits in sight, he was on the verge of giving up.

The Admiralty became concerned that D'Arcy might sell off his concession rights to a rival foreign power. France and Russia were both interested in asserting their presence in the region. The Admiralty intervened in its trademark stealthy fashion, sending a British spy named Sidney Reilly,* disguised as a priest, to meet with D'Arcy. The

———————

* Reilly, known as the "Ace of Spies," had a storied espionage career, including operations in Germany, the Middle East, and Russia. The German intelligence apparatus was equally robust at this time and included an operative named I.T.T. Lincoln (a Hungarian whose birth name was Ignácz Trebitsch), who, while working undercover in Britain, won a seat in Parliament in January 1910 and became a close friend and confidant of future prime minister David Lloyd George. Several other German operatives embedded within the UK were able to deliver information regarding prewar preparations of the Royal Navy to the German High Command in 1913. Churchill, with an eye already to counterintelligence, was aware of many of these German assets and pragmatically allowed the communications to proceed unmolested, reasoning that had he captured the foreign spies "others of whom we might not have known would have taken their place."

"priest" convinced D'Arcy to sell the majority of his concession to "a good Christian company"—in this case the British firm Burmah Oil.

This concession syndicate, soon renamed the Anglo-Persian Oil Company (APOC), kept the exclusive rights to prospecting in Persia within British control. Newly capitalized and with the support of the Admiralty, APOC continued prospecting for petroleum. At 4 a.m. on May 26, 1908, a fifty-foot-high gusher shot up from an oil rig in the city of Masjed Soleyman in Khuzestan Province of modern Iran.

Immediately after the discovery, the British government directed APOC to negotiate rights to obtain land on nearby Abadan Island for petroleum operations, including a refinery, depot, and storage tanks. APOC built the refinery and began operations in 1912.

In 1913, Winston Churchill, holding the office of First Lord of the Admiralty, directed the British government's acquisition of 50.0025 percent of APOC,* bringing one of the world's largest reserves of petroleum under state control of the British Empire. In 1914, the Admiralty confirmed a thirty-year contract with APOC for the supply of oil to the Royal Navy at a fixed price.

One-half of Churchill's hedge was in place.

———

While securing reliable access to petroleum addressed one immediate need, Churchill understood that British industry and its military would quickly become noncompetitive without access to world-class expertise in building and maintaining the Diesel engine.

Vickers and Mirrlees, reputable firms maintaining a long-standing relationship with the British government to deliver armaments, engines, and ships of all sizes, had both proved to be second-tier manufacturers of Diesel motors. There was no British firm in the same league as Sulzer Brothers, Nobel, Polar, or Burmeister & Wain, and

———

* In 1935, APOC was renamed the Anglo-Iranian Oil Company, then in 1954 renamed the British Petroleum Company (BP), which is presently one of the world's seven oil and gas "supermajors," along with Chevron, Eni, ExxonMobil, Royal Dutch Shell, Total, and ConocoPhillips.

certainly not in the league of the three dominant German firms M.A.N., Deutz, and Krupp.

To close the gap in Diesel engineering expertise, Churchill needed the best. According to Knudsen, Nobel, Sulzer, and Busch—all of whom in the years between 1908 and 1912 had actively collaborated with Diesel on technical hurdles to deliver groundbreaking new technology—the "best" was still clearly Rudolf Diesel himself.

On March 7, 1912, six days after Churchill walked the engine room of the *Selandia*, and about a week before Churchill and Diesel gave near-simultaneous London speeches, each speech an echo of the other, a new venture, the Consolidated Diesel Engine Company, was incorporated in Ipswitch, England.

George Carels, a Belgian who was known to be sympathetic to the British, was a founder of this new British-based Diesel company. Listed as director and cofounder of the new English company was Rudolf Diesel.

Rudolf's participation in the Busch-Sulzer Brothers company in America a few years prior had provoked litigation from Augsburg. His new involvement with Britain, the kaiser's chief rival and antagonist that was only five hundred miles from Berlin, was far more worrisome to the German High Command. Rudolf Diesel had publicly declared that his engine could be the savior of Great Britain. The Admiralty intended to give him the chance to prove it.

The second half of Churchill's hedge was in place—an alliance with the creator himself, Rudolf Diesel.

CHAPTER 21

The Great Light to the West

RUDOLF DIESEL SPENT a busy March in England working on the establishment of the new UK-based Diesel engine company, and he celebrated his fifty-fourth birthday there on March 18, 1912. On March 26, he and Martha sailed for the United States aboard the Hamburg America steamship *Amerika*. Over the last few years his admiration had grown for the scrappy upstart nation that was far more a meritocracy than the nations of Europe. As the *Amerika* entered the open sea Rudolf wrote in his diary, "When the shores of Europe disappear, so somehow, and surely for good reason, do the class distinctions of Europe." Hardworking and self-made, Rudolf saw something of himself in this rising power in the New World.

American industry and press eagerly awaited the arrival of the great man. He appreciated his astounding change in fortune from only five years before when he'd taken his family on a trip to Paris in 1907 to see exhibits of the designs of Denis Papin, the seventeenth-century physicist who'd built a forerunner to the steam engine. At that time, Diesel lamented to his family that he, like Papin, was "born too early for his work."

But now Diesel's invention was celebrated around the world. A few months before Rudolf sailed for America, Thomas Edison had called Diesel's engine "one of the great achievements of mankind."

W. T. Stead, the famed British journalist, had written in March, in connection with the arrival of the *Selandia* in London, that Rudolf Diesel was "the master magician of the world."* In the same piece, Stead had predicted that coal in its crude form was doomed, and that in England "all our coal mine towns will become gas-works, yielding tar. The gas [coal gas] will drive dynamos supplying towns with electricity. The coke will remain, but the motive force for the ships of the world will be fed by pipelines from the coal mines to the ports . . . the invention of [the Diesel engine] has doubled the power of man over Nature [as it requires half the fuel to deliver the equal work of other engines]."

Diesel had crossed the threshold to become a household name. The American press greeted his and Martha's arrival in New York with a barrage of questions and explosions of flash bulbs. Rudolf wrote happily to his son Eugen that his reception in America showed a level of reverence that might have been reserved for the likes of James Watt.

The Diesels boarded a train in New York bound for St. Louis, and the press was waiting for them there as well. American media were interested to hear the German inventor's remarks on industry and the rising apprehensions of war in Europe.

———————

"Houn' Dog" cocktails (bourbon, ginger, lemon, peach, and mint) were the signature drink to start the evening at the Engineers' Club of St. Louis. Busch spared no expense for the banquet in honor of his friend's visit. Mushrooms *sous cloche* followed by broiled squab guinea hens *au cresson* provided a foundation for the endless supply of cognac, cigars, and cigarettes.

———————

* Stead was a passenger on the RMS *Titanic* and perished along with more than fifteen hundred others on April 15, 1912, while the Diesels traveled from St. Louis back to New York. Stead was an ardent believer in the Diesel engine and correctly forecast its future dominance, though the oil trusts managed to ensure the Diesel engine would burn petroleum derivatives rather than coal tar as Stead had assumed.

Diesel rose to deliver remarks to a well-plied audience. Much of the speech pulled from his remarks in London the month before, though he tailored his message for the Americans, and included specific analysis as to the military advantages of adopting Diesel power for ships of war.

He touted his engine's proved efficiency. Of the 365 commercial and military Diesel-powered ships in service around the world per statistics as of November 1911 (approximately 140 submarines, 40 warships, 60 passenger or freight merchant vessels, 30 oil tankers, and the rest a mix of smaller craft), Rudolf relayed that the average improvements over prior engines were an operational range that was four times greater, a reduction in fuel weight of 80 percent, and a reduction in the engine crew of 75 percent.

The opportunity for fuel savings was even greater for military ships than commercial because the comparative efficiencies of Diesel power were even more pronounced when the engine ran at slow speeds or when idling. While commercial ships have predetermined routes to cover at speed, military craft often patrol a zone at slow speed or remain idling near a strategic location.

Rudolf presented a chart of calculations prepared by English naval engineers for replacing the steam engines of a British destroyer with Diesels. While Diesel engines are heavier than the Otto engine (which cannot meet the power requirements to drive a capital ship), Diesel engines are far lighter than the steam engine of comparable power. The overall efficiencies deliver an improved radius of action that would render steam power militarily obsolete.

	STEAM	DIESEL
Weight of engines	*449,000*	*317,000 lbs.*
Weight per B.H.P.	*64*	*44 lbs.*
Radius of Action at 10 knots and 120 tons of fuel	*1,700*	*10,000 knots*[*]

---

[*] 1 knot = 1.15 mile

	STEAM	DIESEL
Radius of Action at 28 knots and 180 tons of fuel	950	6,302 knots
Engineers and stokers	56	21
Fuel consumption in one year (20,000 marine miles)	2,100	350 tons
Cost of Fuel	3,040	924
Cost of engine crew labor	4,300	1,920
Cost of repairs	2,000	400

Diesel then presented a design diagram made by engineers of the Royal Navy that compared two destroyers currently under construction in Britain—one with steam power and one with Diesels. Though the engines were still on the machine shop floor, news of the destroyer represented yet another startling leap ahead for the Diesel engine, this time moving from oceangoing merchant ships to powering large surface ships of war. It could not have been lost on the American audience that Diesel made his calculations and designs for warships in collaboration with engineers of the Royal Navy—this during the height of the prewar naval arms race with Germany.

Rudolf noted that the Diesel engines took up only half the space of the steam engines. Further, "in the steamship the steam engines and boilers reach up nearly to the upper deck," making the engines vulnerable to the rain of enemy shells. But the diagram of the Diesel destroyer showed the engines fully to the stern and below the waterline, under the armored plating of the deck, which made "the ship invulnerable from the enemy fire as far as the engines are concerned."

The Diesel warship had greater offensive capability with its guns as well. Rudolf Diesel showed the next diagram from Royal Navy engineers—the comparison of a steam versus a Diesel battleship. The diagram of the traditional steam engine battleship showed the deck surmounted by smokestacks. Because the Diesel engine required no

Rudolf Diesel presented this design sketch during his American lectures of 1912. On the left is a battleship with steam propulsion; on the right is a battleship with Diesel engines. The battleship under Diesel power has ten guns of 30.5 cm, which the gunners can direct to all points of the horizon, as opposed to the steam battleship, which has four big guns with limited maneuverability. Of note, this design sketch was created by engineers of the Royal Navy under direction of First Lord Churchill.

chimney apparatus for the engines, the entire expanse of the decks of the Diesel ship could be open and free. A freighter could stack cargo. A battleship could stack more big guns. And these guns would have no obstructions in the way of rotating turrets. Diesel remarked to an enthralled American audience, "Due to the absence of funnels, each of these ten guns can be directed nearly to every point of the horizon, for instance, all ten can be directed towards one side, which does more than double the fighting capacity as compared with the steam ship."

The implications of Diesel's analysis had spread through the Royal Navy—the revelation that under Diesel power the guns of a battleship could have double the value while the ship would have a radius of action five times greater, a more useful deployment of crew, a reduced fuel cost, and a far better record of engine repair and maintenance that could keep the ship in service.

The evidence that the Royal Navy was already in feverish pursuit of Diesel is not only apparent in the fact that an engineer of the Royal Navy had drawn the presentation sketches Rudolf showed in St. Louis but is also reflected in confidential letters written by First Sea Lord Fisher. On August 28, 1912, Jackie Fisher wrote an internal memorandum to First Lord Churchill, "The . . . enclosed report points to the accuracy of the newspaper report I sent you yesterday of the construction of a German cruiser with Diesel Engines. The boast made some time ago was that she would be capable of going round the world without re-fueling! What an Alabama!!!"

In a separate memorandum, Fisher echoed what Rudolf had said in his London address in March—that the benefits of the Diesel engine were greater for Britain than for any other country. He concluded that if the kaiser ever came to fully appreciate this, Rudolf Diesel could be in grave danger. "Krupp has a design for a cargo-ship with Internal Combustion Engines to go 40,000 miles without refueling.* It's vital for the British Fleet and for no other Fleet, to have the [Diesel] oil engine. That's the strange thing! And if only the Germans knew, they'd shoot their Dr. Diesel like a dog!" Fisher recorded this observation only twelve months before Rudolf Diesel disappeared.

On September 20, 1912, Fisher sent an excited confidential letter to Lord Esher, a Liberal politician and diplomat: "All the drawings and designs [for a British battleship with Diesel engines] quite ready . . . Owing to our apathy the last two years, [the Germans] are ahead with internal combustion engines! I have it from an eye-witness of part of the machinery for her at Nuremberg, that a big German oil engine Cruiser is under weigh! We must press forward . . . A *greater than the*

---

* During the Great War, as both sides suffered losses to commercial shipping beyond what even the submarine advocates had predicted, Germany experimented with building massive submarines for the purpose of delivering cargo. The engine design emphasized reliability over speed and performance. On March 28, 1916, Germany launched the cargo submarine *Deutschland*, powered by a nonreversible 450-horsepower Diesel, capable of carrying 791 tons of cargo. The ship had no armaments. As it approached a hostile blockade, it submerged and cruised safely beneath the enemy ships. On the first round-trip to the United States, still a neutral power, the sub carried 163 tons of dyestuff, then returned with 348 tons of rubber, 341 tons of nickel, and 93 tons of tin for the German war effort. She made two trips during the war carrying a total of 1,800 tons of cargo.

Dreadnought' is here! Imagine a silhouette presenting a target 33 per cent less than any living or projected Battleship! No funnels—no masts—no smoke—she carries over 5000 tons of oil, enough to take her round the world . . . Imagine this set loose in a sea fight! WE HAVE GOT TO HAVE HER" (Fisher's emphasis).

In his St. Louis lecture, Rudolf moved from military matters to economic ones, reminding the audience that the Diesel engine delivered similar operating efficiencies to inland industrial use, where a total of two million Diesel horsepower was currently at work around the world. By 1912, Diesel motors already accounted for 30 percent of the total inland horsepower in Germany.

Rudolf extended this discussion to the use of alternative fuels, explaining that his engine could ably burn coal tar or vegetable and nut oils in addition to a petroleum-derived fuel. He declared, "The use of vegetable oils for engine fuels may seem insignificant today. But such oils may become in the course of time as important as petroleum and the coal tar products of the present time."

Diesel argued that the flexibility of his engine with regard to the fuel it burned meant that his technology could break any fuel monopoly and provide a measure of political stability to any country, no matter its natural supply of fuels. "Some [countries] are exclusively coal-producing, others exclusively oil-producing, still others produce coal and oil, like the United States. It is difficult to predict what development will take place in a given country." With Diesel engines, it didn't matter. Every country possessed workable fuel. Diesel noted that the abundance of fuel in the United States was a reason for lagging Diesel adoption in America.

He then declared that because the Diesel engine gave European nations the option to use coal by-products as fuel that Europe was largely able to "prevent the increase of prices for the natural liquid fuels and the establishment of trust or monopoly companies."

Upheaval and competition in the Caucasus and discoveries of petroleum elsewhere on the continent meant that Europe had no equivalent of Rockefeller. Nor could it now that the adoption of the Diesel engine was on the rise. Rudolf added that "in Europe we have definitely broken the monopolies in liquid fuel oil, not by law or other artificial means [clearly a reference to the actions of the Supreme Court the year before against Standard Oil under the Sherman Antitrust Act] but by the invincible force of scientific investigation and industrial progress before which the mightiest must bow." From his office in New York Rockefeller surely read these boasts, which were published in newspapers around the country. He had no intention of bowing to Rudolf Diesel.

To conclude his speech, Rudolf reflected on the geopolitical implications of his discussion, and made the point that was also then top of mind for Churchill, Rockefeller, and Wilhelm II—that fuel is the decider of the fate of nations.

Diesel made three predictions. First, he insisted that pollution, largely ignored in industrial nations, would become an important consideration in engine design. Second, despite the slow start of Diesel power in America, he believed America would come to utilize the Diesel-powered locomotive more than any other nation in the world. Third, while America was presently "monstrously" rich in its domestic supplies of fuels, eventually economic efficiencies would transcend wasteful habits.

His predictions proved to be prophetic.

He made one other prediction. As a young scientist in the 1880s Diesel had sketched a solar-powered engine. He theorized that the sun would heat the engine chamber, providing the fuel for the engine to deliver work. His quick calculations in the four-page sketch estimated that the engine could deliver a maximum of 1/50th horsepower, and so, at the time of his drawing with nineteenth-century metalworking constraints, the engine was "too weak for any kind of efficiency." But he never fully gave up on the idea.

In the way that da Vinci had the gift of vision that could span centuries and penetrate the obscuring limitations of his own time to draw an uncannily accurate future reality, Diesel could see around corners to a new reality.

Thirty years after he made those sketches, Diesel again referenced his idea for solar power in his St. Louis speech. He predicted that the noxious, polluting effects of coal and oil engines would eventually surpass what the earth could absorb, but that "motive power can still be produced from the heat of the sun, always available, even when the natural stores of solid and liquid fuels are exhausted."

———

At that moment in Europe, the locomotive engines Rudolf had designed with Sulzer were beginning test runs. During his St. Louis remarks, Diesel expressed his fascination with the expanding rail network in America. He was especially envious of the American opportunity to design a road and rail network from scratch, to build what ought to be built for the specific purpose, rather than the situation in Europe where engineers designed transportation networks to fit the ancient pathways of the Romans and other civilizations.

Though there was, as yet, no commercially successful rail line running Diesel power, he boldly asserted in his address that "one thing is certain—the Diesel locomotive will come sooner or later." When asked by a reporter about his chief ambition in America, Diesel responded, "To drive my own thermo-locomotive from New York to St. Louis—fueled with nothing but butter, if you will kindly spare me the butter."

At the conclusion of the two-hour lecture, the audience of midwesterners leapt to their feet for an embarrassingly long ovation. Diesel smiled, the first of the night since his Houn' Dog cocktail. Meier saw in the man before him the same humility he'd first observed in the inventor fourteen years earlier. Rudolf was never lured off his course by his growing wealth and fame but remained unwaveringly devoted to science and the advancement of humankind.

Rudolf bowed to his audience, turned from the wooden podium, and passed directly through the side exit. Waiting for him in the alley was the chauffeur hired by Busch, standing next to the open door of the latest model Benz, engine warm and running.

————

Between speaking engagements, Rudolf and Martha traveled the American West by rail, again going as far as San Francisco.* During various stops, the press sought Diesel's views on Germany and the prospect of war. While he generally avoided specific comments regarding German foreign policy, he declared emphatically that he deplored extreme nationalism. He also went so far as to deny being German, saying that he preferred to be called Bavarian, though his first choice was to be a "citizen of the world." He informed the reporters that he had Slav ancestors, was French-born, and Bavarian-naturalized. He concluded, "I am from everywhere."

At one interview a reporter told Diesel that the German Imperial General Staff had recently embedded personnel with the Ringling Brothers Circus in order to study how the circus provisioned and mobilized such a large operation across distances. Diesel responded that the "Imperial German Staff would do better in circuses than anywhere else."

Later writings of Eugen Diesel illuminate Rudolf's negative feelings toward Germany during these years. "Many were the journeys we took together on which [Rudolf] would teach me to observe the characteristics of the different nations; the problem of Germany was a continual source of both interest and anxiety to him." Rudolf and his son observed of the turn-of-the-century Germans, "The military manners and bearing per-

———————

* Diesel traveled the "Frisco" railroad when returning to St. Louis from California. He stopped for the night in the Ozarks of Arkansas where a youth, helping his older cousin who was the local reporter, greeted him on the platform. The youth, Charles Morrow Wilson, coauthored a biography of Diesel fifty-three years later. In it he recounts the pleasant evening he spent with Diesel during which the tall and "exceptionally handsome" traveler was generous with his time. Curious about the local farms, he traveled with the boy to meet his family and shared a cream soda. He had invited Diesel to join the family for dinner, but Diesel "graciously declined the invitation . . . explaining that he was obliged to take medicine before meals and that his medicine kit was at the hotel." It was an enameled pillbox that could fit in the palm of one's hand, and apparently Diesel didn't typically keep it on his person.

meate the people, so that even the civilian learnt to click his heels together and bow with the requisite stiffness. The conversational tone became loud and brusque; arrogance and ostentation were to be met with every-where. Life took on the blaring pomposity of a military march."

In an eerie foreshadowing of Germany's fate years later under Nazi rule, Eugen continued, "The military spirit often usurped the place of the political. And this was the cause of much of what was called 'militarism' and what, together with certain other qualities, made the Germans so hated. These hosts of individualists grew into willing subordinates, and this welding together of individualists under the pressure of impersonal service was really the characteristic feature of German military service."*

In sharp contrast to his remarks to the American press about Germany, Diesel had wonderful things to say when asked for his observations of the United States. He called America "the great light to the west," and that the young nation was "the haven and heaven for all inventors."

After sharing his opinion that America had already become the world's leading power and that America's industrial and financial supremacy would continue to grow, Paul Greer of the Omaha *News-Bee* asked, "What do you like most about Americans?"

Diesel answered:

> *There are four American virtues which I believe basic. First, I would name the absence of any durably fixed classes. Your poor and rich, laboring and professional classes are quite readily inter-changeable. . . . Next, I would say that the distribution of intelli-gence and charity among everyday Americans is very fair and generous. My third point is great respect for American inventive*

---

* Eugen Diesel became a member of the resistance movement during the Nazi re-gime. He published these observations of turn-of-the-century Germany in January 1931, prior to Hitler's rise. It is interesting to note his foreshadowing of the commonly used defense of Nazi soldiers after World War II: "I was just following orders."

talents, also exceptionally well distributed among all kinds of
workers. And finally the modesty of important Americans. Modesty
of important people invites more of its kind.

When reporters asked about the rumor that Diesel was assisting the Royal Navy to build a Diesel-powered fleet of submarines, Diesel demurred.

———————

Martha wasn't spared a blitz by the press either. She handled the incoming questions with grace and discretion that bordered on the comedic. When asked for her views on women's suffrage, she replied, "It is an interesting development." When asked for her views on Teddy Roosevelt, who was then fracturing the Republican Party in another run for the presidency, she answered, "He is an interesting development." Her views on the growth of the Lutheran church in America? "Lutheranism is always an interesting development."

Perhaps she had a firm understanding that her husband had plenty of enemies and that the press was not looking to make friends but headlines. She managed to give any pitfalls a wide berth.

———————

Rudolf and Martha arrived in Ithaca, New York, two days early for Diesel's lecture at Cornell University scheduled for the evening of April 18. Stunned faces passed by them on the streets, people shouted the impossible news. Only when they had bought a newspaper and read the headline for themselves did the event seem real. The information came by Marconi telegraph. The unsinkable RMS *Titanic* had gone to the bottom.

The Diesels shared the universal sadness and shock, perhaps more acutely as, if not for the earlier obligation with Adolphus Busch in St. Louis, they might have been among the 1,517 dead. Rudolf clipped the newspaper headline and pasted it into his diary.

Compounding this distressing news was the fact that during the overnight ride in the Pullman railcar, Diesel's gout (an arthritic condition that causes pain and swelling) had flared up. His inflamed right foot was half again the size of his left. Nevertheless, determined to go on with the lecture, Diesel instructed the student reception committee to find a black shoe large enough to fit. Hours later, in white tie and tails, he delivered the second of his major lectures in America.

The couple then traveled to New York City for medical treatment and, conveniently, a visit with Rudolf Jr. The eldest Diesel child had recently taken a job in the city, then promptly fallen in love with and married a New Yorker, Daisy Weiss. The two just had a son, whom they named Arnold.

After this brief respite, Diesel traveled to Annapolis to speak before the US Naval Academy, then returned to New York for his final lecture on April 30. Hours prior to the speech, the American Society of Mechanical Engineers held a ceremony to celebrate their esteemed guest. The chairman of the society bestowed an honorary membership on Rudolf and delivered a speech summarizing Diesel's significant place in history. The chairman began by declaring that civilization became possible when man first discovered how to make and use fire, and that "the ancient world deified this unknown [discoverer] as Prometheus." The chairman then reminded the audience that two thousand years earlier the Egyptians learned to use the medium of heated steam to open and close the massive doors of their temples. This technology was improved when "less than two centuries ago, James Watt first applied the same power to the useful arts [and developed] means of transportation, mining, metallurgy," though Watt's limitation was that a "scarce two per cent of the power locked up in the fuel could be utilized." Then in more recent history, "[Alphonse] Beau de Rochas, Otto, [William Dent] Priestman and other engineers, abandoning the intermediary of steam, produced explosive engines in which the direct conversion of heat into power reached a useful effect of twenty per cent."

The chairman brought the speech to a crescendo by anointing Diesel as the deliverer to the world of the power source that would bring civilization into a new era. "Rudolf Diesel presented to the engineering profession an internal combustion engine in which *controlled* combustion replaced explosions, from which ignition troubles were banished, and which reached . . . efficiency of thirty-five per cent." In the final judgement, "Rudolf Diesel is the great conservator of the precious fire."

During his two American trips (1904 and 1912), Rudolf traveled the American rail system for a combined total of twenty thousand miles, and his opinion of the country greatly improved the second time. During his first visit he had been taken back by the poor civil engineering of even the major cities, the impermanent and vulnerable wooden housing of all towns, the extreme focus on making a "quick dollar." But America was growing strong at a breakneck pace, and Rudolf admired the social, political, and economic freedoms. By late April 1912, he had a distinctly positive view of America.

When asked by reporters if he would consider American citizenship, he replied that it would be a "great honor" but that he had immediate work in Europe.

In connection with his travels to the "great light," both the Pennsylvania Railroad and Henry Ford tried to hire Diesel in 1912, requesting his assistance with the Diesel motor in their respective businesses. Both companies offered Diesel a consulting position and fee. To conquer the locomotive and the automobile were among his remaining life's ambitions, but Diesel declined both offers, which came as a surprise to his friends and family. Rudolf had decided there was more urgent and all-consuming work in Europe, though he hadn't made clear to anyone what the work might be that could be more pressing than these grand American offers that were so closely aligned to his personal ambitions.

Rudolf's private diary records the astounding pace he kept during his trip, as well as the degree to which the most prominent businessmen in America sought an audience with him. He had lunch with George Westinghouse, a meeting with George Merck (whose family emigrated from Germany to New York and founded Merck pharmaceuticals as well as the shipping conglomerate Hamburg America and H. J. Merck & Co., a merchant bank in Hamburg), and with various admirals and submarine commanders of the US Navy. The entire executive team of Baldwin Locomotive Works traveled from Philadelphia to Baltimore for the opportunity of a brief meeting with Rudolf.

His typical day consisted of meetings over lunch, then meetings over tea followed by a separate dinner meeting, then drinks after dinner, or (when in New York) a visit to the theater with Martha. He punctuated this pounding routine with his four major lectures before upward of a thousand people, corporate board meetings, factory tours, and lengthy train rides between cities. Though he wrote that his gout flared up a few times, he also noted the pleasurable visits he had to several museums and Ellis Island. Diesel's boundless energy and enthusiasm to share his vision, as well as his deep appreciation of the finer things, leap from the pages of his diary.

He took meals at the Metropolitan Club in Washington, D.C., the posh Sunset Country Club in St. Louis, and during his time in New York he visited the famous Sherry's restaurant on Fifth Avenue, the New York Yacht Club, the New York Athletic Club, and even rode the subway to the Bowling Green station for lunch at the exclusive Whitehall Club, Manhattan's premier maritime club of the era.

He stayed in America's fanciest hotels: the historic Planter's Hotel in St. Louis, the Iroquois Hotel in Buffalo, the Clinton House in Ithaca, and while in Annapolis at the home of Commander Reed (who oversaw the Naval Academy visit), after which Diesel made a note of Reed's "charming wife."

Among other Broadway shows, Rudolf and Martha enjoyed the new play *Disraeli* at Wallack's Theatre on Forty-Second Street, and *Typhoon* at the Hudson Theatre.

After this exhausting schedule, on his final full day before sailing from New York Harbor, Germany's most esteemed inventor called upon his most celebrated American counterpart.

———

The legacies of Thomas Edison and Rudolf Diesel will outlast those of kings and presidents. More than a hundred years after their achievements, people around the world pass these names with such frequency each day (on a car, a light bulb, a utility bill) that the names are now disembodied and attributed to common nouns.

The two men had much in common: a veneration of science, a slavish devotion to work, and fame in their own time.

At the conclusion of Diesel's American lectures, he accepted Edison's invitation to visit West Orange, New Jersey. On May 6, 1912, Rudolf and Martha arrived at Edison's home for a meeting of titans. They found the two men had more differences than similarities.

Thomas Edison greeted Martha and Rudolf outside the modest cottage that was also his home laboratory. Inside they sat on uncomfortable chairs to eat a light breakfast next to tables piled high with gear parts and sections of models and a large roll-top desk that was overwhelmed by untidy stacks of papers and drawings. The expansive workroom was the dominant feature of the cottage, and the walls were lined with wooden partitions creating separate workspaces for a variety of projects. In a corner that was slightly less cluttered was a metal-framed cot, and nearby, bizarrely, an armchair made of cement.

Edison was sixty-five, eleven years older than Rudolf. Diesel quickly came to feel that Edison assumed the role of being not just the elder but also the wiser as he dispensed his insights on life and science to his guests.

Edison told them that his wife had recently "dragged" him on a trip through Italy, which he found very boring. His wife apparently took him to cathedral after cathedral until he refused to set foot in another. He had no interest in the murals, tapestries, or sculptures, and he detested religious-inspired art.

Edison stated with pride that he was "self-educated." Diesel felt this was a questionable asset, though he kept the opinion to himself. Diesel certainly admired the drive for self-improvement, but believed advanced science required formal training, and at the turn of the century it was hard to find such training in America at all. The best and most prestigious technical schools were all in Europe where Rudolf had paid his dues.

Their different educational backgrounds led to entirely different methods of invention. Innovation can be achieved by scholars and tinkerers. Edison was more of a field scientist, tinkering with vaguely formed concepts and sharpening his focus through trial and error, as did Marconi.*

Diesel, and inventors like Charles Parsons and Hugo Junkers, believed that the prize rose from the theoretical analysis performed up front. Diesel was a skilled mathematician and physicist, and he worked out in detail what was theoretically possible before he proceeded to the "field." As an inventor of a combustion engine, for which materials are expensive and require skilled metallurgy to make the component parts, trial and error can become prohibitively costly.† Before Diesel touched a single piece of metal, he satisfied himself through a complete study of the thermodynamics of his design that the engine would work. When he encountered obstacles in his testing, it was his supreme confidence in the correctness of his calculations that made his determination unshakable. Certainly, he made tweaks and optimized his invention during the test phase, but that was not a time meant to alter the main premise of the work or make a significant new discovery.

---

* Guglielmo Marconi was homeschooled by tutors and, like Edison, who was homeschooled mainly by his mother, had no formal higher education. Around 1890, he read published articles about the telegraphy experiments of Heinrich Hertz and attempted to replicate these in the attic of his family's estate in Italy. Marconi made a breakthrough in 1895 when he moved the experiments outdoors, believing that if he raised the height of the antenna he could transmit a radio signal over a much greater distance.

† Detractors of Rudolf Diesel point to the fact that the commercial engine he delivered in 1897 fundamentally differs from the famous patent he filed in 1892 (patent No. 67207), which is true. Diesel's first patent described a "constant temperature engine," referring to the high temperature in the engine chamber. However, in 1893, Diesel reorganized his engine concept to a "constant *pressure* engine" and filed a new patent in November (granted in July 1895 as Reich Patent No. 82168) prior to embarking on the expensive testing phase that began in late 1893. Diesel wrote of the detractors, "I was persecuted by a number of critics with almost unbelievable hatred. The deviation from the theoretical ideal, which was unavoidable in practice, was denounced as a crime against science, and the new engine was denounced with moral indignation."

The men differed on the very definition of the word *inventor*. Edison argued that a successful inventor was more a coordinator of prior inventions. As a voracious reader and relentless tinkerer, he manipulated the innovations brought to him with his homespun genius to find a new direction and reimagine market usefulness. For example, on July 18, 1877, Edison was testing an automatic telegraph that had a stylus to read coded indentations on paper. Perhaps due to an increase in voltage, the stylus began to move much more quickly, which resulted in greater friction and a sound. Edison determined to make the sound intentional, eventually refining the stylus over indentations to reproduce the human voice, and so invented the phonograph. Diesel never wandered into an invention in this way, and he was appalled by this view of an inventor as aggregator and modifier. The discussion turned into barbs traded between the men.

After Edison shared his lengthy reflections on engines (which Diesel found to be no more than "froth on beer"), he summarized by imagining an "accumulated" engine whereby the work of a dozen or more engineers might be "composited" together in one "light and practical machine."

To Diesel, this was absurd. The various engine designs were distinct ideas, and simply to mush them together was embarrassingly naive. Having left Edison's comments on art and homeschooling alone, he now felt provoked, and on this point he broke his silence, asking his host whether he thought engine makers were worth a dime a dozen?* Edison responded with amusement, saying that the main worry was whether "what a dozen engine inventors bring together [was] going to be worth a dime when brought together."

The differences didn't stop there. Edison, in a haughty way, or so Diesel thought, denied having confined himself to any "speciality." Diesel, for his part, not only found Edison to be inadequately learned

---

* There is no archival material to provide Edison's perspective of the meeting. The only source material is the published writing of Eugen Diesel, who recounts what Rudolf and Martha told him.

in the basic scientific building blocks of mathematics and physics but took pride in declaring himself to be an engine specialist.

And though Diesel didn't say it out loud, he took satisfaction in the observation of another fundamental difference—that while Edison built machines that were power-consuming, Diesel built engines that were power-producing.

Of their wives, Edison remarked, perhaps enviously, "The girls appear to get along just fine."

The whole visit might have been more bearable but for one other irritating difference between the men. Edison abhorred alcohol, and this polarity of opinion led to another round of barbs with Diesel. When Edison proclaimed that "swilling alcohol is unnatural," Diesel pointed out that *Homo sapiens* had been consuming alcohol almost as long as he had been consuming bread and meat. Edison wanted to know why Diesel had said "almost as long." Diesel laughed and said, "Only because fermentation takes a little time."

Diesel had commercially fruitful and personally fulfilling relationships with many of the leading inventors of his day, but he felt no great affection for Edison. Their backgrounds and working methods were widely disparate. Their mutual respect for hard work and achievement was not enough to cross the gulf between the two faith-like approaches to invention.

The Diesels retreated to the Waldorf-Astoria Hotel in New York City. On May 7, 1912, Rudolf and Martha rode in a limousine to the Thirty-Fourth Street pier on the Hudson River to board the *Victoria Luise* of the Hamburg America Line. Aboard the ship Diesel was fascinated to meet two survivors of the *Titanic* disaster. Oberst (Colonel) Alfons Simonius-Blumer and his secretary, Max Stähelin-Maeglin, attempting to recross the Atlantic less than a month after being fished out of the cold sea, recounted the harrowing adventure to a rapt Diesel.

On May 15 the passengers disembarked in England and Rudolf immediately resumed his bustling pace. At 2 p.m., he attended a meeting in London of the board of directors of the new Consolidated Diesel Engine Company, for which the Admiralty had high hopes.

As was the way of the Renaissance man, from the board meeting he met Martha for a fine dinner then attended London's Kingsway Theatre to enjoy George Bernard Shaw's *Fanny's First Play*.

CHAPTER 22

Rising Pressure

THE DISRUPTIVE FORCE of Diesel technology was no longer abstract. The engine performed better than any other engine in the world. Leaders of political and industrial empires needed to come to terms with the impact that the emergence of the Diesel engine had in an already fraught and dynamic environment.

In 1912, John D. Rockefeller was seventy-three years old and once again found himself on the ropes. The trust-busting efforts begun during Teddy Roosevelt's administration had finally caught up with the tycoon. On May 15, 1911, the Supreme Court issued a landmark ruling in *Standard Oil Co. of New Jersey v. United States*, with Chief Justice Edward White writing for the majority that Rockefeller's trust was participating in "restraint to trade and commerce in petroleum." White's written opinion went on to declare that Standard Oil's attempt to eliminate competition and control the free market through fixed pricing, monopolies, and combinations was *unreasonable* and *illegal*. The cornerstone of the prosecution's case was the rebate scheme that Standard Oil had created with the railroads.

The court ruled 8–1. Justice John Harlan, who wrote the lone dissenting opinion, agreed with the resulting breakup of the trust but objected to the court's more far-reaching definition of "restraint of trade," which he believed would set too onerous a precedent on American businesses.

Many Americans had agreed with Rockefeller's legal defense— not only fellow industrialists but laypersons as well. Standard Oil's advantage was fairly won, they felt, and the business tactics, though ruthless, were no more ruthless than the tactics of the competing integrated oil empires in other countries. A government overreach to force an impairment on America's most powerful trust, which no other oil firm in the world would suffer, was an impairment to America's international standing and influence.

In fact, by the time of the court's ruling, Standard Oil's stranglehold on the petroleum market was already loosening. New entrants, right in Standard Oil's backyard, included Texaco, Gulf Oil, Sun, and Union Oil. These were relatively small firms, but as a result of the court's ruling, so now was Standard Oil. The court broke the trust into "Baby Standards"—thirty-four geographically separate and eventually competing firms.*

To make matters worse for Rockefeller, future growth in demand for petroleum was uncertain. While demand for kerosene continued to plummet due to the adoption of the light bulb, the rise in demand for gasoline to fuel the automobile's combustion engine did not yet show signs of filling the void. In 1909, Ford sold only 10,000 autos. By 1913, the number was up to 265,000 but this was nowhere near enough. (By comparison, today there are 6.5 million vehicles in Los Angeles County alone.) Rockefeller had lost his monopoly power. With his oil trust broken and the arrival of new competitors, he could no longer control the supply-side and manipulate prices.

---

* Some of these Baby Standards went on to be among the highest-revenue-generating companies in America. Standard Oil of New Jersey became Exxon; Standard Oil of New York became Mobil, later combining with Exxon in 1999 to form ExxonMobil; Standard Oil of California became Chevron; Continental Oil became Conoco, then Phillips 66; Standard Oil of Ohio became Sohio, later acquired by British Petroleum in 1987.

In the immediate term, the breakup of the trust actually increased Rockefeller's wealth. These thirty-four separate companies were now independently traded stocks, and the stock prices went up. It turned out that the whole was *not* greater than the sum of its parts; the parts were worth more on their own. By some estimates, Rockefeller reached the peak of his wealth in 1913. In that year, the GDP of the United States was $39.1 billion, and Rockefeller was worth $900 million, or 2.3 percent of the GDP.

But there was a difference between this paper wealth and the real power to control the petroleum market and global events that he had enjoyed with a unified Standard Oil. As a result of the court's decision, Rockefeller was wounded, and, like any animal, therefore unpredictable and more dangerous. The future of Standard Oil rested entirely on the rapid adoption of the gasoline-burning internal combustion engine and the conversion of the steam engine from coal to fuel oil, which would increase the demand for petroleum and avoid a glut of supply and a ruinous collapse in the price of oil.

Rockefeller had no interest in boosting agrarian economies through the use of oil engines that ran on vegetable and nut oils, as advocated by Rudolf Diesel. He had no interest in bailing out Great Britain and petroleum-poor nations of Western Europe with an oil engine that burned coal tar derived from their own mines. He must have read with fury the newspaper reports of Rudolf Diesel's boasts to break the American fuel monopoly by means of his new engine. Rockefeller's success required the world to be addicted to crude oil. As long as Diesel technology was on the rise, petroleum's position as the dominant source of fuel for the world was uncertain.

———————

Kaiser Wilhelm II was also in a desperate struggle to exploit the evolving capabilities of different types of engines and to obtain the fuels needed for each. Wilhelm's engine manufacturing contracts with M.A.N., Deutz, and Krupp constituted big bets on the Diesel engine for his submarines and, in the near future, his entire surface fleet. But at present, Wilhelm needed reliable access to fuel oil and gasoline. He determined that getting quick access to the abundance of crude oil in the regions of the Persian Gulf was a better strategy than building an agrarian economy to produce alternative fuels, and better than investing in a refit of his domestic coal production to refine coal tar on the scale he required.

In 1910, Germany began construction of the Berlin-Baghdad Railway, a thousand-mile rail line to run through Turkey, Syria, and Iraq, connecting the German capital with the oil-rich and Ottoman-controlled city of Baghdad. Wilhelm wanted a direct supply of oil to Germany that was not affected by British-patrolled shipping lanes.

This German action in the Persian Gulf, previously the domain of the British Empire, set off a cascade of international threats and tense diplomatic discussions among the Great Powers.

Wilhelm enjoyed close relations with the Islamic world, dating back to an official state visit he made to Turkey in 1889 (a visit that Bismarck opposed, arguing that it would needlessly alarm Russia, a traditional enemy of the Turks). Wilhelm tightened his embrace of the Ottoman Empire, making another state visit in 1898, and continuing to nurture a Turkish connection to Germany as a counterbalance to the strengthening alliances of Great Britain, France, and Russia.

Russia, already fearful of the rising power and belligerence of Germany, immediately protested the railway. Russia saw the new rail line as a dangerous extension of German influence into petroleum regions close to the Russian fields in the Caucasus. To compound Russia's concern, the rail line would bring an enormous boost of commerce to strengthen a weakened Ottoman Empire. The combined German and Ottoman interests in the railway put Russia on high alert.

Great Britain was alarmed as well. Understanding that Wilhelm wanted the railway to fuel the Anglo-German arms race, the British had good reason to want to block its construction. Additionally, Britain was unsettled by the capability the railway would give Germany to move military assets in close proximity to India, a prized colony of the British Empire.

Germany's design for the rail line anticipated the violent opposition of the British that surely would come. Though a coastal route for the railway would have been far cheaper and easier to build, it would also have been within shelling range of the British navy. Therefore, Wilhelm selected an inland route for the line, even though it was far more challenging and expensive to build. The land buffer of this route provided a measure of safety from the British but required the Germans to blast several tunnels through the Taurus Mountains in southern Turkey and the Amanus Mountains (today called the Nur Mountains), a range in the Hatay Province of south-central Turkey.*

Map of Berlin-Baghdad Railway, *extending German influence east toward the Russian oil fields of the Baku region and toward British-controlled India.*

---

* By the outbreak of war in 1914, Germany had built four hundred miles of the line. The Treaty of Versailles in 1919 addressed the project, canceling all German rights to the railway. Germany later reacquired the project, and finally completed the thousand-mile line in the years 1938–40 under the Nazi regime. Ultimately engineers blasted twenty-seven tunnels for the railway. At present, the railway is still intact and most stations are original.

Morris Jastrow Jr., a scholar writing at the time of the Great War, observed of Wilhelm's ambitions in the Persian Gulf, "It was felt in England that if, as Napoleon is said to have remarked, Antwerp in the hands of a great continental power was a pistol leveled at the English coast, Baghdad and the Persian Gulf in the hands of Germany would be a 42-centimeter gun."

For Wilhelm the project was worth the risk of antagonizing Britain. He believed in the rise of Germany as an imperial power, and he was counting on German mastery of the oil engine (both Diesel's and Otto's) to power his military. Success required two things: Wilhelm needed to secure reliable access to fuel for his military and his economy, and he needed to make sure that the engineers in Germany, particularly those with Diesel expertise, remained one step ahead of those in the rest of the world. The Berlin-Baghdad Railway pushed diplomacy with Great Britain to the brink.

On February 9, 1912, the elaborately mustached Kaiser Wilhelm drew back the largest of three chairs at the small, narrow table in the private study of his Berlin palace. He deftly stepped aside and waved his good arm toward the chair at the head of the table. His guest, Great Britain's war minister Richard Haldane, took the seat.

Wilhelm directed Admiral Tirpitz to a smaller chair at Haldane's left, and the emperor took the chair to Haldane's right. The three men had just finished lunch in the palace with Wilhelm's wife the kaiserin, their daughter Princess Victoria Louise, and Chancellor Theobald von Bethmann Hollweg, but at the conclusion of lunch Wilhelm had dismissed the others. He wanted a private audience with the member of the British cabinet. The kaiser smiled at Haldane, leaned forward, and lit his guest's cigar for him.

Wilhelm was quite charming when he wanted to be. Handsome and regal in bearing, by 1912 he had recovered much of his standing both at home and abroad after his string of gaffes between 1905 and 1909. This recovery was in part because he had quietly assumed the role of one of Europe's elder monarchs. England's Edward VII, always in the position of the older and wiser relation, had passed away in May 1910. Bertie, also fondly known as "Europe's Uncle,"* was no longer around to hog the spotlight.

The kaiser considered himself to be a skilled diplomat and manager and frequently shared his views on the full spectrum of matters. With the unshakable self-belief that he was the Universal Man, he reworked theater productions and symphony orchestras, often contradicting Germany's most revered conductors on their own stage. He involved himself directly in the works of painters and sculptors, adjusted the arrangement of parade routes, altered military ship designs, directed military budgets and the deployment of troops. And when it came to diplomacy, Wilhelm inserted himself into official channels and negotiated directly with the foreign ministers of other nations, often to the chagrin of his diplomatic corps.

By 1912, both Germany and Great Britain were skittish about massive military budgets that strained governments and episodes of diplomatic brinksmanship occurring around the world. Wilhelm's ministers knew Germany was bankrupting itself, but he and Tirpitz felt that if they could not close the gap of naval power with Britain, then nearly fifteen years of Risk Theory would have been for naught.

Wilhelm believed he had a solution satisfactory to both empires. Not disarmament, but a slower pace of building arms. He had a plan to reduce the Reichstag budget, reduce the British Parliament's budget, and still manage to close the gap in naval power between the nations without alarming the British. His plan involved a sleight of hand.

As the men sat in the palace, Wilhelm apologized to Haldane, saying that because Admiral Tirpitz spoke poor English, the conversation would have to be in German. Then he placed a hand on Haldane's arm and reassured him that as Haldane was in the important chair at the head of the table, Wilhelm had found a way to "balance the power" for his guest.

---

* Bertie was uncle to both Wilhelm II and Tsar Nicholas II.

Wilhelm contended that a reduction in arms spending would benefit both nations. Haldane countered that Germany must then modify its planned construction expenditure by a proper ratio. Haldane promised that for every dreadnought Germany built, Great Britain would build two. Wilhelm already knew this. He knew that he could not spend his way to catching Great Britain's fleet of dreadnoughts while maintaining his land-based military. But he knew something else that he thought the British did not yet fully appreciate. Germany's greater command of Diesel power offered Wilhelm a new approach—one that elevated the critical value of Rudolf Diesel himself.

Rudolf was the key to a German submarine advantage because not only did the kaiser need to enhance his nation's expertise with Diesel technology, but it was equally important that Great Britain not enhance its own.*

Tirpitz continued to push back on Haldane's position, likely according to a pre-agreed script with Wilhelm. The admiral fought hard to convince Haldane that Britain should build at a similar pace to Germany rather than at a two-to-one ratio, but Haldane didn't budge. The two men were at an impasse until Wilhelm intervened with his strategic concession. The kaiser agreed to a dramatic reduction in the pace of new German dreadnoughts and allowed a ratio between the powers that was agreeable to Haldane. Following his kaiser, Tirpitz conceded, and the British war minister was triumphant. Wilhelm redrafted the proposed naval laws for the Reichstag, a highly technical document written in German, and passed an advance copy to Haldane on the day he departed.

---

* Two years later, in June 1914, a large contingent of the British fleet made a friendly visit to the Kiel Regatta, including the flagship *King George V.* Tirpitz attended and Wilhelm arrived aboard the *Hohenzollern.* Churchill was not invited. During the fraternizing between the Germans and the British, Commander Erich von Müller, the German naval attaché in London, was heard whispering to his officers of the British guests, "Their object of this visit is only spying. They want to see how prepared we are. Whatever you do, tell them nothing of our U-boats!" During the week of this regatta, at 2:30 p.m. on June 28, a telegram arrived announcing the assassination of Archduke Franz Ferdinand.

On February 12, Haldane reported in a cabinet meeting in London that Wilhelm "had been delightful to me . . . I am sure he wants peace most genuinely, but he has Germany to deal with." There was broad enthusiasm among the cabinet at the prospect of making deep cuts to the current estimates of spending on dreadnoughts given Wilhelm's new conciliatory stance. At the end of his report, Haldane passed the advance copy of the redrafted German naval laws to the First Lord.

Churchill scrutinized the document. What he found in the details of the proposed law laid the kaiser's plan bare.

Wilhelm had abandoned going dreadnought for dreadnought with Britain. The race was unwinnable, so he chose a different path. Churchill discovered in the document that would go before the Reichstag that despite the welcome reduction in dreadnoughts, Wilhelm was asking Germany's parliament for a 20 percent increase in active-duty naval personnel. Churchill recognized that this capacity would create an "extraordinary increase in the striking force of ships of all classes immediately available through the year." Rather than three thousand new men to join the German High Seas Fleet, as Churchill had anticipated, Wilhelm requested fifteen thousand.

And while Wilhelm had reduced his planned dreadnoughts, for which the Germans assumed a commensurate reduction in British dreadnoughts, Churchill's analysis concluded that, "From the fact that 121 additional executive officers are required for [the German submarine] service alone by 1920, we may infer that between 50 and 60 submarines are to be added."

Though Britain is an island nation, much of the coastline is menacing rock cliffs or treacherously high banks of sand that inhibit easy transition from sea to land. The bays and inlets that subdue the raging seas to calm waters for safe passage of the navy and seaborne trade to inland ports are surprisingly few. Churchill was contemplating the very real threat that a U-boat fleet of this size could surround the British Isles and seal off every port, locking in even his battleships, and bringing Britain's commercial marine and naval activities to a standstill.

Here was Wilhelm's ploy to close the gap of naval power, within his obtainable budget and without provoking a budget increase from the British.

Instead, the First Lord detected the kaiser's attempted sleight of hand. Churchill reported his findings to the cabinet after his review of the proposed German naval laws. Wilhelm had played the character of peacemaker with Haldane, but Churchill concluded that the kaiser's ambition was anything but peaceful. The arms race reached new levels of urgency. There was a tonal shift in thinking about the possession of military might as a foreign policy tool, to the increasingly likely deployment of actual force.

CHAPTER 23

The Final Months

THE DIESELS HAD a cheerful beginning to 1913. Rudolf had completed work on his book *Die Entstehung des Dieselmotors* [The Origin of the Diesel Engine], which was published at the beginning of the year. Then, as Rudolf and Martha entered their thirtieth year of marriage, they vacationed in Sicily, Capri, Naples, and Rome. They rode in first-class train accommodations, stayed at posh hotels and spas, dined in the finest restaurants. Rudolf kept up his professional correspondence, but otherwise the pair enjoyed some restorative vacation time with each other after a year of stressful work and travel.

Returning north by train, they made a detour to Säuling, a mountain in the Bavarian Alps along the German-Austrian border. Diesel was familiar with the area, having summited the mountain in his youth. Säuling is a twin-peak mountain reaching an elevation of nearly seven thousand feet with a steep, almost pillar-like, incline. The view from the top offered spectacular vistas of the surrounding lakes.

At fifty-five years of age, Rudolf elected to spend his free time attempting to climb mountain slopes as steep as roofs. He was clearly no longer suffering from the gout that had plagued his American travel. Rudolf kissed Martha goodbye at the trailhead and set off with a guide on the route to the peak that was still snow-capped during the early spring season. Diesel kept a robust hiking pace, determined to match his youthful effort on the mountain.

The guide later reported that Rudolf stayed an unusually long time at the summit, quietly absorbing the Bavarian view, lost in deep contemplation. The two then began the decent and reached Martha just as the last daylight faded.

———

The Diesels traveled the fifty-six miles from Säuling back to Munich. Martha resumed the routine of her life at home while Rudolf continued his travels alone. First, he went to see his younger sister Emma, recently widowed in August 1911, in Ragaz, Switzerland. He then paid a visit to his old friends the Sulzers in Winterthur, where they discussed the future of Diesel power for the rail system, submarines, and the ongoing Sulzer efforts to fulfill their contract with the kaiser for a Diesel engine to drive a battleship.

Rudolf rounded back from Switzerland to Germany, where he attended the Internationale Baufach-Ausstellung (International Architecture Exhibition) in Leipzig. Up to that time, Diesel had refused to board airships, believing them to be too dangerous—this despite his long friendship with Graf von Zeppelin. Diesel was aware that most of von Zeppelin's early flying machines had been destroyed in accidents within weeks of their initial launch, though by 1910, Luftschiffbau Zeppelin had worked out the root causes of their fledgling disasters (which made Diesel's early engine struggles seem like a walk in the park) and founded the world's first passenger airline, DELAG (Deutsche Luftschiffahrts Aktiengesellschaft).

At the 1913 exhibition, DELAG offered two-hour sightseeing

flights aboard the newest Zeppelin ship, LZ 17 *Sachsen*.* Diesel took a ride on the massive dirigible that was 518 feet long (a Boeing 747 is 232 feet long) and had boasted Orville Wright and the crown prince of Germany as recent passengers.†

From Leipzig, Rudolf returned to Munich in late springtime. He gifted his son Eugen 10,000 marks (approximately $75,000 in 2022), which Rudolf called a study fund, as the young man set out for Winterthur and an engineering internship with Sulzer Brothers. Rudolf and Martha then commenced hosting a series of lavish dinner parties at Maria-Theresia-Strasse 32, primarily for foreign dignitaries.

In early June, Rudolf and Martha entertained more than one hundred American engineers who had come to see the Augsburg plant. Afterward, Diesel happily led a tour for this troupe of enthusiastic mentees through the grounds of his home and, in a style more gracious than Edison, up to his second-floor workshop where he'd papered the walls with the sketches of new engine designs.

The impetus for this surge of American interest in Diesel's operations was the American naval appropriation act of March 4, 1913, which declared "the unobligated balances under appropriation 'Steam machinery' . . . are hereby reappropriated and made available for the development of a type of heavy-oil engine . . ." The American navy was pulling back from steam power and moving behind Diesel.

---

* *Sachsen* was transferred to the German Imperial Army on August 1, 1914, and saw service on the Western Front. Refitted with machine guns fore and aft of the control cabin, the airship conducted several bombing raids on Antwerp in 1914. The ship was damaged during a landing and dismantled in 1916. The *Sachsen* made a total of 419 flights and was one of the most successful airships.

† Nearby in Berlin in May 1913, Wilhelm hosted the wedding of his only daughter, Victoria Louise. King George V and Tsar Nicholas II attended the event, which also included tours on Zeppelin airships. It was the last prewar meeting of the monarchs. Many then thought an Anglo-German war to be inevitable, including Jackie Fisher, who, with the powers of a mystic, in 1911 had predicted that war between England and Germany would occur on October 21, 1914 (his prediction was less than three months off). Still others at this time, most notably the sovereigns themselves, believed that for England to enter a war against Germany was impossible.

Diesel walked at the head of the sprawling procession of engineers, who stopped for long moments to gawk at the component parts
of engines in the workshop and the inventor's drawings of locomotive,
submarine, and automobile engine installations.

At the reception after the tour, the delegation presented Rudolf
with a prestigious invitation. In connection with the upcoming San
Francisco World's Fair of 1915 (the Panama-Pacific International Exposition), the Americans asked Diesel to be the guest of honor for a
ceremonial passage through the Panama Canal. He'd make the trip
aboard the *Fram*, under Diesel power, the same ship that had carried
Amundsen on his successful polar expedition to Antarctica.

Among the Americans were representatives of the Pennsylvania
Railroad, who renewed their offer of employment to Diesel (which he
again declined). But it was another of these visitors who would come
to play an important role in the future of the Diesel engine.

———————

Chester Nimitz rose to the rank of fleet admiral during World War II
and became one of the most decorated and celebrated officers in the
history of the US Navy. At the start of his naval career in 1905, Nimitz
distinguished himself as an engine and submarine specialist.* The
navy dispatched Nimitz to Augsburg in 1913 for a summer apprenticeship with Diesel technology. The top brass instructed Nimitz to
observe the "manufacture and operation of submarine Diesels" with
the hope that he would return to the New York Navy Yard to refit the
American submarine fleet with Diesel power.

Lieutenant Nimitz, twenty-eight years old and recently married,
traveled to Germany with his bride and several naval engineering as-

———————

* In 1913, Nimitz earned $300 per month in the navy. Upon his return to America
that fall, Busch and Colonel Meier attempted to hire Nimitz for the Busch-Sulzer
Brothers Diesel Engine Company and offered the young lieutenant a $25,000 annual
salary. He turned them down. Nimitz's heart remained with the navy and submarines throughout his career. When he assumed command of the Pacific Fleet on December 31, 1941, the ceremony took place in Pearl Harbor on the deck of the
submarine *Grayling*, from which the crew hoisted his four-star flag.

sistants. The curious American, eager to get into the guts of the engine technology, did not come away unscathed.

Touring the Augsburg plant, Nimitz approached a large Diesel motor in test operation. He observed the "[engine chamber air pressure] was about 800 pounds per square inch." Explosions of fuel hammered the pistons in perfect time. Nimitz marveled at the engine's easy rhythm and compact design. He reached his left hand forward to aid his inspection of the moving gears, and in his exuberance, he reached too far. The cuff of his coat caught in a rotating gear, pulling his arm farther into the motor. The hot, heavy gear fired around again, this time crushing the ring finger of his left hand and pulling his arm yet farther into the cast iron beast. Nimitz yelped in pain and those around him rushed to his side but were uncertain how to save the young man. The gear came round again to crush more of the finger, and would have eventually taken his whole hand, but this time the gear came to a thudding stop.

Nimitz jerked free of the motor. In agony, he held up his hand for a look. The finger was mutilated, all the way down to his heavy Annapolis class ring, which had saved the hand from further damage. Nimitz sought treatment for the injury. Doctors amputated what remained of his ring finger. (Soon there would be no more visits to M.A.N. for Americans or the engineers of any other nationality. In October 1913, only months after the Americans visited and weeks after Rudolf disappeared, the German Empire forbade M.A.N. from any foreign communications. The kaiser was plugging the Diesel leak.)

In June, Sir Charles Parsons crossed the channel to visit with Rudolf for a dinner party at his Munich home. Amid the merriment, there was a note of concern about the looming threat of European war. The two inventors discussed the First Balkan War, which had concluded only weeks earlier, in which the Balkan League (comprised of Serbia, Bulgaria, Greece, and Montenegro), with the support of Russia, roundly defeated the Ottoman Empire (supported by Austria-Hungary), as well as the Second Balkan War, which had just begun, in which Bulgaria, only weeks after the armistice of the first war, attacked its former ally Serbia due to its dissatisfaction with the previous victory's peace terms. A disquieted Europe watched the blaze in the Balkans knowing that it could spread with the slightest provocation.

It was during the First Balkan War, on December 9, 1912, that the Greek submarine *Delfin*, running Carels-built Diesels, became the first-ever submarine to launch a self-propelled torpedo at an enemy ship, though the attack was unsuccessful due to the torpedo malfunctioning. Amid this blood-soaked conflict of competing land grabs in the Balkans, news of the *Delfin* portended the wider use of this fearsome application of Diesel's engine, which was enabling the use of a stealth weapon capable of sending combatants as well as innocent men, women, and children to horrifying deaths, adding a new dimension of terror to the already steady stream of mutilated bodies carried back from the front lines to overwhelmed makeshift hospitals. Diesel and Parsons wondered how thousands of years of civilization and reason could not prevent such madness.

Parsons and Diesel shared the belief that these Balkan nations were merely pawns in a game of interests between the Great Powers of Europe. And it was not lost on the two scientists what a critical role they each played in this game. Parsons was the father of the world's most efficient external combustion engine; Diesel was the father of the world's most efficient internal combustion engine.

At the same moment that these two sympathetic friends sat side by side at the dinner table at Maria-Theresia-Strasse 32 in June 1913, the Royal Navy was installing 75,000-horsepower Parsons turbines into five *Queen Elizabeth*–class battleships, the fastest and most heavily armed battleships in history. Concurrently, the German navy was installing pairs of the 800-horsepower M.A.N. Diesels into the four submarines *U-19* to *U-22*.

European peace was on a knife's edge. Parsons and Diesel were uneasy. War had never seen such weaponry, and though the creation of munitions had never been an intention for either man, each had

Diesel engine at the M.A.N. works in Nurnberg, Germany, that was inspected by then Lieutenant Chester Nimitz in 1913. The engines Nimitz later assembled at the New York Navy Yard in 1913–14 closely resembled this one. (Photograph from the personal collection of Chester Nimitz)

done as much to increase the military capacity for destruction as any scientist before them.

George Carels traveled from Belgium to join Diesel's Munich dinner parties that month. Colonel Meier came from St. Louis for what he called "our wonderful little June shindigs at Diesel's house." During Meier's return trip to St. Louis, he wrote a "thank you" letter to Diesel from Philadelphia in which he told Rudolf, "In a long and foot-loose life you are the most gracious host I ever met." This was an extraordinary compliment coming from one who had worked more than two decades at the side of Adolphus Busch.

After a dinner party on June 28, Parsons and Carels persuaded Rudolf to join them for events in England in the fall. Diesel agreed to meet Carels in Ghent at the end of September so the two could cross the English Channel together. From there, Diesel would address the

Royal Automobile Club of London on September 30, then attend the ground-breaking ceremony of the new British Consolidated Diesel Engine Company (of which both Diesel and Carels were board members) in Ipswich on October 1, followed by dinner at Parsons's home.

The men parted company that night, bolstered by fellowship, only to have optimism dashed two days later on Monday, June 30, when the Reichstag passed the 1913 Army and Finance Bills that authorized 1 billion marks in additional military spending. As the Second Balkan War raged on, this new German military budget exceeded that of any other of the Great Powers. By this time, the Germans had abandoned the attempt to match Britain's fleet of dreadnoughts. The focus of the new spending was for the German army and the fleet of submarines.

The festivities of the summer season began to wind down.* On the first of September, Martha traveled to visit her mother in Remscheid in northwest Germany. From there she planned to rendezvous with Rudolf by mid-September at Hedy's home in Frankfurt, to spend a week with their daughter and newest grandchild. From Frankfurt, Martha and Rudolf intended to travel by train to Ghent and make the channel crossing together with Carels.

As soon as Martha left for Remscheid, Rudolf escorted Eugen to the train station to make his journey to Sulzer Brothers in Winterthur.

---

* Elsewhere in Munich during the busy summer of 1913, just two miles from the Diesel home, Adolf Hitler entered the boardinghouse at Schleissheimer Strasse 34 and paid rent of 3 marks per week, listing himself as an "architectural painter" on his lease. The twenty-four-year-old stayed in Munich from May through September, religiously painting one watercolor each day to sell to tourists, converting the proceeds to pretzels and sausage. He attended an artistically controversial Munich exhibit by the thirty-one-year-old Spaniard Pablo Picasso. Separately, September in this small Bavarian city saw the arrival of Sigmund Freud and Carl Jung for the Fourth Congress of the International Psychoanalytic Association (September 7–8), the first time the two men saw each other since their professional split in the spring. Attendees immediately partitioned themselves in alignment behind one or the other of the rivals. Freud and Jung would never again see each other after this.

Then Rudolf returned home and gave the entire household staff an immediate vacation of several days.

Alone in the house, he invited his eldest child, Rudolf Jr., to visit with him for a long weekend. Rudolf Jr. was back from New York and living nearby but had become increasingly withdrawn. When the young man arrived at the family home, Diesel presented him with a large key ring. He then escorted his son through the home and explained what each key opened and instructed him to try the keys in the various doors, drawers, and lockers. He told his son where he kept all his most important papers.

Father and son then took a day trip to Starnberger See, only a few miles outside Munich. While there, Rudolf Jr. mentioned the fact that Ludwig II, a Bavarian king of the previous century, had drowned himself in the very lake in their view. Rudolf Jr. further remarked that the easiest way to end one's life would be by jumping off a fast-moving ship.

At home alone again in Munich, Diesel gathered many of his landmark documents related to the origins of his engine and traveled to Berlin, where he donated the items to the national museum. From there, he went to Frankfurt and his beloved Martha.

When the staff returned to the Munich mansion days later, they discovered that Diesel had burned many papers in one of the downstairs furnaces, though there had been no cold weather nor other apparent reason for building a fire.

———

Rudolf had planned to spend only a week at Hedy's home, but the visit was so enjoyable that he extended his stay by a few days. He played joyfully with his toddler granddaughter and newborn grandson, and reportedly charmed the parents of his son-in-law, Arnold.

Arnold von Schmidt was a very successful businessman. Having started his career at the side of Diesel himself (he and Hedy even lived at the Munich mansion for a time when first married), he had set out on his own and by 1913 was director of the firm Adler Werke, which manufactured stationary Diesel engines, as well as pioneered early Diesels for the automobile.

During the visit, Rudolf took the wheel of an Adler test car powered by a Diesel motor and tore along the local roads at speeds that Martha, who watched from a distance, thought to be a little reckless. Feeling the strength of his engine on the open road gave Rudolf the taste of new successes he knew must come.

Arnold came from a high-born family. His grandfather Friedrich had been ennobled by Austrian emperor Franz Joseph in 1886 in recognition of his renovations to the Sistine Chapel and the rebuilding of the south tower of St. Stephen's Cathedral in Vienna. Arnold's father, Heinrich, was a professor at the Technische Hochschule Munich, Rudolf's (and Arnold's) alma mater. Arnold himself was a devout German patriot and fully in stride with the strain of nationalism that fueled the country's burgeoning industry.

Rudolf was proud of his son-in-law, and happy for the stability the marriage brought to his daughter, but Rudolf and Arnold were never intimates. The distance was likely the result of their unequal degrees of patriotic fervor. Rudolf's disdain for nationalism strained the familial connection to his daughter's new family.

Eugen Diesel described the way Germany viewed men like his father in the immediate prewar era: "People of original creative ability were felt to conflict with the Prussian ideal, and therefore to be suspect in their patriotism. Great inventors were regarded with a smile of toleration."

Arnold von Schmidt was a patriot first. Though his career relied on the success of Diesel's motor, his connection to Diesel the man was secondary.

Diesel was long resigned to the idea that his daughter's marriage would distance her from him, even under the best of circumstances. At the time of Hedy's wedding, he had reflected that a girl's love for her father must eventually give way to the more consuming love of a romantic partner. But during the wedding, he also took to referring to Arnold as *Dieb schöne Töchter* (a "pretty-daughter stealer").

By September 26, Diesel needed to depart from Hedy's home for Ghent to meet Carels. At some point between the end of June and the end of September, Rudolf and Martha had changed plans and determined that Martha would not accompany Rudolf on the crossing to England. She decided to remain behind in Germany—a few more days in Frankfurt, then back to Munich.

During his last days in Frankfurt, Rudolf had gone shopping for his wife. He purchased an elegant leather overnight bag as a parting present and had it wrapped. He gave the gift to Martha with the instruction that she should not unwrap it until the following week.

Rudolf also gifted inscribed copies of his just-published book, *Die Entstehung*, to Eugen and Martha.

Eugen's inscription had a strange tone:

> *My beloved son Eugen. This book contains only the bare, clear technical side of my life's work, the skeleton. Perhaps sometime you can mould on this skeleton the living body through the addition of the genuine humanness that you perhaps more than anyone else have witnessed and know with understanding.*
>
> *Your Father.*

Martha's inscription was more unsettling:

> *My Wife,*
> *You were everything to me in this world, for you alone have I lived and struggled. If you leave me, then I want to be no more.*
>
> *Your 'Mann.'*

The couple had a lengthy goodbye that Hedy observed to be especially affectionate. Then Rudolf boarded a train for Ghent.

Rudolf sat alone in the luxurious first-class compartment. The rail line to Ghent followed the scenic Rhine for a stretch, and to pass time on the slow train he thumbed a book by the pessimistic German philosopher Arthur Schopenhauer.

But Rudolf had much to be happy about. On September 20, 1913, *Scientific American* had just published its conclusion, citing various rigorous tests, that the Diesel engine had succeeded for the railways and would eventually become the dominant form of locomotive power. The article was an enormous boost for one of his chief remaining ambitions and signaled that his collaborations with Sulzer were bearing fruit. Other ambitions also looked promising.

On September 15, around the time Diesel had arrived at Hedy's home and exactly two weeks before his disappearance, he wrote to his brother-in-law, Hans Flasche, who was still working in Russia for the Nobels, "I still have a firm conviction that the automobile [Diesel] engine will also come, and then I will consider my life's task finished."

George Carels wrote of Diesel at this time: "I have known [Rudolf] intimately since we were very young men. He has the calm thoroughness of a high-class German, and the culture, modesty and self-control of a high-class American. . . . He insists he has at least twenty years of work still to complete and is straining at the leash to get on with it."

Rudolf was also excited to visit the ongoing Ghent exhibition of 1913, at which Carels was demonstrating his firm's new Diesels, which burned Mexican crude oil, a much lower-quality and less-expensive crude that, if successful in Diesel motors, could circumvent the monopoly of the world's oil trusts that controlled reserves of richer premium fuels, such as those of the Rockefellers and Rothschilds. Early tests by Carels were very promising.

Once in the river port city of Ghent, Diesel checked into the upscale Hotel de la Poste located on the Place d'Armes near the opera house. He immediately penned a meandering—but tender and affectionate—letter to Martha, dated September 27. He wrote alternately in French and German. He informed Martha that he had already telegraphed ahead to London to reserve a room at his favorite London hotel, De Keyser's, and that he hoped to hear word from her there. He talked of the warm welcome from Carels and his excitement to tour the exhibition with his friend the following day. He closed the letter, "I love you, I love you, I love you. Your 'Mann.' "

On the twenty-eighth, Rudolf penned a second letter, this one heartfelt and poetic. In it he wrote:

> *Do you feel how I love you? I would think that even from a*
> *great distance you must feel it, as a gentle quivering in you, as the*
> *receiver of a wireless telegraph machine.*

On September 29, Diesel wrote a letter to Rudolf Jr. that complained of gout and insomnia. The letter had a joyless tone, yet in the same sitting he wrote a separate, delighted letter of an entirely different topic and tone to Martha. In the last hours before the *Dresden* departure, Rudolf penned his third and final letter from Belgium to his wife, postmarked that day from Ghent. In it he recounted his pleasant adventures with Carels at the exhibition, and the tremendous impression his partner's Diesel engines had made on the audience. "The highlight [of the entire exposition] is, and this is no exaggeration: Carels' Diesel engines, which are considered by the people as the main attraction, as I have been told repeatedly."

Diesel went on to convey lighthearted and fanciful observations of the fair. As he and Martha had first met and lived in Paris, he took particular note of the French exhibits. He wrote the following passage in German. "There are some exquisite things there, these mostly being from the French (furniture, bronzes, undergarments, you know those, or rather you don't know those yet: from the top to almost the belt, everything is visible, from the bottom up to the belt also everything visible, only veiled with a thin chiffon." Then Diesel playfully switched to French for the next line: "The less there is, the more expensive!"

Rudolf went on to critique the art at the fair, and, as an aficionado of the grander fairs of old, lamented that the event had drawn a mostly local Flemish audience with few foreigners. He then told Martha that he had spent that morning at the Carels Brothers' Diesel plant, where his partner had recently expanded the factory to double the size, but business was worryingly slow. Revealing that Rudolf and Rockefeller were actively working at cross purposes, Rudolf identified the culprit responsible for the headwinds. "There is considerable setback in the production of Diesel engines because of the manipulations of the petrol trust." The Diesel engine performed equally well with the lower-quality, lower-cost petroleum from Mexico, presenting yet another existential threat to the established trusts.

In the next sentence, writing again in German, Rudolf transitioned back to his social activities and repeated a request, with seeming urgency, for information from Martha:

> *After dinner at Carels I returned to my hotel and am writing you these lines. Then I will travel to Harwich—Ipswitch [sic]—London.*
>
> *I received your message with greetings from the Fabers, that is about all I got so far from you and I hope to receive some more information from you in London.*

Then, returning to French:

> *While waiting, I love you, I love you, I love you.*
> *Your husband.*

After indicating that he would remain "waiting" in London for Martha, Rudolf closed with a postscript of three lines in poetic form:

> *We have warm summer weather.*
> *Not a breeze.*
> *The passage promises to be a good one.*

CHAPTER 24

SS *Dresden*:
September 29, 1913

GEORGE CARELS AND his chief engineer, Alfred Laukman, met Diesel on the ground floor of the Hotel de la Poste in the early afternoon of the twenty-ninth. They sent their luggage ahead to the docks with a porter, then enjoyed a relaxed cup of coffee together at the hotel before walking the several blocks to the *Dresden* in port.

As predicted, the day was warm and windless, though the city of Ghent was still bustling from the exposition that would run until November 3. It was a pleasant stroll, and the three men boarded the *Dresden* at 5:30 p.m. Each had taken a private stateroom.

The men agreed to receive their luggage in the staterooms, freshen up, then reconvene in the dining salon for dinner. The three met as planned for a meal and cheerful conversation. Diesel ate lightly and had only a bit of wine. Carels was the most enthusiastic of the bunch, declaring to his celebrity friend that the Diesel engine would soon "command a following so strong that the Diesel name alone would certainly take him beyond any debts and make [Diesel] rich."

Following the meal, the friends took a walk, as was Diesel's habit, though they were limited to the promenade deck. The ship had entered service in 1896 as a British passenger ferry for the Great Eastern Railway.* She was three hundred feet long and thirty-eight feet wide with a maximum speed of eighteen knots. The ship had traveled up the Scheldt to the estuary, where the river released into the North Sea along the coast of Belgium and northern France. From the deck at the stern of the ship, Diesel looked back at the coastal estuary scene that was the subject of a painting by Franz Courtens that hung on a wall in his living room.

The sea was flat. Black plumes from the twin chimney stacks of the old steamer darkened the air high above the passengers, then dissipated into the darkening night sky. The three men enjoyed one another's company during the pleasant voyage until 10 p.m., when they decided to return to the quiet solitude of their staterooms. They made plans to reunite for breakfast, and Diesel put in a request for a wake-up call at 6:15 a.m.

The next morning Rudolf's traveling companions arrived for breakfast and waited for their friend. After a few minutes, Carels went directly to Diesel's room and knocked on the door. Once he heard there was no sound from within, he entered. He found that Diesel's bunk had not been slept in, though someone had laid out a night shirt on the mattress. The luggage seemed untouched. Diesel was gone.

———

Carels hurried to the bridge to report his friend's disappearance. Captain H. Hubert, the ferry master, immediately ordered the craft held at sea for search. The crew scoured every inch of the ship but found no trace of Diesel.

---

* In an ironic twist, the *Dresden* was pressed into naval service by the British in 1915 and renamed the HMS *Louvain*. On January 21, 1918, *UC-22*, a submarine of the Imperial German Navy, torpedoed the *Louvain*, sending her to the bottom of the Aegean. Two hundred twenty-three British sailors perished. Twin five-hundred-horsepower M.A.N. Diesel engines powered the German U-boat *UC-22*.

Hubert interviewed the two crewmen who'd been posted on the overnight watch. They reported seeing "nothing out of the ordinary," though there had been the unusual discovery during the early-morning hours of a hat and coat, neatly folded and placed beneath the rail of the afterdeck (the promenade deck at the stern of the ship). Carels confirmed that the hat and coat were Diesel's. The placement of the hat and coat seemed deliberately to mark Rudolf's point of egress from the ship.

The *Dresden* docked at Parkeston Quay, Harwich, one hour late on September 30. Hubert delivered a formal missing-at-sea certification for the "esteemed Dr. R. Diesel" to the port master, but according to port officials the captain "refused steadfastly to issue a death certificate or to comment on the appearance of suicide on Diesel's part." The crew manifest and passenger list accounted for all other people on board, and there was no record or testimony of anyone being on board who was not listed on the roster.

One day later, on October 1, British authorities notified the German vice-consul in Harwich that Diesel was missing. The Germans immediately dispatched investigators to the *Dresden* in an urgent search for their country's most famous inventor. The investigators combed the *Dresden*, but the effort yielded no further evidence. They brought Carels and Laukman in for interviews, but Diesel's traveling companions only repeated their identical dead-end stories.

———

Back in Diesel's stateroom, his key ring still hung from the lock of his suitcase, his steel-cased pocket watch still rested on a side table where it could be seen from the bed. His enameled pillbox, his eyeglasses case, coin purse, and penknife were nowhere to be found. Diesel's notebook was turned open on the desktop. The page was empty except where he had penciled the date, September 29, 1913, and below the date he had drawn a cross.

Diesel's disappearance had taken place in international waters where there was no status of jurisdiction. There was no governing body to pursue the matter, and, as such, there are hardly any official records of the event. There was no ship's company hearing nor official coroner's report.

As a criminal investigation, the matter was dropped. But the media set the story ablaze. A century later, the name Rudolf Diesel fetches only a curious look, but in 1913 he was one of the most famous men in the world. Major newspapers around the world jumped on the beat of his mysterious disappearance. The confused and conflicting reports of his disappearance that would follow reveal much about the true nature of his disappearance.

———

Back in Munich, Martha unwrapped the beautiful leather overnight bag Rudolf had given her the week before in Frankfurt. Inside the bag he had stuffed twenty thousand marks.

PART IV

VANISHING ACT

CHAPTER 25

The World Reacts

HERE THE FOOTPRINTS vanish from the trail. There are no more Diesel diaries, letters, speeches, dinner parties, or personal interactions. The narrative must pull back to the wide-angle lens of reported history.

Newspapers around the world covered the Diesel disappearance from day one. At first, the articles relayed the simple and undisputed fact that Diesel was missing, augmenting the reporting with the testimony of Carels and Laukman, the last-known people to have seen Diesel alive.

Dateline: September 30, 1913—London
[Diesel: one day gone]

Reports appeared in newspapers around the world by Marconi Wireless Telegraph. The *New York Times* covered Diesel's disappearance at length, including detailed testimony from George Carels that recounted a cheerful dinner with Diesel, the walk on the ship's deck in sight of the Flushing coast, and the 10 p.m. return to the cabins, at which point Rudolf had said to him, "I will see you tomorrow morning."

The *New York Times* related the state of Diesel's cabin once he was discovered missing in the morning—the nightshirt placed over the turned-down sheets of the bed that he had not slept in, the key ring dangling from the lock of his suitcase.

Carels conjectured that the cause of death was most likely an accident and that the notion of suicide was inconsistent with the man. Carels told reporters that "[Diesel] was quite jolly in humor when I parted from him overnight. . . . He was most abstemious, did not smoke, and, so far as I know, did not suffer from giddiness."

The global media as of September 30 seemed satisfied with the "accident" theory. Like most papers around the world that were running the same basic reporting off Marconi's Wireless Telegraph, the *New York Times* included in its coverage that:

> It is conjectured by his friends that Dr. Diesel fell overboard. He complained to a friend some time ago that he was occasionally troubled by insomnia, and it is possible that when his friends retired to their cabins he decided to continue to stroll the deck.

The article did not name the friend of Diesel who testified to his history of insomnia, though all other testimonies in the piece were sourced. The overall message of the reporting out of London was that Diesel was optimistic about his future, in high spirits, and in good health with occasional bouts of insomnia. Those closest to him determined that his disappearance was due to a tragic accident, a far more dignified way to go than the inglorious alternative theory. But the media's acceptance of the "accident" theory lasted only about a day.

Dateline: October 1, 1913—London
[Diesel: two days gone]

The annual meeting of the Consolidated Diesel Engine Company took place the next day, on the morning of October 1 in London, as scheduled, but without Rudolf. Instead, the directors spoke of his absence, and the mystery of his disappearance. All who knew him con-

tinued to declare that suicide seemed grossly out of character for
Diesel. But there was no getting around the fact that his passage occurred on a night with flat seas and no wind, aboard a ship with a
railing that was four feet, six inches high encircling the promenade
deck. Stumbling overboard, even for a sleepwalker, was unlikely. Another oddity of the story was that anyone would neatly fold his coat
and place it with his hat by the rail then fall over.

The *New York Times* stayed on the beat. The subhead of the *Times*
piece of October 1 read "German Inventor Was a Millionaire and His
Home Was Happy." The reporting included more testimony from
friends and colleagues: "The conclusion [at the annual meeting] was
that Dr. Diesel must have fallen overboard. . . . Dr. Diesel's friends are
greatly mystified. While on the one hand the probabilities of an accidental fall overboard seem remote, on the other hand they cannot con-
ceive any motive which might prompt a suggestion of suicide."

The article goes on to tout Rudolf's business success, that the Diesel engine had already emerged globally triumphant, that he had
amassed a fortune in excess of $2.5 million, and that he was growing
richer all the time. None of Diesel's friends and colleagues challenged
the reporting of Diesel's great wealth.

The *Times* article further bolstered Diesel's image in America by
closing with a mention that Diesel had recently "struck up a great
friendship with Thomas A. Edison."

As far as establishing a legacy for the man, it was quite a nice piece.
It was an article that Diesel, who very much valued his legacy, would
have appreciated.

And yet, there was something fishy. An accidental fall overboard
seemed implausible—more like a cover-up. The press smelled a story
and didn't let go.

Suppositions of foul play began to circulate—that German agents had
murdered Diesel before he could share a revolutionary submarine engine
design with the Royal Navy. Perhaps the German General Staff had
learned what Jackie Fisher already knew of the British Diesel designs and
had followed through on Fisher's conjecture and shot Diesel "like a dog."

Another theory held equal weight—that the oil trusts had hired assassins to eliminate a threat to their monopoly. W. T. Stead, Britain's most famous journalist, had argued that the Diesel engine, running on coal tar, would be the engine of the future. Rudolf had advocated for his engine to be run on coal tar, vegetable or nut oils. And though the Diesel engine could also run on petrol-Diesel, Carels had proved that it could run on the cheapest crude oil from Mexico or other regions. As Rockefeller precariously hovered between the fading market for illumination and the uncertain market for the combustion engine, Diesel's invention could have been the death knell for Standard Oil.

———

Separately, also with a dateline of October 1, a bizarre bit of news appeared out of Munich. Two sentences were buried inside the British newspaper *Binghamton Press & Leader*:

> *A telegraphic denial from London of the disappearance of Dr. Rudolf Diesel, the motor inventor, while on the voyage across the English Channel from Antwerp to Harwich was received today by Dr. Diesel's family [in Munich]. Dr. Diesel is now in London.*

By this time, the Diesel story was among the biggest news items in the world. Did a telegraph operator send the message from London (that was intended to be private and for only the Diesel family) and then deliver this major scoop to a friend at the newspaper? Or did the family receive the message and alert the press to placate reporters? Perhaps the telegram was a hoax, not from Rudolf or anyone connected to him. Or perhaps the reporting was erroneous and there was no telegram at all. No matter. Major papers picked up the surprising news item, which fueled wild media speculations. And there was much more fuel to come.

Dateline: October 2, 1913—Antwerp
[Diesel: three days gone]

A shocking claim upended the competing narratives of murder, suicide, and accidental death and presented a new possibility. The Associated Press, and therefore nearly every paper in America and around the world, picked up the headline from Antwerp: "SAILOR DENIES INVENTOR WAS LOST AT SEA—Member of Crew Says German Did Not Even Make Cross-Channel Trip."

This head-scratching twist had readers around the world on the edge of their seats. The mystery had developed a new layer. A crew member of the *Dresden* testified that "Dr. Diesel went on board the steamer at 5:30 pm, but on learning that the vessel was not to start until 7:30, went ashore and was not seen again."

The crewman went on to express his certainty that Rudolf did not cross the channel on the *Dresden*, and added the significant detail that the ship's steward did not enter Diesel's name on the cabin list, which was another indication that Diesel was not aboard the ship at the time of departure.

There was no subsequent reporting that challenged the claim that Diesel's name was not on the steward's cabin list. If Diesel didn't make passage on the *Dresden*, was he perhaps snatched and murdered in Belgium before he could reboard? Or was his initial boarding a deliberate misdirection so that he might quietly disembark and otherwise leave Belgium of his own volition, possibly by way of Geneva?

And if the sailor's testimony was to be believed, then the story told and retold by Carels about dinner, wine, talking, observing the Flushing coastline, saying a heartfelt good night at 10 p.m. with plans for breakfast had to be a complete fabrication. The contradictory testimonies of Carels and the sailor would have been easy to settle had Captain Hubert or any of the numerous other people on board the *Dresden* come forward as eyewitnesses to confirm Diesel's presence at dinner, on the promenade deck, or anywhere else on the ship after its departure. But this never happened. There is no record of anyone coming forward to confirm Diesel's presence during the crossing except for the testimonies of Carels and Laukman.

About the only thing not in dispute was that Diesel's luggage, pocket watch, and notebook were placed in his stateroom, and that his hat and neatly folded coat were placed by the rail of the afterdeck.

However, what no one could establish was whether Rudolf Diesel was the person who put the items in those places.

With the crewman's testimony, the story of Diesel's disappearance went from merely juicy to the kind of front-page fodder that reporters dream about. Unanswered questions, conflicting testimony, the disappearance of the inventor of the century's most disruptive technology against the backdrop of an industrial boom and war in Eastern Europe.

On the same day, the London *Daily Mail* added the intriguing revelation that only one week prior, "Dr. Diesel bequeathed a valuable collection of drawings and documents relating to the origins of his patents to the German National Museum in Munich."

––––––––––

The British Board of Trade opened an official inquiry into Diesel's disappearance. As reported in the *New-York Tribune*, when the Board of Trade was asked on October 2 whether it was satisfied that Dr. Diesel had fallen overboard, a government official replied, "Dr. Diesel has simply disappeared. We cannot at present say anything further."

The accident theory was gone by the wayside. The suicide theory was quickly losing credibility. Reporters were looking for a new angle and explored theories of foul play and deception.

Hedy and Arnold von Schmidt seemed to feel as the press did. From London, also with a dateline of October 2, the *New York Times* reported, "Baron Schmidt, Dr. Diesel's son-in-law, declares that the theory of suicide in a sudden fit of aberration is entirely unsupported."

Arnold didn't believe that Rudolf committed suicide, nor did he believe Rudolf just stumbled overboard. Arnold was convinced something nefarious had happened.

Dateline: October 12, 1913—Berlin
[Diesel: thirteen days gone]

The press had scoured the landscape of possibilities for more than a week, torpedoes looking to acquire a target, exploring the motives of

Rockefeller and Wilhelm II in particular. Could Pinkerton thugs have killed at the behest of big industry, or German agents acted to recover vanguard submarine designs? Could Rudolf be alive somewhere, a prisoner or in hiding?

———

Then intimate details of Rudolf's personal circumstances began to appear in articles, which had the effect of reinforcing the prior narrative of suicide.

By special cable from Berlin on October 12, the *New York Times* ran an article with the headline "DIESEL FAMILY IN STRAITS— Missing Inventor Said to Have Left Them In Extreme Need."

Despite the unresolved contradiction in testimonies that Diesel crossed the English Channel on the *Dresden* at all, the *New York Times* (and most papers around the world) reported: "It is alleged that Diesel had money invested in a number of manufacturing companies which have not proved successful, and that a realization of his position is responsible for his disappearance."

SAILOR DENIES INVENTOR DIESEL WAS LOST AT SEA

Member of Crew Says German Did Not Even Make Cross-Channel Trip.

By Associated Press.

ANTWERP, Oct. 2.—The mystery of the disappearance of Dr. Rudolph Diesel, the German inventor, when on his way from Germany to England, was deepened today by the assertion of a member of the crew of the cross-channel steamer Dresden, who said that Dr.

Diesel went on board the steamer at 5:30 p. m., Sept. 28, but on learning that the vessel was not to start until 7:30, went ashore and was not seen again.

The sailor declared he was convinced that Dr. Diesel did not cross the channel. The steward did not enter his name on the cabin list.

The London Daily Mail says that in Berlin a week ago Dr. Diesel bequeathed a valuable collection of drawings and documents relating to the origin of his patents to the German National Museum at Munich.

Official of Company Says Diesel Did Make Trip.

LONDON, Oct. 2.—The statement made by a sailor that Dr. Rudolf Diesel did not travel on board the steamer Dresden is contradicted by George Carels, an official of the Diesel company, who says he dined with Dr. Diesel on board the Dresden and left him on the ship's deck at 10 o'clock Sept. 29.

The Associated Press reported the testimony of a Dresden crewman that Rudolf Diesel was not aboard the ship for the crossing of the English Channel, nor was Diesel's name on the cabin list. From London, George Carels contradicted this testimony.

As with the friend who spoke of Diesel's insomnia, the article included no sourcing of the personal information about Diesel's financial circumstances. Also noteworthy is the unwillingness to write the word *suicide*. It's an uncomfortable topic today and was even more so then. A suicide story doesn't sell papers on a serial basis. It's big news for a day, then everyone wants to move on. Yet there seemed to be momentum in the media to conclude the matter as a suicide.

Despite George Carels being among the first people interviewed more than a week earlier, it was only at this point that he offered the press the additional information that his dinner conversation with Diesel during the *Dresden* passage included the topic of Rudolf's debt, and that Carels had suggested to Rudolf that the prospects of the Diesel engine were so bright that he would likely earn enough money to lift himself out of debt and become rich.

New intimate details trickled into the press coverage. Rudolf's medical history with gout, stress, and overwork. His angst over prior patent lawsuits, his acrimony with rival engineers. The press gathered, or was handed, all this personal history and in turn presented these elements to the public as the clear markers of a candidate for suicide.

Yet there were still three pesky matters. News of the telegraph to Diesel's family in Munich that he had safely arrived in London had been plastered in newspapers across the globe. No one had recanted the story. Second, the crewman of the *Dresden* maintained his absolute certainty that Diesel disembarked and never returned, and that the *Dresden* had crossed the English Channel without him aboard. No one had come forward to confirm Diesel's presence on the ship during passage, other than Carels and Laukman. Third, the steward's cabin list did not include Rudolf's name. No one had stepped forward to explain why this should be the case.

How could anyone reasonably conclude that Diesel committed suicide by jumping from the ship without first establishing he was on the ship to begin with? The world wanted an answer to the question: Where was Rudolf Diesel?

Dateline: October 13, 1913—Amsterdam
[Diesel: fourteen days gone]

Then came the coup de grâce. News flashed around the world. The *New-York Tribune*, which had stayed on the Diesel beat almost daily, ran the headline "DR. DIESEL'S BODY FOUND—Boatman Loses It After Securing Clothing."

With the discovery of the body, the rampant speculation that Diesel was still alive could be put to rest. Now the press had their corpse. The *Tribune* printed:

> *A body, evidently that of Dr. Rudolf Diesel, the German motor inventor, was picked up in the mouth of the Scheldt on Saturday by a boatman,* * *who, after removing the valuables, was forced to throw it overboard again, owing to encountering heavy weather. The objects found and the clothing were identified to-day by a son of Dr. Diesel as belonging to his father.*

According to these reports, the sailors of the Dutch steamer *Coertzen* took the curious action of returning the body to the water during an age when the custom was for sailors to go to staggering lengths to recover bodies lost at sea and bring them home for proper burial. When the *Titanic* had sunk the year before, recovery efforts had been monumental. The SS *Algerine*, one of four ships chartered by the White Star Line to search the area for bodies, remained furiously circling the disaster site for *three weeks* despite finding only a single body

---

* The reporting of who found the body conflicts. Some reports indicate a small rowboat with a single man aboard found the body, others indicate that a pilot steamship found the body. Still others indicate it was one, and then days later, the other. The correct account appears in early newspaper accounts that reported a steamer found the floating corpse on Saturday, October 11 (twelve days after Diesel reportedly went overboard), and dispatched an oarsman on a small lifeboat to approach the body. In any event, all accounts are consistent in reporting that personal items were removed from a clothed and badly decomposed corpse and that the corpse was returned to the sea.

The pin marks the Scheldt estuary of the Belgian coast where the Coertzen *reported discovering the corpse of Rudolf Diesel.*

in all that time. Yet in the case of Diesel, these steamship sailors pulled the rotted but "finely dressed" body alongside their craft then plucked an enameled pillbox, coin purse, eyeglasses case, and penknife from its pockets. The sailors then committed the corpse back to the sea due to the rough weather and the state of decomposition, apparently unaware of the media sensation of the last eleven days. This time the body disappeared for good.

From the port of Vlissingen where the *Coertzen* next called, authorities brought these items to Eugen Diesel, who confirmed that each belonged to his father. Eugen, Martha, and Rudolf Jr. offered immediate and identical conclusions: Rudolf Diesel had committed suicide. The sailors' names never reached the public record. The fact remained that there still wasn't a body in evidence, but of the family members, only Hedy and Arnold continued to publicly discount the suicide theory.

The confirmation of personal items eliminated the three pesky inconsistencies played up by the press. The telegraph claiming Diesel was safe in London had to be wrong. He was dead in the North Sea.

Sailors of the Coertzen *reported discovering the corpse of Rudolf Diesel in the Scheldt estuary of the Belgian coast. Diesel had planned to travel from Belgium to port in Harwich, England, then on to Ipswich for a meeting of the Consolidated Diesel Engine Company.*

As for the *Dresden* crewman, he had either missed seeing Rudolf return to the ship on the evening of the twenty-ninth, or else he was looking to get some attention from the press. And the steward had made a simple oversight with his cabin list. Diesel had indeed freshened up in his cabin before dinner with Carels and Laukman.

There it was, a neatly wrapped story.

Dateline: October 14, 1913—Munich

[Diesel: fifteen days gone]

Having established Diesel's death with the discovery—and subsequent disappearance—of his corpse and the acquisition of four of his personal items, the media piled on the story for the next several days with coverage of his financial ruin and strained mental state, though firm details remained murky.

The *New York Times* ran the headline "DIESEL WAS BANKRUPT; He Owed $375,000—Tangible Assets Only About $10,000." New revelations of Diesel's financial obligations appeared in print, accompanied by damning and leading description. The *Times* wrote, "The meeting [of Diesel's creditors] found itself unable to take definite action regarding the administration of Dr. Diesel's wrecked fortune, as the exact state of affairs remains to be cleared up. . . . Figures laid before the meeting showed a state of confusion in the tabulation of Dr. Diesel's supposed assets."

Actual financial details remained obscure, and there was no hard evidence to fully conclude the case. Though the facts seemed to be either inconsistent or expedient, the prevailing winds of opinion blew strongly toward suicide, and there were no fresh tidings still to come. The press had already sucked the nectar from the delicious tale. The newspapers, and therefore the world, while not convinced they had learned the whole truth, began to shift focus. The mystery of Rudolf Diesel's disappearance drifted away. But it wasn't gone—it merely lay dormant.

CHAPTER 26

———

The Available Theories

THE EVENT OF Rudolf Diesel's unnatural death on September 29–30, 1913, allows for three possible causes: accident, suicide, or murder. There are sufficient facts from his life and the circumstance of his disappearance to make a determination on each.

ACCIDENTAL DEATH THEORY

The idea that Rudolf Diesel's death was accidental never warranted serious consideration or press coverage. Faced with the unyielding fact that he was not aboard the ship on the morning of September 30, his friends tended to offer the possibility of an accidental fall because it was the most polite and least incendiary thing to say. But no one actually believed it.

Rudolf had said his good nights, closed his cabin door, and gone to bed after 10 p.m. Even if he had gone back on deck, the passage was on calm seas and a windless night. The deck had a safety railing four and a half feet high. If he had been sleepwalking (and he had no history of sleepwalking at all), he would have had to leave his room, emerge on the deck, take off his coat, neatly fold it and place it on the deck, take off his hat and place it on top of the coat, then hoist himself up and over the rail. The theory of accidental death was absurd and correctly dismissed.

SUICIDE THEORY

The idea that Rudolf Diesel committed suicide has prevailed for more than a century, but most of Diesel's close friends and colleagues (apart from Martha and Eugen's endorsement) never believed this theory either. In newspaper report after newspaper report, friends and family offered consistent testimony that Rudolf had never in his life attempted or even mentioned suicide. Fellow board members in Britain, such as Sidney Whitman, were in disbelief of the suicide theory, and Diesel's professional and personal friends felt that self-harm was inconsistent with the man they knew.

While contemporaneous newspaper reporting pointed to Rudolf's poor health as a contributing factor for suicide, his health was robust enough to allow him to summit the snowcapped Säuling. A person feeling either physically or emotionally weak doesn't make plans to climb steep mountains. In addition to the 1913 vacation with Martha, Rudolf regularly took lengthy walks as a form of exercise and was not a gluttonous eater or drinker. Photos of Diesel in his last years show a trim, erect, healthy man.

In keeping with robust health, Rudolf's work and travel schedule from 1910 through the time of his disappearance was extremely active. From San Francisco to Saint Petersburg and points between, Diesel gave lectures, advised colleagues, developed new engine designs, and vacationed. He enjoyed the benefits of his wealth and success, dining with friends at fancy restaurants, or hosting them at his home. He visited museums and attended the theater whenever possible and nourished his passion for music and the arts. Diesel engaged life ravenously. There was no sign of isolation or withdrawal that would indicate suicidal tendencies.

Rudolf's conversations and written correspondence with colleagues and Martha indicate that he was highly motivated to continue his work far into the future. He already knew the Diesel engine was the only engine suitable for submarines, and there was ongoing and rapid technical advancement. The sensation of the *Selandia* only one year before changed the game for surface marine, and Diesel was aware of the successful tests of his engine for locomotives, which indicated it would come to dominate the railways. The Diesel-powered automobile, the other achievement he required "to consider his life's task complete," according to his September 1913 letter to Flasche, was nearly in his grasp. As icing on the cake, Junkers was working to expand the applications of the Diesel engine to include metal aircraft. There was an enormous amount of work and innovation yet to go, as his Munich study, wallpapered with sketches, indicated. Diesel wasn't suffering the postpartum blues that come with sated ambitions and an absence of new goals. The most exciting work, the crowning applications of his engine atop each category of industry, was still ahead. And rather than engage this work with the financial burdens and headwinds that he faced in the 1890s, Rudolf enjoyed the open doors, red carpets, and tailwinds that come to those with fame and fortune. Diesel was in his prime.

Throughout the same period, Rudolf spent freely on lavish parties, first-class travel, the maintenance of a large household staff, and sizable monetary gifts to his children—all apparently without any creditors knocking on his door. The initial newspaper reporting after Rudolf's disappearance was that he was rich and growing richer. It was nearly two weeks after his disappearance that the first reports of his financial distress, presented as a motive for suicide, began to bleed into the press and quiet the alternate theories.

Diesel's biographers, with many years' hindsight and the presumption of his suicide, look back on the years 1910–13 as a time when Diesel's intellectual powers were failing him, his debts were mounting, and he was in a state of despair. The evidence for this description of him through 1913 is either absent or wholly contrary. Diesel achieved his greatest fame and praise in this period. His engine emerged triumphant for the oceans, and he already had the practical confirmation that his engine would do the same for railroads. With a request for consultation from Henry Ford, the automobile seemed a likely next conquest.

————

The posthumous revelation of the supposed poor condition of Rudolf's finances has always been murky. Some biographers point to the large expense of building his Munich mansion in 1900–01, unsound investments in Galician oil fields (near the modern-day border between Poland and Ukraine), which also occurred around 1901, the dissolution of the General Society for Diesel Engines (which was effectively defunct by 1908, then officially liquidated on February 27, 1911, at which point shareholders did receive a payment, approximately 10.25 percent of the original investment), and various legal defense fees related to his patents (also mostly resolved by 1908, five years before his disappearance). There is little contemporaneous evidence of financial struggle and none that discussed bankruptcy prior to October 1913. The absence of this evidence is explained away by the suggestion that Diesel might have hidden these facts because he wanted to protect his family from the discouraging truth, but there are no letters to business colleagues or correspondence with his bankers to support this theory. Other than the price tag of his mansion and bad investments that had happened more than ten years before his 1912 trip to America, there is no evidence that would indicate a lost fortune in 1913, even though much else in his life by this time is well documented. The picture of his life in financial ruin seems to appear out of thin air, and only after his disappearance.

Even if this posthumous picture were accurate—that bad investments and expenses had wiped away his entire fortune—in 1913 Diesel was well positioned to make another fortune in short order. He could have had his choice of plum assignments in the public and private sector, anywhere in the world. Given his fame, he could simply lend his name to corporate boards and make a fortune while barely having to work for it.

But the main and most compelling point is that he *did* want to work. He hadn't yet met his goals. There was much more to do, and he had every means at his disposal to do it. By the end of 1913, Diesel was securely at the pinnacle of the engineering world.

Diesel's enthusiasm for the next chapters of his life is staunchly confirmed by Hedy and Arnold, who had just spent more than a week with him during an intimate family gathering in Frankfurt in the days immediately prior to the *Dresden* passage.

And what of the curious items that Diesel decided to bring with him as he leapt to his death? A pillbox, an eyeglasses case, a coin purse, and a penknife. It makes no sense to place these particular items in his pockets when planning to drown himself.

Moreover, Diesel had prepared no last will and testament. For a man as rigorously prepared in every other detail of his life, this is bizarre. And he left no note for his family—only the strange pencil drawing of a cross on the open page of his notebook. For a man who clearly loved and was devoted to his family, depriving them of any closure as to his fate and leaving them embroiled in a mystery seems completely out of character for Rudolf. Perhaps keeping the four uniquely identifying items on his person was his design to provide his family with closure, but he could hardly have counted on these items, or his corpse at all, being found.

MURDER THEORY

Certainly Rockefeller had motive, means, and a pattern of behavior to give rise to the suspicion that he murdered Diesel. In 1913, when coal miners at his Ludlow, Colorado, mine had gone on strike to press for better labor terms, Rockefeller hired the Baldwin-Felts Detective Agency. For the job in Ludlow, these "detectives" developed an early form of armored assault vehicle named a "Death Special." In what came to be known as the Ludlow Massacre, an event contemporaneous with Diesel's disappearance, the detectives shot to pieces the canvas-tented community of miners and their families, then set fire to the camp, killing dozens of women and children. Diesel's engine posed a greater threat to the security of Standard Oil than did the eight-hour workday.

The kaiser also had motive, means, and a history of deploying deadly force when he felt it was in the national interest. Royal Navy designs of submarines and battleships under Diesel power, Rudolf's advocacy of Diesel power as the savior of Great Britain's energy needs, and his public jabs at the German General Staff could not have gone unnoticed. Certainly, Churchill and Admiral Fisher noticed.

But the facts don't support a murder theory. First, there is Rudolf's odd behavior in the weeks prior to his disappearance. Premeditation in murder is not on the part of the victim. Yet Rudolf seemed to know something in the days leading up to his disappearance. During his September weekend at the mansion in Munich with Rudolf Jr., Diesel had the household staff leave the home, then escorted his son around various locked cabinets and closets, and at the end of the weekend he burned a stash of papers in what seemed a literal and metaphorical cleaning of house. He made the decision to gather all his important documents regarding the origins of the Diesel engine and deliver them to the Deutsches Museum before meeting Hedy in Frankfurt. Then his strange inscriptions and letters to Eugen and Martha in the final days before the *Dresden* passage, capped by his gift to Martha with the enigmatic instruction not to open the gift for a week—a gift that turned out to be an overnight bag stuffed with cash. All of this indicates that whatever caused Diesel's disappearance at the time of the crossing, he knew something about it.

The possibility that Diesel was murdered is also subject to the same constraints as the accident and suicide theories when it comes to the requirement of the victim's presence in the sea. Therefore, the same three contradictions—the London telegraph, the *Dresden* crewman, and the steward's cabin list all challenge the murder theory. Again, not one person, other than Rudolf's alleged companions, addressed the conflict presented by the cabin list and the crewman. Captain Hubert never came forward to clear up the matter, and further, Hubert's September 30 testimony, which declared only that Diesel was not present at the time of the search that morning, was so limited as to arouse greater suspicion. Why would Hubert go to such lengths to avoid saying whether Diesel was present for dinner on September 29?

———————

Lastly, the choice of the *Dresden* as the place of the hypothetical murder makes no sense. It's implausible that the oil trusts or the kaiser would select an English-owned passenger ferry from which an assassin would have no means of escape after killing Diesel. Once Diesel was discovered missing, the ship was of course held at sea, and in this case, Captain Hubert did confirm that all others on board were accounted for and that there was no one on board who was not on the ship's roster.

———————

As much as Rockefeller and the kaiser had motive, the evidence is against murder. And although several of Diesel's actions prior to his disappearance indicate premeditation, which could support the theory of suicide, as we eliminate suicide, murder, and accidental death as possibilities, then a single explanation emerges. The same conditions that led to Rockefeller's and Wilhelm's motives also suggest the motive behind another theory. The story of the corpse is a fiction. Rudolf Diesel didn't die on September 29, 1913.

CHAPTER 27

Operation Rudolf Diesel

ONLY ONE THEORY resolves every contradiction and inconsistency and satisfies the threshold for motive and opportunity. Rudolf Diesel defected from Germany to move secretly into the fold of the British Admiralty. The *Dresden* crossing was part of a larger deception. Seen in this light, the many peculiar actions and facts surrounding his last days make perfect sense.

Diesel's antagonistic relationship with M.A.N. from 1907 onward, and his public remarks, especially during his trip through America in 1912, show his antipathy for Wilhelm II and the German government. In addition, his admiration of Great Britain, and in particular his friend Charles Parsons, was on display on numerous occasions at events in London and in each other's homes. Not only did he offer consultation to Vickers, but Rudolf went so far as to serve as a cofounder of a new British Consolidated Diesel Engine Company, the focus of which was submarine Diesel engines.

It is widely known today that British intelligence of the era used contacts at newspapers to influence the media. Reporting on Churchill's early intelligence apparatus has revealed the frequent manipulations of British media as an operational tactic. The rapid spread of erroneous details about Diesel's health and financial status appears to have been contrived to establish a narrative for suicide. This narrative overwrote the startling revelations of the crewman's testimony and the steward's cabin list, especially when combined with the discovery (and immediate loss) of a body. And with regard to the corpse, there was no follow-up investigation to determine why Diesel's body was not returned to his family or authorities. Who were these sailors? Their names are lost to history, and perhaps were never known at all, but the newspapers didn't chase these leads. The hands-off approach by the press to these open questions, together with the new emphasis on Diesel's poor health and financial troubles, helped the suicide theory become the suicide conclusion.

Martha, Rudolf Jr., and Eugen's swift acceptance of the suicide theory is equally suspicious. Rudolf's family had intimate knowledge of his distaste for Kaiser Wilhelm's policies, and his quarrels with the ruthless oil trusts. It seems peculiar that these family members wouldn't pause for a moment over the prospect of foul play. Especially when his daughter and her husband so publicly declared suicide to be an impossibility. Perhaps Rudolf tipped his hand to Martha, Rudolf Jr., and Eugen in some way, maybe even asked for their assistance in the deception, whereas with his more patriotic kin, Hedy and Albert, those inclined to be loyal to the kaiser, Rudolf felt he could not.

The choice of Antwerp as the point of departure would have given the British an operational advantage, as Belgium was sympathetic to Great Britain. (Less than a year later, Belgium and England joined the war effort against Germany.) The *Dresden* sailed under the British flag, again useful for cooperation with a British operation; for example, in the matter of testimony from the ship's captain.

And there was the fortunate detail that the disappearance occurred in international waters, where there was no investigative jurisdiction. An important element of the testimony from Carels was his claim, painstakingly spelled out in the public record through his interviews with reporters and the authorities, that he was with Diesel until 10 p.m., because by that time the ship had definitively reached international waters. Even the anecdote from Carels that the ship had passed through the Scheldt estuary and that the friends observed the European coast from the vantage of the open water was very convenient in establishing this lack of jurisdiction. Because of this detail, confirmed by Laukman, authorities determined that *whatever* happened to Diesel must have happened outside the bounds of any national investigative authority.

Carels played a key role. He was a Belgian, known to be sympathetic to the British. His firm, Carels Brothers, had worked jointly with Vickers for almost a decade to fulfill engine contracts for the Royal Navy, and Carels was also the other cofounder with Rudolf of the new British Consolidated Diesel Engine Company in Ipswich.

The investigation of Rudolf's disappearance by the German consul in Harwich was dropped almost immediately. Perhaps the investigators decided that, after inspecting the ship and hearing the testimonies of Carels, Laukman, and the *Dresden* crewman, the disappearance was clearly the result of a British operation. For Germany, the suicide theory would be a far preferable public narrative to the national embarrassment of having lost their most valued scientist to Churchill. On this point, the Germans and the British would have been perfectly aligned. Each would have preferred to settle the matter as a suicide, and let secret operations remain secret.

Even small details such as the strange placement of Rudolf's hat and coat beneath the rail of the stern deck now appear so contrived as to be less a marker of suicide than a prop for deception. Further, one stops to wonder why a person would carry items in his pockets so useless for committing suicide as medicine, eyeglasses, money, and a knife when leaping from a ship. And indeed, which pockets was he to have used, given that Rudolf's coat was not with his body but neatly folded and placed on the afterdeck?

The only thing useful about the items in Diesel's pockets was that each was unique and personally identifying. As objects linked to Rudolf, these would be helpful in a deception to fool the press and public that his corpse had been found.

Equally revealing that these items were actually part of a ruse is the extreme improbability that each would have remained in the corpse's clothing after eleven days in stormy seas. As officers of the NYPD explained to me, "floaters," meaning bodies that wash up in the waters surrounding the city, that have been in the water more than a few days tend to wash up with their clothing shredded, sometimes completely naked. The clothing deteriorates in the salt water and is torn by currents and coastal wildlife. Given Diesel's body was allegedly discovered in the Scheldt estuary, it would certainly have been subject to birds and other coastal wildlife that would have shredded his clothing.

Additionally, the tumult of the sea, especially a stormy North Sea, tends to empty pockets in the way that a washing machine dumps coins from pants pockets during a laundry cycle. The pillbox was nearly the size of the palm of a hand (see photo insert), and it is nearly impossible that it could have remained inside a pocket at sea. Moreover, Diesel typically didn't carry the pillbox with him. But as part of a deception, the ornate, enameled box made it a convincing identifier.

Other odd behaviors on Diesel's part become more logical in the light of a premeditated deception. Diesel's dismissal of his household staff while he escorted his eldest son through all the locked compartments in the mansion, then the burning of many documents in the cellar furnace, suggests a man settling his affairs. Likewise, in the next days, Diesel gathered his most important papers and documents and donated them to the national museum.

And the mysterious overnight bag to Martha stuffed with cash makes more sense if Rudolf was concerned Martha might not make the same trip soon after him. And Rudolf did seem very concerned about Martha joining him.

A second look at his final correspondence, through the lens of Rudolf's defection from Germany, gives new meaning to his words. The inscription he wrote to Martha in his book reads:

> *My Wife,*
> *You were everything to me in this world, for you alone have I lived and struggled. If you leave me, then I want to be no more.*
>
> *Your 'Mann'*

Those who endorse the suicide theory focus on the word *were*, arguing that Diesel's use of the past tense is a Freudian slip that indicated a preexisting resolution to leave the world behind. But perhaps he wasn't determined to leave the world behind, only Germany.

Furthermore, who has all the agency in this inscription? Who has yet to make a decision regarding the continuity of their relationship in September 1913? Martha. "If you leave me," he wrote. Rudolf seemed to be making a request that she not leave him, or perhaps he was making an invitation for her to join him. It's unreasonable to conclude that he was inviting her to a couple's suicide at the bottom of the North Sea. But he was asking her not to leave him, to go with him, somewhere.

On March 24, 1872, at age fourteen, Rudolf Diesel selected a passage to read for his Lutheran confirmation. He chose Genesis 12:1:

> *Go from your country and your kindred and your*
> *father's house to the land I will show you.*

This portentous command has eerie meaning almost forty-two years later. A part of the evidence regarding Diesel's fate exists in what is not there. An examination of what is missing reveals as much as what's in plain sight.

Simon Mann—former Scots Guardsman, member of Special Air Service (SAS), soldier of fortune—has planned and executed many covert operations. Captain Mann reviewed the evidence of the Diesel case and concluded, "Not only did the Naval Intelligence Division [NID] have the motive, capability, and opportunity to carry out the operation, but the case has all the familiar tactics and fancy footwork of British operations of that era. Given the volume of circumstantial evidence, one can reasonably eliminate each of the alternative theories. A British deception operation is the only conclusion that makes any sense."

The lengthy period of eleven days between the time of disappearance and the discovery of the corpse (while newspaper reporting ran wild), as well as the inelegant choice of personal items discovered in the clothing, indicate that using a corpse (or the story of one) was not part of the original deception. The British had likely initially hoped that the story of insomnia leading to an accidental fall would pass muster. As a fallback plan, the suicide theory would suffice. The planners hadn't counted on the reporting of the telegraph to Diesel's family, the testimony of the *Dresden* crewman, or the disclosure of the steward's cabin list.

But what a simple fix! The planners needed only a few items known to belong to Rudolf and a person willing to say he found them on a sharply dressed corpse floating in the North Sea. If Rudolf handed over his enameled pillbox, eyeglasses case, coin purse, and penknife to his British handlers, all confirmed to belong to Rudolf by his son Eugen, then the newspapers would run it. Barring closer review of the underlying improbabilities, the public could go for it.

The truth is that not only did Rudolf Diesel not cross the English Channel on the *Dresden*, but there was never a corpse at all.

CHAPTER 28

Fingerprints

I F RUDOLF DIESEL lived beyond September 1913 and contributed to Churchill's war preparations, it's quite possible that reports would surface of his whereabouts in British territory.

Dateline: March 15, 1914—Berlin
[Diesel: one hundred sixty-nine days gone]

Reporting by special cable from Berlin, the *New York Times* ran the extraordinary headline "REPORTS DR. DIESEL LIVING IN CANADA— Munich Journal Hears Inventor, Supposedly Drowned, Has Begun Life Anew—Disappeared from a North Sea Steamship Last Fall— Body Supposed to be His Recovered."

Canada was a part of the British Empire. Was it possible Diesel had found his way to London after all, then slipped away to Canada, away from prying eyes, where he might play some role for Churchill?

The *Times* continued, "The *Abend Zeitung* [a newspaper] of Munich publishes a statement that Dr. Diesel, who was reported drowned in the North Sea last Fall, is not dead, but, according to letters received in Germany, has begun life anew in Canada."

Who wrote these letters? Who received them? Were the letters written by Rudolf to Martha, still hoping that his beloved would join him, then the letters fell into the wrong hands in Munich? Or were the letters from someone in Canada who recognized the face of the famous German national, and reported back to the Fatherland?

Dateline: March 24, 1914—Munich
[Diesel: one hundred seventy-eight days gone]

Then Martha went missing. Newspapers in Germany reported that none of Martha's closest friends was able to find her, and that there was not a trace of her in either Munich or Berlin.

On March 24 the British newspaper the *Daily Citizen* published an article claiming that for a five-month period Martha, still living in Munich, had been in frequent written correspondence with Rudolf, living in Canada, but that she had now disappeared. Could Rudolf have been living in Canada and carrying on a correspondence with Martha? The paper noted that "this is the question which is perplexing the whole of Germany to-day. The newspapers have devoted considerable space to the story which emanates from Munich."

It was a one-off news report in Britain, and the fantastic story soon stalled in Germany as well. The British papers seemed to be called off the story as though responding to a dog whistle. This suspiciously scarce media reporting in March 1914 that Diesel had reappeared in Canada was compelling to Simon Mann. "The story of Diesel living in Canada was covered in Germany. In America it made the *New York Times*. But an extensive search of British newspaper archives reveals the story barely got a mention there. Only three small, regional papers made a mention, just a few throwaway sentences, and only then probably because they missed the memo from the government. The British press of that era was famously anti-German and was also cooperative with the British government to an extent that would be unthinkable of the press today. This treatment of the story by the British press bears the obvious hallmarks of a D-notice [Defense Advisory Notice] from the government to warn editors off the Diesel news."

A British D-notice is "an official request to news editors not to publish or broadcast items on specified subjects for reasons of national security." The *Guardian* explains, "The *D-notice* system is a peculiarly British arrangement, a sort of not quite public yet not quite secret arrangement between government and media in order to ensure that journalists do not endanger national security." The British War Department created the D-notice system in 1912 (uncanny timing in the Diesel story) for exactly the type of situation Diesel would have presented in the hysterical and paranoid prewar period.

Mann concluded, "The absence of reporting about Diesel in March 1914 is resounding confirmation that there was an intelligence operation to extract Rudolf Diesel."*

Several retired British intelligence officers, who have asked to remain anonymous, spoke with me and concur with Mann's assessment that the likely escape route for Rudolf Diesel in a deception operation was up to Scapa Flow, off the northernmost coast of Scotland. From there he'd have crossed the Atlantic on a military craft. Upon completing any work for Churchill in Canada, the Admiralty would likely relocate him somewhere out to the farther reaches of the empire. Most frequently, operational assets went to Australia, which was considered a sort of witness relocation zone during that period.

Of the operational case files, Mann says, "The Diesel operation is significant enough that it would be a sticky issue between Germany and Britain even to this day. My bet is that NID case files are utterly denuded. This was an off-book operation."

The apparent complicity of the British press in the weeks after

---

* Only a single newspaper anywhere in the English language carried the detail that Martha and Rudolf had apparently carried on an active written correspondence for five months through March 1914. This newspaper, the *Daily Citizen*, a small-circulation paper that published in London and Manchester, did not survive. It shuttered in June 1915. It seems in wartime ignoring a D-notice was not good for business.

Diesel's disappearance had grown to a willingness to completely obliterate the story of his reappearance in Canada. And then came the war.

Four months after the bizarre report of Diesel living in Canada, all hell broke loose.

The world fell into a calamity unlike any other. Eventually thirty-two nations declared war in the largest, most technologically advanced conflict in the history of the world. The subsequent four years and three months of bloodshed claimed forty million military and civilian casualties.

IS DR. DIESEL IN CANADA?

DISAPPEARANCE OF HIS WIDOW.

FROM OUR OWN CORRESPONDENT.

BERLIN, Monday.

Is Dr. Rudolf Diesel, the famous inventor of the Diesel heavy oil engine, who was reported to have been lost from the Great Eastern Railway Company's steamer Dresden on a passage from Antwerp to Harwich on September 29-30 last, alive and well in Canada? This is the question which is perplexing the whole of Germany to-day   The newspapers have devoted considerable space to a story which emanates from Munich. Briefly, it is alleged :—

That Herr Diesel is in Canada;

That for the past five months Frau Diesel has conducted a heavy correspondence with someone in that country ;

That Frau Diesel, without wishing her friends " good-bye," has suddenly disappeared from Munich, and all efforts to find her destination have proved futile.

Soon after Herr Diesel's disappearance (he was last seen at 11.45 p.m., when the vessel was one and three-quarter hours' run from Flushing) it was stated by a Belgian newspaper that Herr Diesel never set sail in the Dresden.

On October 13, however, the Amsterdam correspondent of the Central News reported that the missing man's body had been washed ashore on the Isle of Walcheren, and had been identified by the inventor's son.

Interviewed by a representative of *The Daily Citizen* yesterday, officials of the Consolidated Diesel Engine Manufacturers' Company, Limited,

The March 24, 1914, report from the British newspaper the Daily Citizen *announcing that Martha had disappeared from Munich after maintaining a months-long correspondence with Rudolf Diesel, who was alive in Canada.*

In the frenetic pace of war when an hour has the value of a peace-time week, the sheer volume of news from the conflict was overwhelming and squeezed the mystery of Diesel's disappearance out of the papers. But buried within all the chaotic war reporting, there was a trace of peculiar activity regarding the development of the Diesel engine.

And again, this peculiar activity involved a covert British Intelligence operation for the Royal Navy, this time in Canada. Churchill was working to close the gap in submarine power.

Dateline: August 15, 1915—Washington, D.C.
[Diesel: six hundred eighty-seven days gone]

The *Washington Post* ran the headline "15 U-BOATS CROSS SEA—Parts Made in United States and Put Together in Canada—NOW PART OF THE BRITISH FLEET."

The Bethlehem Steel Corporation, an American company led by Charles M. Schwab, fabricated the submarine parts in America, then shipped the parts to a secret location in Montreal, Canada, on January 1, 1915. There, a group of foreign engineers working in extreme secrecy at the direction of Winston Churchill and Jackie Fisher, took the parts from the Americans and got to work.

The *Post* article made clear that the role of the American company to assist the Royal Navy "involved no violation of neutrality," as Bethlehem Steel delivered to Canada unassembled component parts only. Per American neutrality laws, American firms could provide raw materials but not completed armaments or war assets to belligerent nations. The engineering and assembly of the submarines took place on Canadian soil.

The mysterious band of engineers in Canada miraculously completed the first five of these submarines by May and was busily fulfilling the rest of the order. In August, the *Washington Post* reported that "the fifteen submarines crossed the Atlantic under their own power

THE MYSTERIOUS CASE OF RUDOLF DIESEL

and are now doing duty in the North Sea and in the Dardanelles." The *Post* confirmed the submarines' engines were Diesels.

Acquiring the raw material was a diplomatic feat that required the great determination of Schwab, Churchill, and Fisher, as well as the assistance of members of the US Department of State to finesse the neutrality laws.

A more remarkable feat was the mysterious engineering that secretly took place in Montreal. Many years after the war, archival documents revealed a bit more about what went on.

Britain's Great War Archive tells a piece of the story. On New Year's Day 1915, a team of engineers accompanied by armed personnel from the Admiralty took over the Canadian Vickers shipyard and stopped all other work happening on the grounds.

The regular employees of the yard were escorted out and the engineering team brought in to replace them began work on a new project. The project was kept secret. The Admiralty built a high fence surrounding the property and placed military personnel around the perimeter. The Admiralty issued identity cards to the workforce and rigidly enforced security at the gates.

Even the Canadian government had no idea of the action taking place. The Diesel submarine project was the kind of British cloak-and-dagger operation that its intelligence service would become known for. Shortly after the war, upon discovering Churchill's project in their territory, the Canadian government and local personnel found his secrecy and circumvention to have the typical imperial disregard for Canadian authority but were powerless against the Admiralty.

The news reports of Britain's new Diesel submarines came in the fog of war. America was still neutral, and the nation's potential entry into the war was the hot topic at home and abroad. Therefore, the main narrative of the clandestine submarine story was about neutrality laws and the fact that the parts were fabricated in America. Rudolf Diesel was never mentioned. None of the press made the connection between the work at Canadian Vickers and the reported presence of Rudolf Diesel in Canada only months before the takeover of the shipyard.

The highly secret operation personally organized by Churchill and Fisher was an impressive success. The stealth operation produced the first five submarines in an unprecedented four months, which was four months faster than the ambitious schedule Fisher had set. Royal Navy submarine commanders after the war testified that the Canadian subs "proved very successful and were the most popular type with the British Submarine Service." Years after the war, independent engineers retrospectively studied the speed and quality of the engineering effort and concluded that "the construction of these submarines was an extraordinary industrial accomplishment and much of the credit must go to the workforce at Canadian Vickers."

But who was this workforce? The English generally, and Vickers specifically, were infamously known to be among the least-proficient members of the world's Diesel community. They certainly had no previous record of building submarines of "extraordinary industrial accomplishment."

Was there anything else about the recent history of Diesel development at Vickers that seemed to have suspicious external involvement? Of course there was.

———

James McKechnie was manager of the Vickers Barrow shipyard in England before the war. For most of his life McKechnie had learned on the job. He left school at age fifteen to apprentice at a sugar mill where he worked with pump engines and hydraulics. By the late nineteenth century, he'd found employment constructing coal-burning steam engines for a small Scottish firm that was acquired by Vickers. He worked his way up and was known as a stern and demanding taskmaster.

By 1906, the Royal Navy completely broke with petrol engines for submarines and firmly committed to Diesel. As discussed previously, the Admiralty gave the sole government contract for submarines and Diesel submarine engines to Vickers. McKechnie brought in C. G. Roberton as engineering manager. Neither McKechnie nor Roberton was a Diesel man.

Vickers began work on the D class of submarine, the first fleet of

Diesel submarines for the Royal Navy. By 1909, the Admiralty had deemed the effort by Vickers an abject failure. The Diesel engineering department at Vickers was unable to surmount the many complicated requirements of undersea engine design.

Then, beginning in 1910, the Vickers Diesel department made a number of mysterious yet highly sophisticated breakthroughs with regard to proposed engine design. The fuel injection system for the engine had previously been a significant obstacle, not only for the British but for the entire Diesel community. Suddenly, this previously wayward group of engineers seemed to have puzzled it out. (Recall that the subject of the 1907–8 lawsuits between Rudolf and his partners at M.A.N. was Rudolf's pioneering patent work with fuel injection systems.) Most mysterious was the attribution, or rather lack thereof, for exactly who succeeded in this endeavor.

British patents No. 24154, No. 26227, and No. 27579, among others, all related to Diesel fuel injection, were awarded from 1911 to 1914. This aligns with the period during which Rudolf was spending much more time in Great Britain and in the company of men like Charles Parsons and George Carels, as well as delivering speeches about the benefits of Diesel technology "particularly for Great Britain."

The accepted story regarding the source of these ingenious breakthroughs with fuel injection systems was that each one came from a group of creative engineers within the department who then, as was not uncommon in that era, acknowledged the boss, James McKechnie, as the inventor named on the patent, despite McKechnie not at all being a Diesel expert.

The McKechnie patent attributions are mysterious enough, but a 1925 technical paper published by the head of Diesel engine design for Vickers at that time, William Rabbidge, reached the truly bizarre. Perhaps the most revolutionary of the British patents of the pre–WWI period led to the common rail system, which enabled an engine operator to have simultaneous control of a multicylinder engine. Though common rail became the global standard, the design was such a bold and pioneering stroke by the Vickers engineers that the broader, worldwide Diesel community didn't catch up and fully accept the concept until almost *eight decades* later.

To whom does Rabbidge attribute the invention of the common rail system? In the 1925 paper, he allowed that it was of course not McKechnie. He recounted the lore passed down through the Royal Navy from the prewar days that the inventor was in fact a handy crewman working in a ship's engine room. Rabbidge spins the tale that an unnamed Royal Navy engine room "Magician" invented the common rail. Within the community of Royal Navy engineers, it was a famously fantastic and improbable story. The true author of the patent has never been named, and even long after the war, when the path of technical development might have been of little interest, the authorship has remained murky.

However, while Vickers was turning out highly sophisticated patent work during the period 1911–14, it was not turning out actual Diesel submarine engines that were worth very much. This poor result in delivering quality engines is further indication of a disconnect between the person who was the source of the patented ideas and the engineering talent that was in the Vickers plant on a regular basis. The ideas seemed to be flowing, perhaps from Diesel himself, but there was nobody on the ground in the plant who could execute the patents into practice to build working Diesel submarine engines.

By 1913, the failure of Vickers to produce the submarines contracted to the Royal Navy in 1910, 1911, and 1912 had the Admiralty in a full panic. This led to an angry and accusing letter from Royal Navy captain Roger Keyes* to Vickers managing director Trevor Dawson on August 20, 1913 (the month before Diesel disappeared):

> *You are several months behind in your* 1910/1911, 1911/1912 *and* 1912/1913 *orders. In three years you will have delivered eight submarines! You must see that if we had continued to trust entirely to you, we should very soon be hopelessly left behind Germany.*

---

* Later promoted to Admiral of the Fleet, Lord Keyes, and head of submarine development.

This dismal track record at Vickers for on-time delivery is in sharp contrast to that of the mysterious group of engineers in Canada only sixteen months later. The domestic inability to build Diesels caused the Admiralty to turn over every possible stone to acquire a Diesel submarine fleet, which included Churchill taking the matter into his own hands.

———————

Without Rudolf, the floor seemed to drop from beneath the new British Diesel company cofounded by him and Carels in Ipswich. The media reported the peculiar and bewildering fate of the Consolidated Diesel Engine Company. Shareholders met in the weeks after Diesel's disappearance and determined to liquidate the firm in November 1913 on the grounds of a lack of progress with the development of the plant, despite photographs appearing in newspapers in October revealing the factory was robust and ready for business.

In February 1915, Vickers Ltd bought the shuttered Ipswich plant and all its contents for the purpose of building submarine Diesels during the war. A strange fact somewhat lost in the rapid demise of the Ipswich firm immediately following Rudolf's disappearance is that the Companies Registration Office in London mysteriously destroyed all details of the company's founding. During the dissolution proceedings, all board meeting minutes and records surrounding Diesel's participation on the board of directors were destroyed.

The most plausible explanation for the strange set of events at Vickers Ltd in the few years prior to the Great War is that by the end of 1913 the firm had gained total access to the most skilled Diesel engineer in the world—the inventor himself.

———————

The tactics employed in the Diesel deception are characteristic of British Intelligence operations of that era, though the world would not come to know this until decades later. There is another British Intelligence operation that used stunningly similar methods. This famous example involved not only the same essential plot device, but included the very same British protagonist, Winston Churchill.

Operation Mincemeat was a wartime deception operation designed by British Intelligence using a corpse that carried false battle plans to fool Hitler in 1943. The British government later declassified details of the operation, though the world might never have learned of this operation at all had not a high-placed politician broken protocol and written a fictionalized version of the events.*

The British based Operation Mincemeat on the Trout memo, a 1939 intelligence document written by Rear Admiral John Godfrey and Lieutenant Commander Ian Fleming (future author of the James Bond novels). The memo contained a number of possible intelligence schemes, and Mincemeat appeared as Number 28, under the heading "A Suggestion (not a very nice one)."

Fleming wrote that "a corpse dressed as an airman, with dispatches in his pockets, could be dropped on the coast, supposedly from a parachute that has failed. I understand there is not difficulty in obtaining corpses at the Naval Hospital, but, of course, it would have to be a fresh one."

Churchill, a lover of the clandestine, had urgent need to deceive Hitler in 1943. The Allies were planning a major offensive and had two options for where to mount the invasion. Churchill could either launch his forces into Sicily and Italy, or he could launch through Greece into the Balkans.

At the Casablanca Conference in January 1943, the Allied planners selected Sicily, even though Churchill was concerned that Sicily was the obvious choice and that the German defenses would be well pre-

---

* The story of Mincemeat escaped classified archives prematurely. Without the blessing of the security services, Duff Cooper, a former cabinet member who had been briefed on the operation, published the spy novel *Operation Heartbreak* in 1950, which had the plot device of British agents floating a corpse that carried fake documents off the coast of Spain to fool the Germans. British Intelligence decided the best response to Duff's unauthorized book was to publish its own version of events. Ewen Montagu, the agent who conducted the operation, published *The Man Who Wasn't There* in 1953, which sold two million copies and was the basis of the 1956 film *The Man Who Never Was*. In 2010, journalist Ben Macintyre published *Operation Mincemeat*, a definitive history of the event.

pared and deadly. He reportedly said, "Everyone but a bloody fool would know that it's Sicily."

And yet the Allies knew that Hitler was worried about defending the Balkans too. The region was a major source of oil, copper, bauxite, and chrome for the German war industry, and Hitler was determined to protect it. He would be susceptible to a feint from that direction.

The Allies launched Operation Barclay, a broad deception operation intended to convince the Germans that Greece and the Balkans were the objective. The Allies set up a fake headquarters in Cairo and sent fictional communications to indicate troop movements in the area knowing that some of the communications would be intercepted. They even produced dummy tanks that were nothing more than inflated balloons, but from a distance were convincing replicas. And they green-lit Number 28 of the Trout memo, Operation Mincemeat.

The extravagant planning of Operation Mincemeat indicates that British Intelligence may have grown the concept from the seed of a WWI operation to deceive the world about Diesel. The planners of Operation Mincemeat faced two challenges that the planners of a hypothetical Operation Rudolf Diesel would also have faced.

First, how could they fool a medical examiner into believing that the corpse was the result of a recent death at sea rather than a body procured from the British naval morgue?

Second, how could they present the corpse and its fake documents in a way that would make the finders believe the discovered information was authentic and not a setup?

Ewen Montagu, the lead agent developing Mincemeat, invented the character William Martin, a captain of the Royal Marines, who was flying with sensitive military dispatches when his plane went down off the coast of Spain where German agents were known to operate. British Intelligence obtained the corpse of a vagrant who had died from rat poison. Montagu consulted pathologist Sir Bernard Spilsbury to learn the factors required to fool a Spanish pathologist who would likely be asked to perform a postmortem on the corpse upon its discovery.

As for the second challenge—the credible presentation of the corpse

and its documents—Montagu went to great lengths of character development, and his techniques shed light on how an Operation Rudolf
Diesel might have happened under Churchill's Naval Intelligence
thirty years earlier. Montagu created a "legend" for his fictional William Martin. He chose to make his character a captain of the Royal
Marines because all inquiries related to the death of a Royal Marine
would be routed through the Naval Intelligence Division, which he
could control. Montagu chose "Martin" because there were several
men of the rank of captain in the Royal Marines with that surname,
and the rank was high enough to be a person carrying sensitive documents but not so high as to be a person more generally known.

The devil is in the details though. Montagu needed to make Martin seem like a real person. He needed to put together the little touches
of a personal life, things that would be carried on the body. Agents in
the trade called this the "wallet" or "pocket litter."

The corpse carried a photograph of an invented fiancée named Pam.
The photograph was actually of MI5 clerk Jean Leslie. There were also
two love letters and a receipt for a diamond engagement ring from a
jewelry shop on Bond Street.

The corpse carried a letter from Martin's father, a letter from the
family lawyer, and a message from Lloyds Bank demanding payment
for an overdraft of 79£ 19s 2d. For these printed documents, MI5 tested
a variety of inks to see which would last the longest in salt water.

Montagu topped off the pockets of the corpse with cigarettes, a
book of stamps, matches, a pencil stub, keys, a receipt for a new shirt
from Gieves & Hawkes, a silver cross, and a St. Christopher medal.

Captain Ronnie Reed filled in for the identity card photograph. He
looked vaguely similar to the dead man and by the time the corpse was
found it would be too far gone to raise much of a question as to likeness.

The corpse carried the critical documents—the falsified battle plans
indicating a forthcoming Allied invasion through Greece and the Balkans—in an official briefcase. Montagu feared that because Roman Catho-
lics have an aversion to tampering with corpses, documents inside the
clothing might be missed, or, even more likely, the documents would come

loose from the pockets while at sea and be separated from the corpse. But a briefcase could be secured to the body and would certainly be investigated.

On April 17, 1943, the corpse in battle dress with all its pocket litter was packed in a sealed canister of dry ice and taken aboard the submarine HMS *Seraph*, powered by twin Diesel engines of 1,900 horsepower each, and commanded by Captain Norman "Bill" Jewell, who gave his crew the story that the canister contained a secret meteorological device to be deployed off the coast of Spain.

At 4:15 a.m., on April 30, the *Seraph* surfaced, removed the body of "Captain Martin" from its canister of dry ice, and lowered it into the water at the stern of the ship. The prevailing winds near Huelva consistently blowing onshore were expected to push the body toward land. To be sure, the captain ordered the engines full ahead and the thrust from the screws pushed the corpse toward the coast. Jewell sent a message to the Admiralty: "Mincemeat completed."

A fisherman from Huelva found the corpse at 9:30 that morning and delivered it to Spanish soldiers, who took the corpse, dressed in the uniform of a Royal Marine, to a naval judge, who eventually notified the British vice-consul Francis Haselden. The hook was set.

On May 14, the Allies decrypted a German communication warning that the Allied objective was the Balkans. Brigadier Leslie Hollis then sent a message to Churchill that read, "Mincemeat swallowed rod, line and sinker . . ."

The fundamentals for an Operation Rudolf Diesel were the same—a floating corpse with pocket litter designed to convince an audience of a false narrative. Some aspects of the 1913 Diesel operation were easier and others harder to pull off.

The deception surrounding Diesel didn't have the luxury of creating a fictional character. The corpse needed to be Rudolf Diesel, a famous and recognizable man. Yet the level of scrutiny of the corpse was much lower. In 1943, Churchill needed to convince Hitler of the authenticity of the body and the plans it carried to the point that he took the remarkable action of reorganizing his armies in Europe.

In 1913, Churchill only needed headlines to sway public opinion a few degrees. To achieve this he didn't need a corpse that would pass a coroner's examination. He needed only testimony that a corpse existed, supported by a few uniquely identifiable personal items allegedly recovered from its clothing. Even if reporters and the German government didn't fully swallow such a story, it could still be enough, given the compliant British media. Churchill didn't need to provoke an action from the Germans other than to have them drop the matter. And soon enough, the two nations had declared war, which consumed any legal or diplomatic recourse the Germans might have brought to bear to recover Rudolf Diesel from Britain.

It is worth restating that Winston Churchill led the naval intelligence apparatus in both 1913 and 1943, and the careers of many senior British Intelligence officials during World War II would have bridged the two operations and provided the origin path for the floating-corpse deception. Admiral John Godfrey, coauthor of the 1939 Trout memo, was one such person. Godfrey was the basis for the fictional character "M," Bond's handler in the Fleming novels.

When taking account of all the information, only one theory satisfies all the curious facts: British Intelligence orchestrated an operation to cover up Rudolf Diesel's defection from Germany. It was a precursor to Mincemeat. Two intelligence operations separated by thirty years.*

---

* It is possible there was an "Easter egg" left behind by British Intelligence in the story of Mincemeat that they published. Montagu ran the operation and wrote the near-true novel and screenplay that recounted the operation. In fact, Ewen Montagu is a named character in the 1956 film *The Man Who Never Was*. In an early scene, he explains the details of the proposed Operation Mincemeat to his superior, Admiral Cross. The admiral responds with the line written by Agent Montagu: "In *thirty years* of intelligence work, I've never heard of anything like it" (my emphasis). Perhaps this is a wink and a nod from Montagu. The admiral's remark in 1943 was precisely thirty years after Diesel vanished and the newspapers reported his floating corpse.

On the eleventh hour of the eleventh day of the eleventh month of 1918, the Great War came to an end after more than four years of bloodshed. At sea, submarines had caused the greatest losses of life and cargo. The Allies used their larger fleet to impose a blockade of the German coast. The Germans attempted a counterstrategy with submarines while keeping their surface warships mostly in port.

The Battle of Jutland in the spring of 1916 was the only major naval engagement of the war in which the prized fleets of England and Germany, which had cost so much of each nation's wealth to build, would face each other. Off the coast of Denmark in the North Sea, Jellicoe's Royal Navy Grand Fleet fought Admiral Reinhard Scheer's German High Seas Fleet in a battle that lasted a day and a night. Jellicoe had 151 ships, including 28 battleships and 9 battlecruisers, while the outgunned Germans had 99 ships that included 16 battleships and 5 battlecruisers. The British lost more ships and sailors than the Germans but forced the German fleet to retreat to port. Both sides claimed victory.

The Germans launched a total of 344 U-boats during the war, sinking approximately five thousand ships (thirteen million gross tons). The fear and carnage inflicted by the U-boats not only caused the Royal Navy to alter strategy and ship deployments, but Allied merchant shipping was so disrupted that Great Britain was nearly starved into submission in the months prior to America's entry into the war in 1917.

During the war, Great Britain launched 137 submarines of her own, and America another 72. More than half of Germany's U-boats were lost, many sunk by Allied destroyers and submarines. (Just one example: the Canadian-built submarine *H-4* sank the *UB-52* off the Dalmatian Coast in May 1918.) Eventually, Allied countermeasures to the U-boat threat (including the rapid construction and replacement of Allied merchant vessels) began to turn the tide of the war.

Late in 1918, the Kaiserliche Marine (Imperial Navy) mutinied against Wilhelm II. Growing unrest forced Wilhelm to abdicate on

HMS H-5, one of Churchill's secret Canadian-built submarines, under the command of Cromwell H. Varley, Royal Navy, has just returned from her patrol in the Bight, where she torpedoed the U-boat U-51, July 14, 1916. This is the first-known photograph of a British submarine flying the Jolly Roger to celebrate her victory. This close-up of the bridge upon the ship's return to Great Yarmouth shows Lieutenant John Byron, Royal Naval Reserve. The Canadian subs were reported to be the best performing of all Royal Navy submarines.

HMS H-5–H-10 group fitting-out and undergoing trials in Montreal. H-7 has laid-off and is preparing to make a test dive. The cruiser HMS Carnarvon is in the Duke of Connaught floating dock undergoing repairs to her bottom received through an accidental grounding. Carnarvon would eventually escort this group of boats to England, May–June 1915.

November 9, 1918, two days before the armistice that ended the fighting was signed.

The Allies decided not to prosecute the kaiser for war crimes, President Wilson arguing that such a prosecution would "destabilize international order and lose the peace." Wilhelm lived the rest of his life in exile in the Netherlands. It was reported that he required sixty railway wagons to haul his fortune of precious art, jewels, furniture, and other treasure.

In the 1930s, Wilhelm hoped that the rising Nazi Party would restore the monarchy to Germany, but Hitler, who had fought in Wilhelm's army in the Great War, held only contempt for the deposed kaiser. Later, in 1938, Wilhelm denounced the Nazis' Jewish pogroms. He died on June 4, 1941, in the Netherlands, aged eighty-two.

One more mysterious account of Rudolf Diesel appeared in the public record. On December 7, 1936, a journalist and trained engineer named Lemuel F. Parton published an article for the *Evening Star* of Washington, D.C., with the headline "Rudolf Diesel, Inventor of Engine, May Be Still Alive."

In the article, Parton recalled working in San Francisco in 1914 on the Panama-Pacific International Exposition to be held there the following year. This was the same event to which the visiting American engineers had invited Rudolf back in June 1913. Parton was building a huge Diesel exhibition that was featured at the fair.

Parton wrote, "Late one night a tall, austere, bearded German came to my home." The strange guest claimed to be a scientist who had consulted in the development of Diesel engines. Speaking in heavily accented English, the man recounted Diesel's career in intimate detail, then told Parton that Diesel did not perish in 1913. He suggested that, as a journalist, Parton should pursue the story in Europe. The following day, Parton told his colleagues working for the fair about the strange German in the night, but "None would tell me more of my visitor."

Parton traveled to Europe where he interviewed "many informed Europeans who believe that Rudolf Diesel is still alive," but none spoke on the record and Parton could never prove the claim. He dropped the story.

———————

John D. Rockefeller lived to just shy of his ninety-eighth birthday. He died on May 23, 1937, at his winter residence in Florida, a mansion in Ormand Beach named the Casements. (The home was the venue of elaborate Christmas parties during Rockefeller's life, and it now serves as a cultural center and public park.) By the early twentieth century, Rockefeller had begun to turn the corporate reins of his empire over to his son John Jr. and to his colleague John Dustin Archbold so that he could devote more of his time and resources to charitable causes. In 1913, he founded the Rockefeller Foundation, to which he gave nearly $250 million over his remaining years (even using 1937, the year of his death, for the entire amount, this adjusts to more than $5 billion in 2022).

At his death his wealth was an estimated $1.4 billion, at a time when the national GDP was $92 billion. (Rockefeller's wealth represented more than 1.5 percent of US GDP while Jeff Bezos's wealth represents about 0.4 percent of present US GDP.) Many of the "Baby Standards" went on to become some of the largest revenue-producing companies in the world.

Skeptics claim his philanthropy was an attempt to distance himself from scandal and to cleanse his reputation and the legacy of the family name so that society would embrace his heirs.

Petroleum became the dominant fuel of the twentieth century and remains dominant, as no nation has built a biodiesel infrastructure capable of supporting Rudolf's version of the engine that won the 1900 Paris World's Fair on a large scale. However, Rudolf's vision does exist on a small scale, as demonstrated by Willie Nelson's tour bus, which famously runs on a Diesel engine fueled by recycled kitchen grease from restaurants. As Nelson said in 2007, "I saw where the farmers

could actually benefit from growing their own fuel and we could benefit by not having to go around the world starting wars over energy."

———

What happened to Rudolf Diesel's family? His parents predeceased
him. Elise died in 1897 and Theodor died in 1901, both before the
meteoric rise of the Diesel engine. Rudolf Jr. married in 1911, had one
son, and died in 1944 at the age of sixty. Hedy and Arnold von Schmidt
went on to have four children and remained together until Arnold's
death in 1947 in Urbach, a German municipality just east of Bavaria.
Hedy died in Munich in 1968. Eugen shifted his professional focus to
writing and published several highly regarded books about the social
and political implications of advancing technology. He married Anna
Luise von Waldersee in 1925 and had three children. Eugen died in
Rosenheim, Bavaria (southeast Germany), in 1970.

There is very little known about Martha after 1913; however, a
few newspapers (in Canada, Spain, and America) ran a single-line
obituary that she died on April 16, 1944, in Austria. It remains a mystery whether Martha ever saw her husband again.

EPILOGUE

At Last

WINSTON CHURCHILL ADVISED, "In wartime truth is so precious that she must always be attended by a bodyguard of lies." More than a century later, the bodyguards are gone and the truth laid bare. Rudolf Diesel can have his due. But how did a man of such global notoriety depart so quickly and thoroughly from the world's consciousness?

First, to the layperson, engine technology was changing rapidly at the turn of the century. The advances in retrospect are clearer, but to the contemporary audience for whom these advances were happening in real time, the changes seemed subtle and complex. Even for Churchill and other leaders, the value of Diesel technology was difficult to grasp and articulate until years after Rudolf's disappearance.

Second, the Allies won the war and, therefore, primarily wrote its history. There was little incentive to glorify a German national, even if he was the inventor of the engine the Allies had learned to use so successfully. Especially if the man was a robbed asset (from the kaiser's point of view), taken in peacetime from a country that would eventually face decades of steep war reparation payments.

Third, wide acceptance of the idea that Diesel committed suicide stymied the reverence and posthumous fame that would otherwise have been his due. Most preferred to move away quickly from the topic of the fallen genius and suggestions of his mental illness. Additionally, several contemporary scientists disparaged Diesel after his disappearance and attempted to usurp credit for the engine's successes, altering the record after Rudolf was no longer around to protect it.

Yet while the man was gone and his image was tarnished and then obscured, the Diesel engine continued its trajectory of market domination across multiple industries related to air, sea, and land. The Diesel engine became ubiquitous through the twentieth century due to the laws of free markets and economic progress. The Diesel motor for trucks and automobiles did come, as Rudolf had predicted. In 1923, both Benz and M.A.N. conducted successful tests of Diesel engines for heavy-load trucks. In 1927, in America, Mack Trucks began testing Diesel engines, and by 1935 was manufacturing and selling its own line of Diesel trucks. By the late 1930s, nearly all new trucks built around the world were Diesel.

A lighter-weight Diesel motor viable for passenger autos took a bit longer, though the American Diesel pioneer Clessie Cummins, who founded Cummins Engine Company in 1919, accelerated the process. Initially Cummins built Diesels for large farm equipment and marine use. In 1929, he refit a marine engine for installation in a Packard limousine (which had a large engine compartment). Amid enormous fanfare, Cummins drove the car from his company headquarters in Columbus, Indiana, to the New York City auto show, some 740 miles, burning a meager $1.38 worth of Diesel fuel (about $20 today).

In 1931, with much wrangling behind the scenes, Cummins managed to enter a Diesel car in the Indianapolis 500. With a mocking chuckle, the race officials permitted entry of the self-made eighty-five-horsepower marine Diesel that Cummins refitted in a Duesenberg Model A. The Cummins Diesel clocked a qualifying speed of 96 mph and, by special exception, secured a place in the forty-car field for the event, though indeed, the gasoline-powered cars clocked qualifying speeds as fast as 116 mph. The heavy Diesel motor delivered high torque for hauling but, as yet, not high speeds, and looked to be nothing more than a marketing stunt for the race.

To the shock of all, with Dale Evans behind the wheel, the Cummins Diesel took thirteenth place. How did Evans manage to beat more than half the field of much faster cars? In a wildly unprecedented performance, the Cummins car ran the entire race *without making a single fuel stop.*

Five years later, Daimler-Benz achieved the first true Diesel automobile with the Mercedes 260 D, a six-seater passenger car with a forty-five-horsepower engine exhibited at the 1936 Berlin automotive exhibition.

In 1928, the Caterpillar Tractor Company successfully tested an Atlas Imperial Diesel engine in one of its tractors. In 1931–32, Caterpillar built 157 Diesel-powered tractors for farm work and earthmoving. In 1932, Caterpillar made a marketing sensation with a demonstration on an Oregon farm. The company hitched a twelve-bottom gang plow (meaning it digs twelve furrows) to a new Diesel tractor. After a continuous run of forty-six days, the tractor had traveled 3,500 miles and plowed 6,880 acres at an average fuel cost of less than six cents per acre, a multiple better than gasoline-powered tractors.

As of 2022, Cummins, Caterpillar, and M.A.N. are among the world's leaders in Diesel engines. The global Diesel market size was valued at more than a trillion dollars in 2022, and the period 2023–28 is projected to have robust 5.65 percent annual growth.

The military applications of Diesel power grew throughout the century as well. The Allies failed in their attempt to limit Germany's access to certain applications of Diesel motors under the terms of the Treaty of Versailles following the Great War. In Part V, Military, Naval and Air Clauses of the treaty, the victors outlined the limits of the future composition of the German navy. Article 181 prohibited any submarines. Article 188 directed that all German submarines remaining at the war's end must be handed over to the Principal Allied and Associated Powers, who further declared in Article 191 that "the construction or acquisition of any submarine, even for commercial purposes, shall be forbidden in Germany."

Despite the agreed terms of 1919, the Diesel engine played an even greater role in the Second World War than it had in the first, and the Diesel-powered German U-boats once again unleashed catastrophic damage on the seas. Diesel engines also powered the flight of German and Russian long-range bombers. On land, the Soviet T-34 battle tank, described by German field generals as "the best tank in the world," ran on Diesel, a reflection of the lasting Nobel legacy of engineering excellence. In 1940, Stalin, whose Red Army had chased Emanuel Nobel from Russia in 1918, began mass production of the T-34, which was faster, more powerful, and simply outclassed the German Panzer (which ironically ran on Maybach gasoline engines).

In 1947, Vice-Admiral E. L. Cochrane declared:

The United States, in this last war, built thousands of ships and 90 per cent of them were diesel powered, and there was no ship that was not equipped with diesel power of some kind . . . The whole landing craft program was diesel powered, and these ships worked under the most strenuous conditions. . . . Diesel engines saved the day. Not a single one failed us in a critical operation.

Though Adolphus Busch died in Germany in 1913 only days after Rudolf's disappearance, the Busch-Sulzer operation continued and built many of the marine Diesels used by the US Navy in World War II.

In the years after the war, Diesel powered global commerce. By 1960, nearly all new commercial ships had Diesel installations. Today, close to 100 percent of the goods traveling the oceans—approximately 11 billion tons annually as of 2021—do so under Diesel power. And when cargo arrives in port, it is loaded onto trucks that are almost exclusively Diesel. The trucks drive the cargo to train depots where the trains, since about 1960, are all running on Diesel power. Nothing seems to move at all today without the aid of Rudolf's wonder technology.[*]

———————

While the engine has gotten its due, now, I hope, so does the man.

Rudolf created the world's dominant power source. He then ensured the technology was not confined to the service of those inside German borders, but this required a great sacrifice. In a sense, Rockefeller and Kaiser Wilhelm II did cause Diesel's "death." Because of the threat he posed to them, he had to leave Germany and complete his work in secret in Canada. Diesel had to abandon his home, his family, his identity, and legacy. When he became an asset of Winston Churchill in 1913, his old life ended.

In numerous ways, Rudolf changed the world. Was he happy with these changes?

That he should have become a prized wartime asset is the terrible contradiction of his life. Though Diesel did support the Royal Navy, augmenting weapons of war was not his life's ambition. He simply viewed the British military apparatus as the lesser of two evils, and as conflict with Germany seemed imminent and unavoidable, Diesel concluded he'd rather build a British submarine than a German U-boat. Seen in this light, Diesel's work with Churchill was not an agreement so much as a coincidence of interests.

The hoped-for utility of Rudolf's engine—to bolster rural economies and the artisan class—never came to be. From the outset of the first patent licensing deals that Rudolf signed in 1897, the fruits of the engine were rapidly co-opted by big industry and the military.

The uncertain application of advancing science, for good or for

———————

[*] The majority of the world's cargo travels by sea. The measurement *tonne-kilometer* captures both the weight and distance traveled of transported goods. "Of the 108 trillion tonne-kilometers [of goods] transported worldwide in 2015, 70 percent traveled by sea, 18 percent by road, nine percent by rail and two percent by inland waterway." Each of these methods is mainly Diesel-powered. A mere 0.25 percent traveled by air ("Global Freight Demand to Triple by 2050," *Maritime Executive,* May 27, 2019).

bad, was a great struggle of Diesel's age, as it is today. The urge to co-opt powerful new technologies for alternate uses has been repeated throughout history; however, the stakes get higher all the time. As Eugen Diesel wrote in a book about his father published in 1960:

> *We have got to strike our bargain with machinery and technology, and we still do not know how to go about it. We are just beginning to make our way in this new age, so full of dangers, and, at the same time, so full of promise.*

Among all forms of life on earth, humans have a unique quality: the conscious ambition to evolve. Is this a quality of our better angels? This question sets the stage for the sad paradox of Diesel's life and work.

Throughout history certain people have developed technologies that deliver conveniences and speed up our lives. The rest of us, for the most part, accept the presumption that progress is inherently good. At a rare crossroads, some stop to reflect that we have come all this way, and for what? Are we truly better off?

Rudolf Diesel wondered this very thing. Was the astounding progress afforded by the Diesel engine for the betterment of humankind? Ironically, nearly every effect of Diesel's wonder motor ran counter to his intention. His engine didn't decentralize economies but rather became a tool of big industry and economic centralization. It enabled terrible new weapons with methods of attack that raised moral questions. And despite Rudolf's advocacy of the engine's capacity to burn alternative fuels derived from vegetables and nuts, the manipulations of the oil trusts won out. Throughout the twentieth century and to the present day, the Diesel motor primarily burns a form of petrol-Diesel. As no nation has overcome the political and investment hurdles to develop the fuel-refining infrastructure for vegetable oils or coal tar, the Diesel engine simply sucks up more crude.

Painfully for Diesel, these ironies were not realized posthumously. Diesel witnessed this paradox unfold during his lifetime.

In the end, Diesel had one last card to play.

"German engineering" threatened to leave the rest of the world hopelessly behind. Rudolf decided to assist the non-German-speaking world. He made a parting gift of himself to Churchill and the Allies as he disappeared from public life.

But he disappeared while still pondering the nagging question that plagued his lifetime of effort and toil, as such a question might for any creator. Rudolf framed the question as well as anyone. He deserves the last word in his own story:

> *It is wonderful to design and to invent in the way that an artist designs and creates. But whether it all has a purpose, whether people have become happier as a result, that I can no longer decide.*
>
> *Rudolf Diesel*

ACKNOWLEDGMENTS

This book required years of research in archives around Europe and America. I had terrific assistance from many of the people working in these archives, especially during the period of the pandemic when I wasn't allowed inside. In particular, I'd like to thank Jana Weber, Julia Oberndörfer, Angelika Pilz, Erich Friedlein, and Michael Melzer at the Historical Archive M.A.N. Augsburg; Anna Krutsch, Matthias Röschner, and Kathrin Mönch at the Deutsches Museum; Stefan Lang at the Historisches Archiv Krupp; Sophie Bridges, Jessica Collins, Amanda Jones, and Katharine Thomson at the Churchill Archives Centre, Cambridge; Alison Firth and John Rigby at the National Museum of the Royal Navy; Jan van Berlo at the Archive & Collection Vereniging Nederlandse Loodsen Sociëteit; Sarah Giersing and Henriette Gavnholdt Jakobsen at the Maritime Museum of Denmark; Andrea Twiss-Brooks at the University of Chicago Library; Susan Krueger and Lee Grady at the Wisconsin Historical Society; Joanne Bloom at the Harvard Library, Faculty of Arts and Sciences; Katherine Terry at the National Archives, St. Louis; and Hywel Maslen, who researched UK newspaper databases and also got inside the archives in Kew during the period of very limited operating hours.

My thanks to Gerhard Reich for translating many letters and other documents from German to English and for the fun conversations about Diesel.

Adrian Kinloch once again did a bang-up job on the site DouglasBrunt.com, as he has done with each of my books. This time around we had some extra fun reveling in the cast of characters of the Diesel period.

My thanks to Jean-Philippe Diesel and Susanne Kropf for sharing in their reminiscences. And my thanks to Peter Romary, Phil Houston, Bill Stanton, and Mike Swain for reviewing evidence with me. Thanks to Andy and Erin Stern for the dining-room table.

My agents, Keith Urbahn, Matt Latimer, and Matt Carlini, shared my enthusiasm for the Diesel story and recognized its importance and relevance to the present day. Not only were they very helpful in crafting a proposal that reflected what the book could become, but they have been a continuous sounding board for ideas.

My editors, Peter Borland and Sean deLone, were terrific. This is a complicated story to tell and the structural work that Peter and Sean contributed to mold this book into a flowing narrative was invaluable. Also at Simon & Schuster, thanks to Libby McGuire, Katie Rizzo, Shida Carr, and Dayna Johnson.

Once again, Megyn is my First Reader and my Chief Supporter—even if that support will sometimes come in the form of telling me: "This one's a dud." In the case of Rudolf Diesel, she matched my excitement. We've had countless conversations about the evidence related to his disappearance as well as Diesel's contributions in the years prior to 1913 that have eerie relevance today. Our discussions frequently included our children, Yates, Yardley, and Thatcher, who also read Diesel's letters, diaries, and theories. As we debated the history of Rudolf Diesel over the long period of my work on the book, he seemed to acquire three dimensions and to walk among us. I'll miss spending my days with him.

APPENDIX

Exhibit 1

Diagram of four-stroke Diesel engine operation

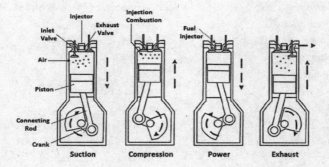

Four-Stroke Diesel Cycle, Compression Ignition Engine

This image shows the four phases of a single cylinder in a four-stroke engine design. In the first image, the piston drops, which draws in the air and fuel mixture. In the second image, the piston rises to compress the mixture. In the third image, the combustion of the compressed air/fuel drives out the piston, which creates the power stroke. In the fourth, the piston rises again to force the exhaust from the cylinder.

Exhibit 2

Diesel Manufacturing Firms, pre-1919

A.B. Diesels Motorer (Sweden)
Allis-Chalmers (USA)
American Diesel Engine Co.
    (USA)
Augustin Normand (France)
Belliss & Morcom (UK)
Benz (Germany)
Brons (Netherlands)
Burmeister & Wain (Denmark)
Busch-Sulzer (USA)
Carels (Belgium)
Daimler (Germany)
Darmstadt (Germany)
Delaunay-Belleville (France)
Deutz (Germany)
Dow (USA)
Dyckoff (France)
Franco Tosi (Italy)
Fulton Iron Works (USA)
General Electric (USA)
Grazer Waggon (Austria)
Güldner-Motoren G.m.b.H
    (Germany)
Haselwander (Germany)
Jastram, Carl (Germany)
Junkers (Germany)
Kaebel, Carl (Germany)

Kolomna Machine-Building
    Plant (Russia)
Körting (Germany)
Krupp (Germany)
Langen & Wolf (Italy/Austria)
Leissner (Sweden)
Leobersdorfer Maschinenfabrik
    (Germany)
M.A.N. (Germany)
Mirrlees (UK)
Nobel (Russia)
Nordberg (Germany)
Sabathe (France)
Sautter-Harle (France)
Snow-Holly (USA)
Schneider et Cie (France)
Ste. De Moteurs à Gaz (France)
Steinbecker (Germany)
Sulzer Brothers (Switzerland)
Trinkler (Russia)
Vickers (UK)
Waffen-u Maschinenfabrik
    (Germany)
Werkspoor (Netherlands)
Westinghouse (USA)
Willans & Robinson (UK)
Worthington (USA)

TIMELINE

March 18, 1858: Rudolf Diesel born in Paris, France.

April 1, 1867: The Paris World's Fair opens, during which Rudolf views the prizewinning Otto gas engine.

January 10, 1870: Rockefeller, Flagler, and Andrews found Standard Oil.

September 5, 1870: The Diesel family flees Paris for London as the French army falls to the advancing Prussian forces at the Battle of Sedan, September 1–2.

November 1870: Rudolf leaves his family behind in London and joins the Barnickels in Augsburg to pursue his education at the Royal County Trade School.

Fall 1875: Rudolf begins studying at the Munich university, Technisch Hochschule München.

July 11, 1878: During a university lecture, Rudolf writes notes in the margin of his notebook speculating about the possibility of a more efficient engine. He later identifies these notes as the beginning of his journey with the Diesel engine.

January 15, 1880: Recovered from typhoid fever, Diesel completes his university exams with the highest marks in the history of the institution.

March 20, 1880: Diesel takes a job with Linde's Paris manufacturing plant.

November 24, 1883: Rudolf and Martha marry in Germany, then return to their Paris home.

November 7, 1884: Rudolf Diesel Jr. born in Paris.

October 15, 1885: Hedy Diesel born in Paris.

May 1887: Rudolf writes a list of the intended uses for his rational heat engine, primarily small businesses like his father's.

May 3, 1889: Eugen Diesel born in Paris.

February 21, 1890: Rudolf moves with his family to Berlin, still working for Linde.

March 20, 1890: Kaiser Wilhelm II forces the resignation of Chancellor Bismarck.

February 27, 1892: Diesel files German patent No. 67207 for the rational heat engine.

April 20, 1892: Heinrich Buz of Maschinenfabrik Augsburg agrees to support the development of Diesel's ideas.

January 10, 1893: Diesel publishes his treatise *Theory and Construction of a Rational Heat Engine.* An early draft that Diesel completed the year before was instrumental in winning the support of Buz.

April 10, 1893: Diesel signs a contract with Krupp to support development of the engine.

October 1896: Diesel completes construction of the third and final test engine.

February 17, 1897: Professor Moritz Schröter conducts the official performance test of Diesel's engine, which reveals 26.2 percent thermal efficiency, and proves the success of Diesel's ideas.

March 26, 1897: With the endorsement of the Lord Kelvin, Mirrlees, Watson & Yaryan obtains the rights to the Diesel patents for Great Britain.

April 15, 1897: Frédéric Dyckhoff acquires the French rights to the Diesel patents.

June 16, 1897: Diesel and Schröter present the results of the February test at a major address in Kassel, Germany.

October 9, 1897: Adolphus Busch acquires the North American rights to the Diesel patents.

February 16, 1898: Emanuel Nobel signs agreement for rights to the Diesel patents.

September 17, 1898: Rudolf founds the General Society for Diesel Engines in Augsburg, Germany, which manages all commercial interests of the technology.

April 14, 1900: The Paris World's Fair opens, during which an eighty-horsepower Diesel engine wins the Grand Prix. The engine runs entirely on nut oil for fuel.

July 2, 1900: Rudolf joins his friend Graf von Zeppelin to observe the first flight of the *Luftschiff Zeppelin 1*, Zeppelin's first dirigible.

October 1, 1900: Winston Churchill wins election to the House of Commons for the first time.

Spring 1901: The Diesel family moves into their Munich home, Maria-Theresia-Strasse 32, Villa Diesel.

November 1902: Ida Tarbell begins her series on Rockefeller and Standard Oil for *McClure's*.

April 1, 1903: Diesel publishes *Solidarismus*.

May 1, 1903: Nobel puts the oil tanker *Vandal* into service on the Caspian Sea, the world's first marine Diesel-powered vessel.

September 29, 1903: Dyckhoff launches the Diesel-powered barge *Petit Pierre* on the French canal system.

March 28, 1904: The French Navy launches the Diesel-powered submarine *Z*, the first-ever submarine with Diesel engines.

May 1904: The Russian city Kyiv installs four M.A.N. Diesels of four hundred horsepower each to power its tramway system. The city soon adds two more.

February 10, 1906: Britain launches the HMS *Dreadnought*, powered by Parsons steam turbines and with Diesels installed for auxiliary power.

April 28, 1906: The Milan International Exhibition opens, at which Sulzer Brothers exhibits a reversing two-stroke Diesel engine.

February 1907: Both M.A.N. and the General Society for Diesel Engines sue Rudolf Diesel over a patent dispute.

December 1908: The German navy places its first order with M.A.N. for a submarine Diesel engine for its U-boat fleet.

August 1909: Anton von Rieppel, an executive at M.A.N., proposes battleship Diesels to the Reichsmarine. Months later, the German navy awards contracts for battleship Diesels to M.A.N., Krupp, and Sulzer Brothers.

September 4, 1909: Russia launches the gunboat *Kars*, powered by twin five-hundred-horsepower Nobel reversible Diesels, for duty on the Caspian Sea.

April 23, 1910: The Brussels International Exposition opens, at which Rudolf wins first prize for his Diesel automobile engine called the "Petite."

August 10, 1910: The *Fram*, powered by a 180-horsepower Diesel built by the Swedish firm A.B. Diesels Motorer (later Polar), departs Norway for the South Pole. Roald Amundsen leads the successful expedition, the completed round-trip to Norway lasting almost four years.

May 15, 1911: The US Supreme Court rules against Standard Oil.

October 24, 1911: Prime Minister H. H. Asquith appoints Winston Churchill to the Office of the First Lord of the Admiralty, the post from which Churchill directs the activity of the Naval Intelligence Division and the overall preparations of the Royal Navy.

March 1, 1912: Churchill tours the engine room of the *Selandia*, the first true oceangoing Diesel-powered vessel, while at the West India Docks.

March 7, 1912: The Consolidated Diesel Engine Company incorporates in Ipswich, England. The company focus is to build large marine Diesel engines. Rudolf Diesel and George Carels are founders and board members of the new firm, which later dissolves under mysterious circumstances just months after Diesel's disappearance.

March 15, 1912: Diesel delivers remarks to the Institution of Mechanical Engineers in London, titled "The Diesel Oil Engine and Its Industrial Importance, Particularly for Great Britain."

March 17, 1912: Churchill addresses Parliament, in an echo of Diesel's speech two days before, declaring that updating the Royal Navy from steam to oil will lift the navy to a "definitely higher level" but would expose Britain to dependence on foreign oil. Overcoming that dependence was critical as "mastery [of the seas] is the prize of the venture." Diesel offered multiple ways to overcome oil dependence. Architects of the Royal Navy had already made detailed designs of destroyers and battleships with Diesel installations, in addition to the Diesel submarines already in service. The Diesel engine, rather than oil, was the true path to the "prize" that Churchill coveted.

April 13, 1912: Diesel delivers remarks to the Associated Engineering Societies of St. Louis, in Missouri.

May 6, 1912: Rudolf and Martha Diesel meet with Thomas Edison in West Orange, New Jersey.

June 24, 1912: Kaiser Wilhelm II tours the *Fionia*, sister ship to the *Selandia*, during the Kiel Regatta.

March 1913: Hugo Junkers develops a four-cylinder Diesel aircraft engine.

June 1913: Chester Nimitz arrives in Augsburg to study Diesel technology on behalf of the US Navy. Visiting American engineers renew an offer of employment to Rudolf from the Pennsylvania Railroad.

June 28, 1913: Charles Parsons and George Carels attend a dinner party at Diesel's Munich home, where the men agree to travel to England for events in early October of that year.

September 29, 1913: The *Dresden* crossing begins, apparently with Diesel aboard.

October 2, 1913: The Associated Press reports the testimony of a *Dresden* crewman that Diesel was not present aboard the ship for the channel crossing.

October 11, 1913: Crewmen of the *Coertzen* allege the discovery of Diesel's corpse floating in the Scheldt estuary.

March 15, 1914: The *New York Times* reports Rudolf Diesel living in Canada.

June 28, 1914: The Serbian nationalist group called the Black Hand assassinates Archduke Franz Ferdinand of Austria while in Sarajevo, sparking the Great War.

January 1, 1915: Bethlehem Steel Corporation completes the fabrication of submarine component parts and ships the assets to a top secret manufacturing location in Canada, fulfilling the agreement between Charles M. Schwab and Winston Churchill.

August 15, 1915: The *Washington Post* reports the story of Churchill's secret submarines, built in Canada, sailing across the Atlantic for the North Sea, under Diesel power.

ADDENDUM

SECRETS AT M.A.N.

Battleship Diesels for the Great War

In August 1909, Anton von Rieppel at the Nuremberg division of M.A.N. had made the audacious claim to the German navy that he was prepared to build a Diesel engine powerful enough for a capital ship. Such a claim was beyond the dreams of any other engine manufacturer. But by the end of the year, he signed a contract with the navy to build six engines, each with six cylinders and capable of twelve thousand horsepower. The engines combined would deliver the seventy-two thousand horsepower required for the battleship. Rumors of battleship-sized Diesels circulated through Europe in the years to follow, but the development work was under such secrecy that details of the design efforts remained unknown until after the war.

This revolutionary Diesel battleship would have the unprecedented range to exert force around the globe without a fuel stop. Diesels of such power also had the frightening prospect of allowing these floating monsters a surreptitious approach. Without the pillars of black smoke issuing from the funnel stacks to paint the sky for miles and mark the ship's progress on the horizon, a Diesel-powered battleship, with all its heavy, long-range guns, could come up on the enemy without giving itself away.

Germany was the only country to seriously pursue Diesel power for the battleship in this period, as it was the only country with the temerity to consider it possible. Hoping to leapfrog the British dreadnoughts in capability, Wilhelm awarded three such contracts in 1909. One each to the German firms M.A.N. and Krupp, and the third to Sulzer Brothers. Wilhelm intended to install the Diesel engines in the SMS *Prinzregent Luitpold*, the fifth and final *Kaiser*-class battleship.

In this century it's difficult to appreciate the value of the range offered by the Diesel engine and the onerous trials of refueling a coal-burning warship, but the flight of the SMS *Goeben*, perhaps the most famous naval chase in history, illustrates these challenges well.

During the first months of the Great War, the German battle-cruiser SMS *Goeben* fled the Royal Navy through the Mediterranean and Aegean Seas. The repeated need for refueling ("coaling") required the terrible risk to put in at island ports or rendezvous at sea with coalers and begin the grueling work coaling the ship. Knowing the British guns were close behind, the entire crew of the *Goeben* worked feverishly. "Through the night sacks of coal were swung across to the warship and clattered down on the steel deck, where shovels began to ply. In the heat the men began to falter. [Admiral Wilhelm] Souchon tried beer, coffee, lemonade, band music, exhortation and the example of officers who stripped off their shirts and worked beside the crew. Nothing could keep the men on their feet. . . . By noon on the second day *Goebben* [*sic*] had loaded 1,500 tons of coal and the crew was exhausted; men lay collapsed on deck, shovels still gripped in their blistered hands." Worse yet for the *Goeben*, once the ship raised steam and again took flight, Souchon strained the engines to the limit of speed. The ship's boiler tubes began to burst, releasing spouts of steam and boiling water onto the bare-chested stokers heaving coal into the furnaces to keep the propeller churning the ocean. As the chase continued, four stokers were scalded to death. Alternatively, on a Diesel-powered ship they might have hooked up a hose to pump fuel to a ready tank that automatically fed the engine.

By modern standards, the scale of the "cathedral" Diesels for the battleship bordered on the absurd—each of the M.A.N. engines was twenty-five feet high. The first test engine from M.A.N. in 1911 briefly delivered the contractually required 90 percent threshold horsepower but failed to maintain that level for the agreed five-day period. A re-designed test engine exploded in January 1912, killing ten engineers and badly injuring fourteen more.

Eventually, M.A.N. completed a seventh and final design in September 1913 and finished construction of the engine in the following February. During initial testing of this design, the engine showed promise, producing ten thousand horsepower over a ten-hour period. However, the outbreak of war slowed the testing phase. Scarcity of fuel to conduct the tests, as well as the skepticism that the engine would be complete in time to see service in the war, reduced the priority of the new Diesel.

Lack of crude oil to produce the derivative heavy Diesel fuel prompted the determined engineers to take the project in the direction Rudolf Diesel had always advocated. M.A.N. modified the engine to burn coal tar, which was in easier supply for Germany than petroleum, and resumed testing in April 1915 on a single cylinder (rather than the full six-cylinder engine). Testing on the full six-cylinder engine began in January 1917, and on March 24 the engine passed acceptance testing. It delivered a whopping 12,200 horsepower, so that the combined performance would deliver 73,200 horsepower. The engine burned 243g of fuel per horsepower per hour. This fuel efficiency delivered a range of operation several multiples greater than any battleship in service. The composition of the fuel was a ratio of 214g coal tar and 29g paraffin oil. For a country like Germany (or England) that had plenty of domestic coal but was vulnerable to foreign dependence on petroleum, the Diesel engine reversed fortunes.

Krupp and Sulzer followed different technical approaches for the battleship engine, though neither approached the success of M.A.N. On December 22, 1914, a delegation of the French Navy visited the Sulzer shop to witness engine tests. A few days later, representatives for the British, German, and Italian navies saw the same engine perform—each at a different viewing.

The colossal engine was a near-mythic scientific achievement by German engineers that would not be matched anywhere in the world for many years, though these engines never saw service. Germany laid the keel of the *Kaiser*-class battleship SMS *Prinzregent Luitpold* in October 1910. As no manufacturer delivered suitable Diesel engines in time, the ship launched on February 17, 1912, with two sets of Parsons steam turbines. Upon Germany's defeat in the war, on June 21, 1919, only one week before Germany signed the Treaty of Versailles, Rear Admiral Ludwig von Reuter ordered the ship scuttled to prevent the Allies from taking possession of it.

———

On March 24, 1949, the *New York Times* ran the story "Diesel Engine Runs on Coal and Oil Mix," touting the apparent accomplishment of a professor at North Carolina State College who had managed to build a Diesel motor that burned a "half-and-half" mix of oil and pulverized coal. The professor felt that in four to ten more years, he'd be ready for commercial use, which was important as, in his words, "In times of war, coal is more plentiful than oil. And with coal, one gallon of fuel does the work of two gallons of oil." This article seems mortifyingly doltish given the engineers at M.A.N. had, in secret, achieved a far more ambitious target ratio of coal to oil all the way back in 1917. Yet another indication of the incredibly advanced work in Augsburg. The M.A.N. engine never left the shop floor and was scrapped under the terms of the Treaty of Versailles.

NOTES

PROLOGUE

4 *"Inventor Thrown into the Sea"*: Tim Harford, "How Rudolf Diesel's Engine Changed the World," BBC News, December 19, 2016. The article recounts the contemporaneous headlines that Rudolf Diesel was murdered by Kaiser Wilhelm or Rockefeller. The same headlines appear in the History. com article "Inventor Rudolf Diesel Vanishes," History.com, November 13, 2009, https://www.history.com/this-day-in-history/inventor-rudolf-diesel -vanishes.

4 *"one of the great achievements"*: *Albuquerque Morning Journal*, February 13, 1912.

4 *"the most perfect maritime"*: Ivar Knudsen, "A Smokeless Marine: Denmark's Recent Development of the Diesel Motor," *The American-Scandinavian Review*, Vol. II. Published by the American-Scandinavian Foundation, New York. 1914. This remark from Churchill is later picked up in other publications.

4 *"the great magician"*: *Mohave County Miner* [Kingman, Arizona], October 5, 1912.

6 *"Do you feel how I love you?"*: Letter in Historical Archive MAN Augsburg, September 28, 1913.

CHAPTER I: AN INTERNATIONAL IDENTITY

11 *One morning while*: Eugen Diesel, *From Engines to Autos: Five Pioneers in Engine Development and Their Contributions to the Automotive Industry.* Chicago: Henry Regnery Company, 1960, 186.

14 *In wide-eyed wonder*: Ibid.

18 *The father and son started*: Robert Nitske and Charles Morrow Wilson, *Rudolf Diesel: Pioneer of the Age of Power.* Norman: University of Oklahoma Press, 1965, 5.

19 *"like the inside of my pocket"*: Ibid.

19 *"quite possibly one of the"*: Ibid., 17.

20 *"Drawing is"*: Diesel, *Engines to Autos*, 187.

21 *I am a liar*: Eugen Diesel, *Diesel: der Mensch, das Werk, das Schicksal.* Hamburg: Hanseatische Verlagsanstalt, 1937, 33.

23 *"a loaf of bread"*: Ibid.

CHAPTER 2: A BRIEF STAY IN LONDON

25 *dragging their boxed possessions through the streets*: Nitske and Wilson, *Rudolf Diesel*, 25.
29 *"more like a mature adult"*: Ibid., 37.
30 *"made a railroad"*: Diesel, *From Engines to Autos*, 189.
30 *"Paris kindled in him"*: Ibid., 191.

CHAPTER 3: A NEW EMPIRE IN EUROPE

34 *"He would be a very pretty boy"*: Robert K. Massie, *Dreadnought: Britain, Germany, and the Coming of the Great War*. New York: Random House, 1991, 27–8.
34 *"The weeping prince"*: Ibid.
35 *"The thought that I should not"*: Ibid.
35 *"Prince Bismarck remains"*: Ibid., 32.
38 *"Germany's lodestar was"*: Eugen Diesel, *Germany and the Germans*. London: MacMillan & Co., 1931, 224.

CHAPTER 4: IS ANYONE TRULY SELF-MADE?

41 *"heard the names of the top executives"*: Diesel, *From Engines to Autos*, 190.
42 *"provisions are diminishing"* and *"I went with father"*: Louise Diesel diary, Historical Archive MAN Augsburg, January 1871.
43 *"Now I shall be"*: Diesel letters, Historical Archive MAN Augsburg, September 11, 1872.
44 *"Didn't she try to awaken"*: Donald Thomas Jr., *Diesel: Technology and Society in Industrial Germany*. Tuscaloosa: University of Alabama Press, 1987, 9.

CHAPTER 5: PETROLEUM UPENDS THE GAME

48 *"I cheat my boys"*: Grant Segall, *John D. Rockefeller: Anointed with Oil*. Oxford Portraits. New York: Oxford University Press, 2001.
48 *"Dr. William A. Levingston appearing"*: Ron Chernow, *Titan: The Life of John D. Rockefeller, Sr.* New York: Random House, 1998.
50 *"the reputation of being"*: Ibid.
52 *George Gardner, you're"*: Ibid., 65.
53 *Markets were active*: Ibid.
57 *"We have a partnership"*: David Leon Chandler, *Henry Flagler: The Astonishing Life and Times of the Visionary Robber Baron Who Founded Florida*. New York: Macmillan, 1986, 73.
57 *"I believe the power"*: Chernow, *Titan*.
58 *A gang of twenty-eight men*: Chandler, *Henry Flagler*, 72.
58 *Once when Rockefeller was riding a train*: Ibid.

CHAPTER 6: PURSUIT OF THE IDEAL

65 *He committed two pages*: Pages from Diesel's notebook, Historical Archive MAN Augsburg.
66 *to keep his single suit*: Nitske and Wilson, *Rudolf Diesel*, 51.
68 *"The wish to realize the ideal"*: Thomas Jr., *Diesel*, 80.

CHAPTER 7: MEANT FOR MORE THAN A SALARY

71 *Linde decided that Diesel*: Nitske and Wilson, *Rudolf Diesel*, 55.
72 *"He is a nice, modest"*: Thomas Jr., *Diesel*, 11–12.
73 *"broadly and voraciously"*: Nitske and Wilson, *Rudolf Diesel*, 61.
74 *"Only two or three more"*: Diesel, *Diesel*, 153.
75 *"I know from experience"*: Thomas Jr., *Diesel*, 12.
76 *"Our goal should not be"*: Ibid.
77 *"How is an idea created?"*: Rudolf Diesel, *Die Entstehung des Dieselmotors*. Berlin: Springer-Verlag, 1913, 1.
77 *"I've had it"*: Thomas Jr., *Diesel*, 16.
78 *"I am tormented"*: Ibid.
78 *The list included*: Ibid., 53.
78 *"I am gone the whole day"*: Ibid., 16.
79 *"To be delayed is"*: Diesel, *Diesel*, 170.
80 *"I must say"*: Thomas Jr., *Diesel*, 17.
81 *"It follows that one"*: Morton Grosser, *Diesel: The Man and the Engine*. New York: Atheneum, 1978, 14.
81 *"I feel myself ready"*: Diesel, *Diesel*, 187.

CHAPTER 8: WILHELM II ENVIES A NAVY

86 *"It is a curious Nemisis"*: Massie, *Dreadnought*, 209.
87 *"criss-cross of commitments"*: Ibid., 82.
87 *"I am the sole master"*: Ibid., 267.
88 *"bent on a return"*: Ibid., 45.
88 *"Wilhelm the Great needs"*: Ibid., 106.
89 *"tried to make excuses"*: Ibid., 284.
90 *"Affairs now are so different"*: Ibid., 241.

CHAPTER 9: THE BIRTH OF DIESEL POWER

92 *"Seeing the tinder begin"*: Diesel, *From Engines to Autos*, 190.
92 *"Now just imagine"*: Ibid.
94 *"It is to be remembered"*: Dugald Clerk, *The Gas and Oil Engine*. Sixth Edition. London: Longmans, Green, 1894.
94 *"I have the pleasure"*: Kurt Schnauffer, *Die Erfindung des Dieselmotors, 1890–1893*. Part 1, unpublished manuscript in the Historical Archive MAN Augsburg, 1954.
94 *"your direction is sharp"*: Lyle Cummins, *Diesel's Engine: From Conception to 1918*. Wilsonville, Oregon: Carnot Press, 1993, 36.
96 *"Publishing my brochure"*: Diesel, *From Engines to Autos*, 206.
96 *"We have carefully"*: Schnauffer, *Die Erfindung des Dieselmotors*.
97 *"Your 3 esteemed"*: Letter in Historical Archive MAN Augsburg, April 20, 1892.
98 *The explosion was evidence*: Lyle Cummins, *Internal Fire: The Internal Combustion Engine 1673–1900*. Third Edition. Wilsonville, Oregon: Carnot Press, 2000, 319.
98 *"The engine never"*: Nitske and Wilson, *Rudolf Diesel*, 210–11.

99 *"The practical application"*: Ibid., 90.
99 *"My heart pounds"*: Nitske and Wilson, *Rudolf Diesel*, 86 and 100.
99 *Robert Bosch later became*: Christopher Andrew, *Her Majesty's Secret Service: The Making of the British Intelligence Community*. New York: Viking, 1986, 383.
100 *"Courage, just for a little"*: Diesel, *From Engines to Autos*, 213.
101 *"My motor still"*: Diesel, *Diesel*, 235.
101 *"In Munich one has"*: Nitske and Wilson, *Rudolf Diesel*, 91.
102 *"Just call it a Diesel"*: Diesel, *From Engines to Autos*, 216.
103 *"Little by little"*: Cummins, *Diesel's Engine*, 126.
103 *"It has been confirmed"*: Letter in Historical Archives MAN Augsburg, January 23, 1894.
106 *"They had been laughing"*: Diesel, *From Engines to Autos*, 219.

CHAPTER 10: LORD KELVIN GOES FIRST

112 *"are almost in agreement"*: Diesel, *Diesel*, 260.
113 *"Diesel's process of heating"*: E. D. Meier's lecture at the Franklin Institute in Philadelphia on May 18, 1898, quoted the Kelvin report.
113 *"How it looks in"*: Diesel, *Diesel*, 293.
115 *"Since the publication"*: E. D. Meier, *Report on Diesel Motor*. October 4, 1897. Copy in Historical Archive MAN Augsburg.
116 *Adolphus inquired as to the "anticipated fee"*: Nitske and Wilson, *Rudolf Diesel*, 125–6.
117 *"It all seems to be"*: Diesel, *From Engines to Autos*, 221.
119 *Rudolf Diesel met Emanuel*: Diesel, *Diesel*, 288–9.
119 *Emanuel oversaw the first*: Nitske and Wilson, *Rudolf Diesel*, 173.
122 *"The broad minded"*: Meier, *Report on Diesel Motor*.

CHAPTER 11: A HICCUP BEFORE THE GRAND PRIZE

123 *"Perhaps I"*: Eugen Diesel, *Diesel*, 260. Copy of letter in Historical Archive MAN Augsburg.
125 *Hedy, thirteen*: Nitske and Wilson, *Rudolf Diesel*, 130.
126 *"At about ten minutes"*: Paul Meyer, *Beiträge zur Geschichte des Dieselmotors*. Berlin: Springer, 1913, 37.
127 *"the development of his engine"*: Diesel, *Diesel*, 318–22.
127 *"There can be no doubt"*: Letter dated July 6, 1899, in Historical Archive MAN Augsburg.
127 *"Everything went quite well"*: Diesel, *Diesel*, 327.
128 *He termed these men*: Nitske and Wilson, *Rudolf Diesel*, 129.
128 *"one real goal of my life"*: Letter in Historical Archive MAN Augsburg, July 16, 1898.
129 *America accounted for*: Nitske and Wilson, *Rudolf Diesel*, 151–2.
129 *he was unsure whether Rudolf's illness*: Letter in Historical Archive MAN Augsburg, July 16, 1898.
131 *Graf von Zeppelin asked Rudolf*: Grosser, *Diesel*, 70–1.
132 *the number of Diesel engines in Germany nearly tripled*: General Society business reports held in Historical Archive MAN Augsburg.

CHAPTER 12: THE TRAPPINGS OF SUCCESS

134 *"intended to build a modest"*: Nitske and Wilson, *Rudolf Diesel*, 157.
135 *Hedy attended a posh*: Thomas Jr., *Diesel*, 25.
135 *"We all gathered to listen"*: Nitske and Wilson, *Rudolf Diesel*, 159.
137 *"You will learn more"*: Thomas Jr., *Diesel*, 37.
138 *"in readiness for the day"*: Nitske and Wilson, *Rudolf Diesel*, 164.
138 *"charged him with excessive leniency"*: Ibid., 145.
139 *"insurance against wars"*: Ibid., 164.
139 *"Solidarism is the"*: Thomas Jr., *Diesel*, 56.
140 *"The results are not"*: Letter in Deutsches Museum, February 11, 1892.
140 *Diesel believed in the concept of*: Thomas Jr., *Diesel*, 56–7.
141 *"The engineer is entering a new era"*: Letter in Historical Archive MAN Augsburg.
141 *"That I have invented the"*: Diesel, *Diesel*, 373–4.
141 *"like so many of its predecessors"*: Thomas Jr., *Diesel*, 65, cites the book review by Karl Figdor.

CHAPTER 13: A STUDY OF THE SLEEPING GIANT

143 *Diesel recorded nearly two hundred*: All quotations from Diesel's 1904 trip to America are from his handwritten diary kept in the Historical Archive MAN Augsburg, translated by Gerhard Reich (professor of German language at the Haverford School, which the author attended).

CHAPTER 14: "THE OLD HOUSE" FIGHTS FOR ITS LIFE

154 *The majority of Pinkerton's revenue through*: Morris Friedman, *The Pinkerton's Labor Spy*. New York: Wilshire Book Co., 1907.
156 *"soft radiance"*: Chernow, *Titan*, 261.

CHAPTER 15: THE KAISER ADOPTS "RISK THEORY"

161 *Royal Navy sailed*: Graham Watson, *Year of the Diamond Jubilee Naval Review: Royal Navy Ship Deployments 1897.* https://www.naval-history.net/xGW-RNOrganisation1897.htm.
165 *"Impossible!"*: Massie, *Dreadnought*.
166 *"commanding position"*: Ibid., 184.
167 *"I am in despair over"*: Ibid., 346.
168 *"present the facts"*: Ibid., 635.
171 *"[Phili] was like a flood of sunshine"*: Ibid., 666.
171 *"It has been a very difficult year"*: Ibid.
173 *"The German Emperor is"*: Ibid., 687.
173 *"Yes, and if they did"*: Andrew, *Her Majesty's Secret Service*, 54.

CHAPTER 16: A PLACE AMONG THE ARMAMENTS OF NATIONS

175 *"War really began to enter"*: Justin D. Lyons, "Churchill on Science and Civilization," *The New Atlantis*, Summer 2010. https://www.thenewatlantis.com/publications/churchill-on-science-and-civilization.
176 *"And since victory by arms"*: Diesel, *Germany and the Germans*, 224.

178 *Nobel launched a nearly identical ship*: Cummins, *Diesel's Engine*, 290.

179 *"breakfast on board"*: Ibid., 478.

179 *"celebrating the momentous event"*: Thomas Jr., *Diesel*, 207.

179 *"the weapon of the weaker"*: Lyle Cummins, *Diesels for the First Stealth Weapon: Submarine Power 1902–1945*. Wilsonville, Oregon: Carnot Press, 2007, 15.

180 *"There is nothing cruel or horrible"*: Thorsten Hordenfelt, "On Submarine Boats," *Royal United Services Institution Journal* 30, no. 33 (1886): 149–173.

181 *"I shall be very disappointed if George"*: Massie, *Dreadnought*, 455.

182 *"The Diesel motor is entering"*: Cummins, *Diesels for the First Stealth Weapon*. Page 38 references the French Naval Ministry report.

183 *During the prewar years*: Ibid., 135, 158, and 175.

184 *The pilot of a ship could crank*: Grosser, *Diesel*, 77.

185 *Dr. M. P. Seiliger*: Ibid., 91.

186 *Robert Scott led a British*: Florian Illies, *1913: The Year Before the Storm*. London: Melville House, 2013.

187 *"Dieselmotor excellent"*: Grosser, *Diesel*, 78.

187 *"If one has come that far in France"*: Cummins, *Diesel's Engine*, 482.

189 *M.A.N. completed successful testing*: Ibid., 485–6.

CHAPTER 17: DAWN OF THE NEW ERA

193 *The board of the General Society dissolved the company*: Thomas Jr., *Diesel*, 193–4.

CHAPTER 18: RUDOLF DIESEL BREAKS RANKS

200 *"Kindly explain to Mr Buz"*: Cummins, *Diesel's Engine*, 308.

201 *"I learned of the work done by"*: Ibid., 325.

202 *"every battleship and cruiser"*: Ibid., 351.

202 *"I made a pretty bad guess there!"*: Ibid., 676.

203 *"[Knudsen is] the man who in the whole world"*: Grosser, *Diesel*, 78.

203 *By the conclusion of the war*: Cummins, *Diesel's Engine*, 619.

204 *"prepare for torpedo attack"*: Robert K. Massie, *Castles of Steel: Britain, Germany, and the Winning of the Great War at Sea*. New York: Random House, 2003, 154.

205 *"Our attempts to copy the German"*: Cummins, *Diesels for the First Stealth Weapon*, 601.

207 *"I will enjoy your"*: Nitske and Wilson, *Rudolf Diesel*, 238.

207 *"Nowhere in the world are the possibilities"*: Ibid., 209.

CHAPTER 19: THE ADMIRALTY BOARDS THE MS *SELANDIA*

212 *"because he saw no smoke"*: Knudsen, "A Smokeless Marine: Denmark's Recent Development of the Diesel Motor."

212 *"The Selandia was often hailed"*: Ibid.

213 *"declared that Englishmen remembered"*: Ibid.

213 *"an advance which will be epochal"*: Grosser, *Diesel*, 80.

213 *In her first twelve years of service*: Ibid.

214 *As Knudsen noted*: John F. Moon, *Rudolf Diesel and the Diesel Engine*. London: Priory Press, 1974, 74.

217 *"effect enormous savings"*: Rudolf Diesel, "The Diesel Oil Engine and Its Industrial Importance, Particularly for Great Britain." June 1912.

217 *"In the case of war"*: Ibid.

218 *"Great Britain, as the greatest"*: Ibid.

219 *"came on board at the head of"*: Knudsen, "A Smokeless Marine: Denmark's Recent Development of the Diesel Motor."

CHAPTER 20: SECRETS OF THE FIRST LORD

221 *"There is nothing else the submarine can do"*: Gaddis Smith, *Britain's Clandestine Submarines, 1914–1915*. New Haven: Yale University Press, 1964, 18.

221 *tasked Mirrlees with developing*: Nitske and Wilson, *Rudolf Diesel*, 207.

222 *"The strength of navies"*: Ibid., 19.

222 *"It is indispensable that"*: Smith, *Britain's Clandestine Submarines*, 23.

223 *in its trademark stealthy fashion*: Diane Cole, "'Sidney Reilly' Review: Spy in His Own Service," *Wall Street Journal*, October 27, 2022, https://www.wsj.com/articles/sidney-reilly-book-review-james-bond-spy-in-his-own-service-11666881695.

223 *Churchill, with an eye already to counterintelligence*: Massie, *Castles of Steel*, 19.

CHAPTER 21: THE GREAT LIGHT TO THE WEST

227 *"born too early for"*: Nitske and Wilson, *Rudolf Diesel*, 198.

228 *"the master magician of the world"*: *Mohave County Miner*, October 5, 1912.

229 *Of the 365 commercial and military*: Rudolf Diesel, *The Present Status of the Diesel Engine in Europe and a Few Reminiscences of the Pioneer Work in America*. A Collection of Lectures Delivered by Dr. Diesel in America. Published by Busch-Sulzer Brothers Diesel Engine Company, Saint Louis, Missouri, June 1, 1912, 27.

230 *"in the steamship the steam engines"*: Ibid.

231 *"Due to the absence of funnels"*: Ibid., 36–7.

232 *"The . . . enclosed report points"*: Letter in Churchill Archive, University of Cambridge, August 28, 1912.

232 *"Krupp has a design for a cargo-ship"*: Lord Fisher, *Memories and Records by Admiral of the Fleet Lord Fisher, Vol. II*. New York: George H. Doran Company, 1920, 191.

232 *"All the drawings and designs"*: Lord Fisher, *Memories and Records by Admiral of the Fleet Lord Fisher, Vol. I.*, 217.

232 *During the Great War*: Cummins, *Diesels for the First Stealth Weapon*, 283.

233 *"The use of vegetable oils for engine fuels"*: Diesel, *The Present Status of the Diesel Engine in Europe and a Few Reminiscences*.

233 *"Some [countries] are exclusively coal-producing"*: Ibid.

234 *"too weak for any kind of efficiency"*: Thomas Jr., *Diesel*, 15. Sketch in Historical Archive MAN Augsburg.

235 *"motive power can still be produced"*: Diesel, *The Present Status of the Diesel Engine in Europe and a Few Reminiscences*.

235 *"one thing is certain"*: Ibid.
235 *"To drive my own thermo-locomotive"*: Nitske and Wilson, *Rudolf Diesel*, 208.
236 *"I am from everywhere"*: Ibid., 223.
236 *"Imperial German Staff"*: Ibid.
236 *"Many were the journeys we took together"*: Diesel, *Germany and the Germans*, 226.
237 *"The military spirit often usurped"*: Ibid., 166.
237 *"the great light to the west"*: Nitske and Wilson, *Rudolf Diesel*, 180.
237 *"There are four American virtues"*: Ibid., 228.
238 *"It is an interesting development"*: Ibid., 208.
238 *Rudolf clipped the newspaper headline*: Diary in Historical Archive MAN Augsburg.
239 *"the ancient world deified"*: Letter from E. D. Meier to James Harris, June 13, 1912. Letter in possession of the Wisconsin Historical Society.
240 *both the Pennsylvania Railroad and Henry Ford*: Nitske and Wilson, *Rudolf Diesel*, 237–8.
242 *Inside they sat on uncomfortable chairs*: Ibid., 231–2.
243 *Detractors of Rudolf Diesel*: Thomas Jr., *Diesel*, 118.
244 *imagining an "accumulated" engine*: Nitske and Wilson, *Rudolf Diesel*, 233.

CHAPTER 22: RISING PRESSURE
253 *the conversation would have to be in German*: Massie, *Dreadnought*, 809.
254 *Two years later, in June 1914*: Ibid., 852.
255 *"extraordinary increase in the striking force of ships"*: Smith, *Britain's Clandestine Submarines, 1914–1915*.
255 *"From the fact that"*: Ibid.

CHAPTER 23: THE FINAL MONTHS
261 *The finger was mutilated*: E. C. Magdeburger, "Diesel Engine in the United States Navy," *Journal of the American Society for Naval Engineers* 61, no. 1 (February 1949): 45–93.
263 *"our wonderful little June shindigs"*: Nitske and Wilson, *Rudolf Diesel*, 236.
264 *Elsewhere in Munich*: Illies, *1913*, 112.
265 *Rudolf Jr. further remarked*: Ibid., 241.
265 *When the staff returned*: Grosser, *Diesel*, 85–6.
266 *"People of original creative ability"*: Diesel, *Germany and the Germans*, 225.
266 *"pretty-daughter stealer"*: Nitske and Wilson, *Rudolf Diesel*, 199.
267 *"My beloved son Eugen"*: Cummins, *Diesel's Engine*, 719–20.
267 *"My Wife, you were everything"*: Ibid.
268 *"I still have a firm conviction"*: Diesel, *Diesel*, 418.
268 *"I have known [Rudolf] intimately*: Nitske and Wilson, *Rudolf Diesel*, 238.
269 *"Do you feel how I love you?"*: Cummins, *Diesel's Engine*, 720.
269 *"The highlight [of the entire exposition]"*: Letter in Historical Archive MAN Augsburg.
270 *"There is considerable setback"*: Ibid.

CHAPTER 24: SS *DRESDEN*: SEPTEMBER 29, 1913

271 *"command a following so strong"*: Nitske and Wilson, *Rudolf Diesel*, 244.

273 *"refused steadfastly to issue a death certificate"*: Ibid., 245.

274 *There was no ship's company*: Ibid., 246.

CHAPTER 25: THE WORLD REACTS

284 *News of the telegraph to Diesel's family*: *Alaska Daily Empire*, January 23, 1919.

CHAPTER 26: THE AVAILABLE THEORIES

295 *in this case, Captain Hubert did confirm*: Nitske and Wilson, *Rudolf Diesel*, 245.

CHAPTER 27: OPERATION RUDOLF DIESEL

301 *Rudolf Diesel selected a passage to read*: Diesel, *Diesel*, 72.

CHAPTER 28: FINGERPRINTS

305 *"The* D-notice *system is a peculiarly"*: Betsey Reed, "The D-notice System: A Typically British Fudge That Has Survived a Century," *Guardian*, July 31, 2015.

308 *On New Year's Day*: J. D. Perkins, "The Canadian-built British H-boats," Great War Document Archive, 1999. www.gwpda.org.naval/cdnhboat.htm.

309 *The stealth operation produced*: Smith, *Britain's Clandestine Submarines, 1914–1915*, 107.

309 *"proved very successful"*: Cummins, *Diesels for the First Stealth Weapon*, 234.

310 *a 1925 technical paper*: William F. Rabbidge, "Some Barrow Light Weight Oil Engines." Trans., Barrow Association of Engineers, 1930. Papers of Philip F. Rabbidge.

312 *A strange fact somewhat lost*: Cummins, *Diesels for the First Stealth Weapon*, 195–6.

318 *Just one example: the Canadian-built submarine*: Smith, *Britain's Clandestine Submarines, 1914–1915*, 132.

321 *"I saw where the farmers could actually benefit"*: Steve Hargreaves, "Willie Nelson's Biofueled Bus," CNNMoney, September 27, 2007. https://money .cnn.com/2007/09/26/news/newsmakers/willie_nelson/.

EPILOGUE: AT LAST

325 *In 1932, Caterpillar made a marketing sensation*: Nitske and Wilson, *Rudolf Diesel*, 259.

325 *robust 5.65 percent annual growth*: "Diesel Market 2023 Research Report Which Shows Huge Growth Rate, Revenue, Progress Insight and Forecast to 2028," Marketwatch, February 3, 2023. https://www.marketwatch.com /press-release/diesel-market-2023-research-report-which-shows-huge-growth -rate-revenue-progress-insight-and-forecast-to-2028-2023-02-03.

326 *"The United States, in this last war"*: Magdeburger, "Diesel Engine in the United States Navy," 91.

328 *"We have got to strike our bargain"*: Diesel, *From Engines to Autos*, 232.

APPENDIX

334 *Exhibit 2*: Cummins, *Diesel's Engine*.

ADDENDUM: SECRETS AT M.A.N.—BATTLESHIP DIESELS FOR THE GREAT WAR

342 *During the first months of the Great War*: Massie, *Castles of Steel*, 39–44.
342 *The first test engine from M.A.N.*: Cummins, *Diesel's Engine*, 663.
343 *On December 22, 1914*: Ibid., 675.

COMMENTS REGARDING THE
BIBLIOGRAPHY

———

RUDOLF DIESEL HAS remained somehow just beneath the surface of history. We see him only when we know to look for him. But once we do, we see that his influence is obvious and widespread.

There is curiously little literature about Diesel, particularly in English. In part, this book rose from the desire to answer this curiosity. He has gotten short shrift. Epic and well-reviewed books like *The Sea & Civilization: A Maritime History of the World* or Yergin's brilliant work *The Prize* (the premise of which is that the quest for oil was the primary geopolitical force of the twentieth century) give only passing mention of the Diesel engine. *The Prize* mentions Diesel in the context of a Panzer division overrunning a Soviet camp and finding the captured fuel to be useless as it was meant for the Diesel engines of the Soviet T-34s. The vast implications of these superior Russian tanks having completely different engines that burned a different fuel was not explored. That Diesel is the greatest threat to the primacy of oil, that Rockefeller identified Diesel as an enemy, is not discussed.

———

In researching the history of Rudolf Diesel and his engine, many of the interesting details come from niche journals published early in the twentieth century. For example, the story of Nimitz losing his finger while in Augsburg in 1913 appears in a 1949 issue of the *Journal of the American Society of Naval Engineers*. Several obscure publications of this type reveal that certain individuals around the world grasped the importance of the Diesel engine long before there was mainstream awareness.

There are only three full-length English-language biographies of Rudolf Diesel, all from a small or university publisher, and mostly for an academic audience (Nitske and Wilson, 1965; Grosser, 1978; Thomas Jr., 1987). All three commit a brief passage of their book to Rudolf's disappearance, and all three ultimately express certainty that Diesel took his own life. Each book relies on the biography published by Eugen Diesel in 1937 as the point of origin for information about Rudolf prior to 1897. The same family stories, cited from Eugen's work, appear in all Diesel lore. Thomas, to his credit, did a bit more original research in Augsburg and Munich archives to find family letters and childhood materials. But Thomas, prejudiced by his misunderstanding of Rudolf's demise, takes a more negative overall tone with Diesel, giving too much credence to the scathing criticisms written after his disappearance by men such as his former assistant Imanuel Lauster, who published a hostile manuscript in the 1930s even though Lauster likely suspected, or knew, that Rudolf had abandoned Germany to aid Great Britain in 1913.

Lyle Cummins, son of American Diesel pioneer Clessie Cummins, has self-published the most comprehensive works on Rudolf Diesel and his engine. Well placed within the Diesel community, Cummins visited archives around the world to compile his rigorous research. The Cummins books are deeply technical for readers interested in learning the engineering details.

None of the biographies gives weight to Eugen's 1931 work *Germany and the Germans*, which is a critical work to establish Rudolf's mindset regarding Wilhelm II's regime prior to the war—what Rudolf and Eugen called "the German Problem."

And none of these biographies places Rudolf Diesel in the strategic context of his time. None addresses the significant juxtaposition of Diesel's London speech with Churchill's speech two days later, Wilhelm's tour of the *Fionia* just after Churchill's tour of the *Selandia*,

Rudolf's 1912 pledge to break any fuel monopoly just as Churchill identifies liquid fuel monopolies as the obstacle before his "prize." None explores the bizarre sequence of media reporting after September 29, 1913, or resurrects the testimony of the *Dresden* crew member, though the article is available in newspaper archives. None explores the extraordinary reports of Diesel's emergence in Canada coincident with Martha's disappearance from Munich. These news reports were indeed difficult to find, but the point is that prior authors didn't think to look for them because none had the conviction there might be something to find. They all thought he died in 1913.

None of the biographies follows the trajectory of the final years of Rudolf's life—from the lawsuit with M.A.N. in 1907 and his falling out with the Augsburg-based company to his tighter embrace of America and Great Britain. There are numerous insights in the Diesel biographies, but with the ruinous presumption of the suicide theory, comprehension of his final decade is unattainable. In the proper context, Diesel's actions and letters from 1907 to 1913 take on an entirely new meaning.

Each prior book takes suicide for granted. None has truly understood the man. But all the clues about Diesel's motivations and his fate are discoverable, obscured by the fog of time and tactics of deception. Only when pulling together the widely disparate and long-neglected threads can we weave the full picture of Rudolf Diesel.

BIBLIOGRAPHY

Andrew, Christopher. *Her Majesty's Secret Service: The Making of the British Intelligence Community*. New York: Viking, 1986.

Best, Geoffrey. *Churchill: A Study in Greatness*. London: Hambledon & London, 2001.

Boyd, Carl L. "The Wasted Ten Years, 1888–1898: The Kaiser Finds an Admiral." *Royal United Services Institution Journal* 111, no. 644 (1966): 291–97.

Carr, Albert Z. *John D. Rockefeller's Secret Weapon*. New York: McGraw-Hill, 1962.

Cave Brown, Anthony. *Bodyguard of Lies*. London: W. H. Allen, 1975.

Chandler, David Leon. *Henry Flagler: The Astonishing Life and Times of the Visionary Robber Baron Who Founded Florida*. New York: Macmillan, 1986.

Chernow, Ron. *Titan: The Life of John D. Rockefeller, Sr*. New York: Random House, 1998.

Clerk, Dugald. *The Gas and Oil Engine*. Sixth Edition. London: Longmans, Green, 1894.

Cummins, Lyle. *Diesels for the First Stealth Weapon: Submarine Power 1902–1945*. Wilsonville, Oregon: Carnot Press, 2007.

———. *Internal Fire: The Internal Combustion Engine 1673–1900*. Third Edition. Wilsonville, Oregon: Carnot Press, 2000.

———. *Diesel's Engine: From Conception to 1918*. Wilsonville, Oregon: Carnot Press, 1993.

Debruyne, Emmanuel. "Espionage." *1914–1918 Online: International Encyclopedia of the First World War*. Berlin: Freie Universität Berlin, 2014.

Diesel, Eugen. *Diesel: der Mensch, das Werk, das Schicksal*. Hamburg: Hanseatische Verlagsanstalt, 1937.

———. *Germany and the Germans*. Translated by W. D. Robson-Scott. London: Macmillan & Co., 1931.

Diesel, Eugen, et al. *From Engines to Autos: Five Pioneers in Engine Development and Their Contributions to the Automotive Industry*. Chicago: Henry Regnery Company, 1960.

Diesel, Rudolf. *Die Entstehung des Dieselmotors*. Berlin: Springer-Verlag, 1913.

———. *The Present Status of the Diesel Engine in Europe and a Few Reminiscences of the Pioneer Work in America*. A Collection of Lectures Delivered by Dr. Diesel in America. Published by Busch-Sulzer Brothers Diesel Engine Company, Saint Louis, Missouri, 1912.

Fisher, Lord. *Memories and Records by Admiral of the Fleet Lord Fisher, Vol 1*. New York: George H. Doran Company, 1920.

————. *Memories and Records by Admiral of the Fleet Lord Fisher, Vol II*. New York: George H. Doran Company, 1920.

Friedman, Morris. *The Pinkerton's Labor Spy*. New York: Wilshire Book Co., 1907.

Fromkin, David. *The King and the Cowboy: Theodore Roosevelt and Edward the Seventh, Secret Partners*. New York: Penguin Press, 2008.

Gilbert, Martin, *Churchill: A Life*. London: Heinemann, 1991.

Grosser, Morton. *Diesel: The Man and the Engine*. New York: Atheneum, 1978.

Harford, Tim. "How Rudolf Diesel's Engine Changed the World," BBC News. December 19, 2016.

Hargreaves, Steve. "Willie Nelson's Biofueled Bus," CNNMoney. September 27, 2007.

Holian, Timothy J. "Adolphus Busch," in *Immigrant Entrepreneurship: German-American Business Biographies, 1720–the Present, Vol. 3*. German Historical Institute. Updated 2013.

Hordenfelt, Thorsten. "On Submarine Boats," *Royal United Services Institution Journal* 30, no. 133 (1886): 149–73.

Hull, Isabel V. *The Entourage of Kaiser Wilhelm II, 1888–1918*. Cambridge, UK: Cambridge University Press, 2004.

Illies, Florian. *1913: The Year Before the Storm*. London: Melville House, 2013.

Knudsen, Ivar. "A Smokeless Marine: Denmark's Recent Development of the Diesel Motor." *The American-Scandinavian Review*, Vol. II. Published by the American-Scandinavian Foundation, New York. 1914.

Langer, William L., ed. *Western Civilization*. New York: American Heritage Publishing Company, 1968.

Levada, C. L., H. Maceti, I. J. Lautenschleguer, and M. M. O. Levada. "Who Wants Rudolf Diesel's Death?" *Discovery Science* 7, no. 17 (2013): 11–14.

Lyons, Justin. "Churchill on Science and Civilization." *The New Atlantis*. Summer 2010.

Magdeburger, E. C. "Diesel Engine in United States Navy." *Journal of the American Society for Naval Engineers* 61, no.1 (February 1949): 45–93.

Marder, Arthur J. *From the Dreadnought to Scapa Flow, The Royal Navy in the Fisher Era, 1904–1919. Vol. 1: The Road to War, 1904–1914*. London: Oxford University Press, 1961.

Massie, Robert K. *Castles of Steel: Britain, Germany, and the Winning of the Great War at Sea*. New York: Random House, 2003.

————. *Dreadnought: Britain, Germany, and the Coming of the Great War*. New York: Random House, 1991.

McCormick, Donald. *Peddler of Death*. London: Holt, Rinehart and Winston, 1965.

Meyer, Paul. *Beiträge zur Geschichte des Dieselmotors*. Berlin: Springer, 1913.

Mohave County Miner. October 5, 1912.

Moon, John F. *Rudolf Diesel and the Diesel Engine*. London: Priory Press, 1974.

Nitske, Robert W., and Charles Morrow Wilson. *Rudolf Diesel: Pioneer of the Age of Power*. Norman: University of Oklahoma Press, 1965.

Perkins, J. D. "The Canadian-built British H-boats," Great War Document Archive, 1999.

Rabbidge, William F. "Some Barrow Light Weight Oil Engines." Trans., Barrow Association of Engineers, 1930. Papers of Philip F. Rabbidge.

Röhl, John C. G. *Young Wilhelm: The Kaiser's Early Life, 1859–1888.* Cambridge, UK: Cambridge University Press, 1998.

Schnauffer, Kurt. *Die Erfindung des Dieselmotors, 1890–1893.* Part 1. Translated by Henry I. Willeke, unpublished manuscript in the Historical Archive MAN Augsburg, 1954.

"Science: His Name Is an Engine." *Time.* December 9, 1940.

Segall, Grant. *John D. Rockefeller: Anointed with Oil.* New York: Oxford University Press, 2001.

Smith, Gaddis. *Britain's Clandestine Submarines, 1914–1915.* New Haven: Yale University Press, 1964.

Thomas, Donald Jr. *Diesel: Technology and Society in Industrial Germany.* Tuscaloosa: University of Alabama Press, 1987.

Watson, Graham. *Year of the Diamond Jubilee Naval Review: Royal Navy Ship Deployments 1897.*

Yergin, Daniel. *The Prize: The Epic Quest for Oil, Money & Power.* New York: Touchstone, 1991.

IMAGE CREDITS

INDEX

submarines *(cont.)*
  M.A.N.'s manufacture
    of, 192, 203–5, 209,
    213, 249, 254, 262
  Nimitz on, 260
  Nordenfelt on limits
    of, 180
  Russian navy's use of, 185
Sulzer, Jakob, 69n, 135,
    138, 200, 225, 258
Sulzer Brothers company,
    183n, 202, 342, 343
  Diesel engines from,
    186, 188, 194, 235,
    258, 268
  Diesel's internship
    with, 69, 259
  Linde ice machines
    at, 71

T
Tarbell, Ida, 57, 156
Tirpitz, Alfred von, 162–
    64, 166, 170, 176, 252,
    253, 254
Tirpitz Plan, 163, 188
Treaty of Versailles, 325–26
Trout memo, 313, 314, 317

V
Vickers firm, 180, 194–95,
    202, 224, 297, 299,
    308, 309–12
Victoria, Princess Royal
    ("Vicki"), 34, 35–37,
    38, 83–84, 87
Victoria, Queen of En-
    gland, 34, 35, 38, 83,
    84, 85, 87–88, 89–90,
    161, 171
Vogel, Lucien, 98–99

W
Waldersee, Count Alfred
    von, 89
Wallenberg, Marcus, 121,
    128

Watson, Sir Renny, 112
Watt, James, 3, 15–16, 61,
    93, 239
White, Edward, 247
Whitney, William, 158
Wilhelm I, Kaiser, 14, 32,
    34, 83–84, 85–86
Wilhelm II, Kaiser, 162–
    74
  Bismarck's childhood
    influence on, 36, 84
  Bismarck's conflict
    with, 80, 81, 85–86
  Bismarck's dismissal
    by, 86, 87
  British minister
    Haldane's visit with,
    252–55, 256
  British perception of
    threat from, 167–68,
    172–73
  childhood of, 34–37
  Churchill and, 175, 177,
    255–56
  death of his father,
    83–84
  desire for exclusive
    access to Diesel's
    advice, 161, 189
  Diesel engines and,
    188, 189, 203–5, 219,
    252, 254
  Diesel's concern about
    military policies of,
    176
  Diesel's disappearance
    and, 4, 283, 295, 327
  Diesel's wariness of,
    189, 297
  Diesel's work with
    England and, 225
  engine fuel issues and,
    234, 249–52
  European foreign rela-
    tions and, 87–88, 167,
    172–73
  Fionia visit of, 219

  Franco-Prussian War
    and, 32, 33
  German military af-
    fairs and, 88–89
  homosexuality rumors
    and scandal and,
    170–71
  naval expansion plans
    of, 89–90, 161–64,
    166, 171, 172–74, 188,
    253
  railway construction
    for oil supply and,
    250–52
  vision for Germany's
    future held by, 84–85
  World War II and,
    318–20
Wilson, Charles, 19
Wilson, Woodrow, 320
World Congress of Me-
    chanical Engineers,
    206–7
World's Fairs
  Paris, 1867, 13–15, 129
  Paris, 1889, 79, 129
  Paris, 1900, 129–31, 181
  Turin, 1911, 206
World War I
  British Intelligence
    during, 317
  British submarines in,
    317–18
  Casablanca Conference
    and, 313–14
  Diesel engines in, 326
  hypothetical Operation
    Rudolf Diesel and,
    317
  news about Diesel
    disappearance and,
    306–7
  Wilhelm II and, 318–20

Z
Zeppelin airships, 258–59
Zeuner, Gustav, 96